THE METAPHYSIC OF EXPERIENCE

THOEMMES

The Metaphysic of Experience
Shadworth H. Hodgson

Volume 1
Book I. *General Analysis of Experience*

Volume 2
Book II. *Positive Science*

Volume 3
Book III. *Analysis of Conscious Action, Chapters 1–5*

Volume 4
Book III. *Analysis of Conscious Action, Chapter 6*
Book IV. *The Real Universe*

Appendix
G. F. Stout
'The Philosophy of Mr. Shadworth Hodgson' (1892)
H. Wildon Carr
'Shadworth Hollway Hodgson' (1912)
G. Dawes Hicks
'Shadworth Hollway Hodgson' (1913)

THE METAPHYSIC OF EXPERIENCE

Volume 3

Shadworth H. Hodgson

THOEMMES PRESS

This edition published by Thoemmes Press, 2001

Thoemmes Press
11 Great George Street
Bristol BS1 5RR, England

Thoemmes Press US Office
22883 Quicksilver Drive
Sterling, Virginia 20166, USA

http://www.thoemmes.com

The Metaphysic of Experience
4 Volumes : ISBN 1 85506 836 2

Series: British Idealism

British Library Cataloguing-in-Publication Data
A CIP record of this title is available from the British Library

Publisher's Note

The Publisher has gone to great lengths to ensure the quality of this reprint but points out that some imperfections in the original book may be apparent.

This book is printed on acid-free paper, sewn, and cased in a durable buckram cloth.

THE

METAPHYSIC OF EXPERIENCE

BY

SHADWORTH H. HODGSON.

HON. LL.D. EDIN.; HON. FELLOW C.C.C. OXFORD; F.R. HIST. S.;
PAST PRESIDENT OF THE ARISTOTELIAN SOCIETY.

*Author of " Time and Space," " The Theory of Practice," " The
Philosophy of Reflection," " Outcast Essays," &c.*

IN FOUR BOOKS.

VOL. III.
CONTAINING CHAPTERS I TO V., INCLUSIVE,
OF BOOK III.
ANALYSIS OF CONSCIOUS ACTION.

LONGMANS, GREEN, AND CO.,
39, PATERNOSTER ROW, LONDON,
NEW YORK AND BOMBAY.
1898.

THE METAPHYSIC OF EXPERIENCE.

BOOK III.

ANALYSIS OF CONSCIOUS ACTION.

CHAPTERS I.—V.

CONTENTS OF VOL. III.

BOOK III.

ANALYSIS OF CONSCIOUS ACTION.

CHAPTERS I., II., III., IV., V.

CHAPTER I.
REDINTEGRATION.

§		PAGE
1.	General Scope of Book III.	3
2.	Some leading characteristics of Redintegration	26
	A. Line of demarcation between presentation and representation	27
	B. The blanks in pure redintegration	31
	C. Time and Space the fundamental forms of the world of objective thought	35
	D. The emotional content of objective thought	42
3.	Spontaneous and volitional modes of Redintegration.—Representation of primary and remote objects	47
4.	The Ego and Personality	59
5.	The Personal Emotions	78

CHAPTER II.
THE LAWS OF ASSOCIATION.

1.	Spontaneous Redintegration, how to be analysed	97
2.	Association in Imagery	100
3.	Association in Emotion	113

§		PAGE
4.	Trains of imagery apparently new	118
5.	Association of elementary perceptions	123
6.	The Limits of Spontaneous Redintegration	131

CHAPTER III.
VOLUNTARY REDINTEGRATION.

1.	Volition	138
2.	Relation of Volition to the Ego	161
3.	The two chief modes of Voluntary Redintegration ;— Desire for Knowledge and Desire for Feeling	170
4.	Relation of these two Modes to each other	180
5.	The main branches of Practice	190
6.	The Sciences of Practice ;—Ethic, Logic, and Poetic	210

CHAPTER IV.
THE FOUNDATIONS OF LOGIC.

1.	Logic and Method	227
2.	Logic and Reality	242
3.	The Material and Origination of Thought	257
4.	The Law of Thought and the Nature of Concepts	275
5	Judgment and Syllogism	314
6.	Hypothetical Judgments and Modal Concepts	336
7.	The Limits of Thought as compared to Perception	356

CHAPTER V.
THE FOUNDATIONS OF POETIC.

1.	Nature and Range of Poetic Imagination	384
2.	Æsthetic and Poetic	400
3.	The Fine Arts	407
4.	The Law of Harmony	428
5.	Relations between Artistic and Non-artistic Imagination	433

END OF CONTENTS OF VOL. III.

BOOK III.

ANALYSIS OF CONSCIOUS ACTION.

CHAPTER I.

REDINTEGRATION.

§ 1. The leading result obtained by the analysis of Book II. consists in this, that we can now bring a definite conception of the real agent and real conditioning in psychology into connection with the previously obtained distinction between consciousness as a knowing and consciousness as an existent. In other words we can now fruitfully combine psychological with metaphysical conceptions and method. Neural processes, as we have seen, proximately condition the stream of consciousness, first in its character of an existent simply, and then in its character of a knowing, that is, of a panorama of objective thought, so far as this depends on the collocation, dismissal, or combination, of parts or moments of the existent stream. The qualities or whatnesses of the ultimate parts or moments, of which the stream and therefore the panorama, as existents, are composed, are (as we have also seen) ultimate data in knowledge, which are not capable of being accounted for by any real condition whatever. Their existence in individual conscious beings is accounted for by neural processes in those beings; but it is in these very qualities or whatnesses themselves, which cannot be so accounted for, that the nature of our consciousness as a whole ultimately consists; and similarly, those of them which are immediately and originally conditioned upon redintegrative processes, I mean more especially the emotions, are the ultimate constituents of the mental and moral consciousness of the individual beings whose neural processes condition their existence, and to whom that consciousness is consequently said to belong.

In the whole of the present Book it will be necessary to keep constantly in mind this double connection of the really conditioning agent and process, first with the actual existence of process-contents of consciousness, and secondly with their nature, so far as this depends upon collocation or arrangement of parts, and not upon the specific and ultimate quality of their constituents. We shall find that this distinction will throw light on several fundamental questions of philosophy, the difficulty of which has rather been increased than lessened by the methods of treating them hitherto in vogue. For instance, the processes which constitute the real action in volition, and consequently the problem of free-will, belong to the purely psychological connection between neural process and the existence of the process-contents of consciousness conditioned by it. Those phenomena on the other hand which constitute the nature and value of actions, as morally right or wrong, belong to the connection between neural process and the nature (not the existence) of process-contents of consciousness, the existence of which, in given cases, the neural process may either condition or fail to condition. The analysis of these phenomena therefore is, in the last resort, not psychological but metaphysical, being an analysis of certain ultimate facts or data of experience.

We are immediately conscious of those features in what is called a conscious action, which constitute it right or wrong; our perception of them is an immediate perception of its moral nature. But of the action itself, that is, the agency at work in it, we are never immediately conscious; this is known to us by inference only, and belongs, as already shown, to the neural mechanism (so to call it) upon which the existence of the concomitant consciousness depends. Both these things, the action which is an object of inference, and the moral nature of the dependent consciousness, which is immediately perceived, enter into, and in fact exhaust, the whole phenomena of conscious action. But of these, the first belongs to the psychology of those phenomena, the second to their metaphysic. To keep these two classes of phenomena, and consequently the two domains of speculation to which they belong, clearly distinct in thought, as the necessary condition of exhibiting their interconnection,—instead of clumping both together as belonging to a single indivisible agent, and consequently bringing both alike under the dominion of psychology,—is the method clearly commanded by the analysis of the two foregoing Books.

It is necessary to bring prominently forward this double distinction, this double connection, between the Subject and his experience, because in the *Analysis of Conscious Action,* which now lies before us, we are in fact returning again to the analysis of consciousness simply as experienced, which we quitted at the conclusion of Book I., though returning to it enriched with the conception of a real agent and agency conditioning consciousness, which was the final result of our excursion into the domain of the positive sciences, which occupied Book II. We quitted the analysis of consciousness simply as experienced, at the point where it was found to yield a knowledge of a material world, and of the individual conscious being as the constant central object therein. We quitted it in order to follow up the clue afforded at that point by the conception of real conditions and the process of real conditioning; and that clue we followed by tracing, in Book II., the operations of material objects *inter se*, and also as real conditions of the panorama of consciousness, with the analysis of which our whole enquiry began, and in which the whole evidence for the existence and nature of the material world was found to be contained. We now return once more to the analysis of conscious experience; but we begin with a different phase of it. We leave behind us the analysis of presented sensations and the material world, and enter upon that of represented sensations and the feelings which arise along with them in redintegration. What redintegration means has been made sufficiently clear in the closing Section of Book II., *The Conscious Being*, to allow of our proceeding at once to the description and analysis of its phenomena, without lingering over its points of contrast with presentations of sense.

At the same time it is evident, that the results reached in Book II. give us an advantage in our proposed analysis, which we did not possess in Book I.; I mean in their providing us with a clear though general idea of the nature and reality of the Subject, as well as of the processes which are the proximate real conditions of his consciousness, both in the domain of redintegration and in that of presented sensation. This advantage we are by no means called upon to forego, in analysing the phenomena of consciousness which now lie before us. Imperfect and general as our knowledge of those real conditions may be, it is an indispensable means of controlling our analysis of the states and processes of consciousness which depend upon them, and thus to some extent of verifying its results, by collateral evidence. Just as in the two former Books we could put side by side and contemplate together the material objects thought of and our own objective thoughts which represented them, so here, in the present Book, we shall be able to contemplate, side by side with our trains of objective thought, the states and processes of the neural mechanism which are, not their objects, but their real conditions. In either case some real objects thought of are the complement of the conscious experience which is our immediate object of analysis. In the former Books (barring their psychological portions) this complement consisted of real objects thought of, which were the remote real conditions of the consciousness analysed; in the present it consists of those which are its proximate real conditions. But in both alike it is the consciousness analysed which alone gives us the true nature, in the sense of the tendency, value, and meaning, of those real conditions upon which it is dependent. They have and can have no other. The tree is known by its fruits.

Moreover it must be noted, that our present analysis, supplemented with an appeal to the real conditions of the phenomena analysed, will have a retrospective value. It will help to fill up with positive knowledge the lacuna which we were forced to leave open, in Book I., when describing the formation of our knowledge of the material world. Redintegration spontaneous and voluntary, reasoning being included in the latter, is a most important factor in the formation of that knowledge. But in Book I. we had to assume this fact as known, leaving the justification and explanation of it for a future occasion. Now in part this justification and explanation have been already given in Book II.; that is to say, so far as to show the reality of the neural processes on which redintegration depends. Partly they still remain to be given, in the present Book, by showing the analysis of spontaneous and voluntary redintegration, so far as they are processes within immediate consciousness. It is enough for the purposes of the present work to bring this fact to notice, without seeking to determine the psychology of the processes by which our knowledge of the material world is either acquired or enlarged, more minutely than has been done already. Advance in this direction depends almost entirely upon advancing knowledge of the anatomy and physiology of the neuro-cerebral system, an enormous field, in which new facts are continually being brought to light by the researches of neurologists.

The present work, which thankfully accepts and endeavours to utilise the results already obtained by physiological psychology, yet excludes from its scope the study of any special science, except so far as its connection with philosophy is concerned; that is to say, except on the one hand so far as it deals with the real conditions of consciousness, in the way just mentioned, and except on the other so far as its own fundamental conceptions or assumptions require the control of the subjective or metaphysical analysis of conscious experience, in order to bring them into systematic harmony. At the point which we have now reached in that analysis we stand between two groups of special sciences. We have left, as it were, behind us the group of positive sciences, treated of generally in Book II., and we have before us the group of practical sciences, originating as sciences of practice, which are sciences dealing with some branch or branches of conscious human action, that is to say, action which is immediately attended with emotion, knowledge, choice, and purpose, and is therefore complex, in the sense that those elements or strains in it which are immediately attended with consciousness of purpose exert an influence in modifying other strains or elements in it, and so contribute to determine the sequence and direction of the whole.

The main division of this group is into Ethic and Logic, the former of which treats of purposive action in its widest scope, that is, including all special branches of practice, so far as the purpose is concerned at which they aim, and by which they are distinguished from one another; and the latter of reasoning, as an action at once directed to the ascertainment of truth of fact, entering into all the other conscious pursuits or branches of practice as the cognitive element in them, and capable in that instrumental character of being rightly or wrongly directed, and of attaining greater or less degrees of perfection. In short Ethic includes Logic, so far as Reasoning is purposive action, and Logic includes Ethic so far as Practice is rational and cognitive action. Not that both kinds of action are not also subject to laws of Nature, for this they must necessarily be, seeing that they fundamentally consist of physiological processes; but they are demarcated as a special class of those processes by the circumstance, that the consciousness, with which they are attended, includes a perception of purpose more or less distinctly apprehended, whereby they become what may most properly be called both forward-looking and self-modifying actions.

Now the characteristic difference of a science of practice from a positive or speculative one lies in this forward-looking and self-modifying attitude of the action which is its object-matter. Like other sciences it is founded in analysis, the analysis of its object matter. A science of practice is one which begins by analysing practice. But since this forward-looking and self-modifying attitude of the action is the essential characteristic which makes it the object-matter of a special science, that is to say, is the special feature of it which that science selects for study, it follows that every science of practice has to consider the aims, ends, or purposes, which are or may be proposed to itself by the practice which is its object-matter, as well as the laws of Nature to which it is subject as a physiological action. It has to consider not only what the practice is and must be *de facto*, as a physiological action subject to laws of Nature, but also what it is best or most desirable that it should be, that is, to what aims, ends, or purposes, it ought to be directed, within those laws of Nature; the consideration being based on previously acquired experience, and on practical precepts thence derived.

In this way and in obedience to this necessity it is, that sciences of practice become themselves practical sciences; that is, their doctrines are the guides to right action. Ideals are part of their object-matter, since they are involved in the practice of which they treat, in its character of a forward-looking action. A positive science is directed simply to the discovery of what is *de facto*, whether in Nature at large, or in human action which is part of Nature. A practical science or science of practice (by whichever name we call it) is directed, over and above this and in combination with it, to the discovery of what is best or most desirable in human action, considered as a forward-looking action the direction or aim of which is still to be determined. A practical science may be described in ordinary language as directed to supply knowledge which may aid in determining the immediately future action of the enquirer in cases where he feels doubt, instead of being directed to ascertain matters of fact, whether past, present, or future, conceived as having an existence independent of his action. In positive sciences the result is conceived as conformity of thought to fact, in practical sciences and in practice, as a conformity of fact to thought. The aim of the former is knowledge of reality, that is, truth; the aim of the latter is realisation of an ideal or of a precept, that is, goodness or right.

From the foregoing contra-distinction we see, that the characteristic of practical science consists in what it has over and above what is contained in positive science, namely, in a mass of experience, drawn from previous cases of practice, which may be brought into consciousness by redintegrative thought, and thereby submitted to subjective or metaphysical analysis. It is from the comparisons and discriminations yielded by this analysis, that the principles of all sciences of practice are and must be drawn. The connection of this mass of experience, or any part of it, with the physiological processes upon which they depend for their existence, does not, in this analysis and the establishment of principles thereby, come into question at all. The analysis of it as a mass of experience, as it is passed in review by representative or redintegrative processes, is here alone concerned.

It follows, that all sciences of practice or practical sciences are, as such and in that character, part and parcel of Metaphysic or Philosophy, as distinguished from Psychology, which is a positive science. To treat any practical science as a branch of psychology, or more generally still, of anthropology, or of (so called) sociology, is a fallacy of the most fatal and destructive kind, because it denaturalises the object-matter with which it deals, namely practice, and transforms it into its opposite, a simply *de facto* process, subject to laws of Nature only, and not subject to laws of conduct, laws prescribing the good and right, forbidding the bad and wrong, laws which, until they are obeyed, or when they are disobeyed, in any given case of practice, have for that case of practice a *de jure* validity only. The whole difference between good and evil is obliterated by regarding practice as the object-matter of psychology or any branch of it. Physiological psychology supplies indeed one half of the whole theory of practice, dealing as it does with its proximate real conditions, but the fundamental conceptions and constitutive ideas of that theory are given by metaphysical analysis, inasmuch as it is an analysis of what practice itself is known as, or as it is in immediate experience.

The two great groups of positive sciences on the one hand and practical sciences on the other divide the whole field of science exhaustively between them. The difference between them is deep and fundamental, inasmuch as it is a difference in the basis on which they stand, and the constitutive principles on which they move. Positive sciences stand on the basis of common-sense conceptions, and move by analysis of common-sense objects. Practical sciences stand on the basis of the subjective aspect of consciousness or experience, and move by analysis of that aspect in the domain of pure redintegration; an analysis which is the continuation and completion of the subjective analysis of experience generally, the less specialised portion of which yields, as we have seen, the explanation and justification of the common-sense

BOOK III. CH. I.
§ 1. General scope of Book III.

perception of an objective Universe and a Material World. Thus, as already said, the practical sciences are part and parcel of Metaphysic or Philosophy, as contradistinguished from Positive Science.

Nevertheless, notwithstanding this circumstance, I propose in one respect to deal with the practical sciences in the present Book in a manner similar to that in which I dealt with the positive sciences in Book II. That is to say, I propose to enter upon them no farther than is necessary to bring their fundamental conceptions (or it may be assumptions) under the microscope of philosophical, subjective, or metaphysical analysis, attempting neither their application in detail, nor even an enumeration of the more specialised branches of practice in which they may be exemplified. To do more than this would carry me beyond the limits of a general treatise on the whole range of philosophy. But to do thus much is indispensable, since without it not only would the whole analysis of redintegration be a mere matter of meaningless curiosity, meaningless at least for philosophy, but also the practical sciences themselves would be cut off from their roots in immediate experience, and fall an easy prey to the assumptions of a random empiricism.

It might perhaps be expected, that the necessity for this treatment would be more readily admitted in the case of the practical than of the positive sciences, seeing that the practical determination of all action rests on an estimate of the comparative value of motives, ends, feelings, or ideas, and that all value is confessedly something essentially subjective, in the sense that it is ultimately and in itself a phenomenon of consciousness alone, that is, of objective thought as distinguished from objects thought of, as the preceding Chapter made evident. Nevertheless, the prevalent treatment both of Ethic and Logic is empirical, quite as much as that of Physics or Psychology. I mean, that the idea is seldom if ever entertained, of bringing the phenomena upon which those sciences are built into connection and comparison with their own context, and considering them as parts of the whole panorama of objective thought as actually experienced. For Ethic and Logic are usually regarded by their professors as sciences which are already constituted on a traditional basis; and this leads naturally to the phenomena which belong to them being disconnected from their own context, and brought into connection, instead, with the objects defined and dealt with by the science as traditionally constituted, and in the same shape and manner as that tradition enjoins. The truth really is, that the sciences themselves can only be properly constituted on the basis of considering the phenomena in their own context, that is to say, as parts of the whole panorama of experience subjectively analysed. At least, until that has been done, the basis or group of conceptions which are fundamental to these sciences, as to others, remains entirely provisional.

The phenomena which belong to Ethic and Logic, and consequently to the practical sciences generally, assume a very different appearance according as they are seen in their own light, or in the light of quasi-scientific assumptions or hypotheses. By the first I mean what I have just called seeing them in their own context, as parts of an immediately experienced and immediately analysable experience, which in other words is taking them as part of the total object-matter of Metaphysic. By the second I mean regarding them as they are necessarily regarded in Psychology, that is, as dependent concomitants of the actions of conscious beings, without previous analysis (and this is the important point) of what they are as parts of the panorama of knowing, and without distinguishing their nature as experiences from their genesis as existents. To take them in this latter way is tacitly to substitute conscious beings for consciousness as the true and ultimate object-matter of the sciences in question, the analysis of which, and not the analysis of consciousness, then determines their constitutive conceptions. For we thereby read the conception of a conscious being into every single analysis which we make, and subordinate all its results to that single conception, which is not an ultimate fact or datum of experience, instead of subordinating that conception itself to the results of analysis without assumptions. By this method we necessarily confine ourselves to giving a common-sense description of the phenomena of consciousness, and bar the road, not only to metaphysical analysis, but to an analytical psychology also, inasmuch as the common-sense conception of a conscious being is taken as the basis of all our explanations, a basis into the true analysis of which we never dream of enquiring.

But if in Logic I thus subordinate the ultimate laws of thought to the real existence of the conscious being who thinks by means of them, I rob them of their universal validity and applicability, since I then regard them merely as ways in which that particular being has been determined to think, in consequence of his particular constitution, history, and development, which might all have been different, and so might have produced a different particular being in his stead. The ultimate laws of thought have an universal and necessary validity because they are essential elements in literally all systematised knowing (and therefore in our conception of a particular being), which systematised knowing is part of consciousness as the subjective aspect of all things; and not because they belong to consciousness as an existent among existents. These two aspects of consciousness were clearly distinguished in both the foregoing Books, and the distinction shown to be both fundamental and unavoidable in philosophy. But these laws of thought, which are formulated subsequently by Logic, govern all thought, and therefore all philosophy and science, so far as these are modes of thinking; and in this way determine our knowledge, so far as it is gained by thinking, of all objects and all existence whatever. To suppose them dependent for their nature on the constitution of particular existents is a self-contradictory notion, since they are thereby conceived as contingent and necessary at once, and in the same respect.

Whoever supposes them so dependent is thereby affecting or assuming to conceive the possibility of other ways of thinking than those governed by what we call the ultimate laws of thought, and of beings who think in some of those other ways.

But both these assumed possibilities are sheer impossibilities, that is, cannot be conceived at all. I can conceive the possibility of other modes of perception than those of time and space, and of other kinds of sentience than those which human beings are endowed with. But just as I cannot conceive myself, or any one else, conscious, and yet not conscious in and for some duration of time, so I cannot conceive myself or others thinking, and yet not thinking in the way formulated by logicians as the laws of Identity, Contradiction, and Excluded Middle. Nor can I frame the thought of any being who can either think in any other way, or avoid being thought of in this way, if he is thought of at all. The connection of consciousness with time-duration, and of thinking with the laws of thought, are instances of inseparable connections, to which there are literally no alternatives. In both cases, take away either element of the union, and the unit into which it enters as a constituent disappears. The idea, therefore, that the nature of the ultimate laws of thought depends upon the constitution of particular beings, who might conceivably have been constituted differently, is a chimera.

Similarly in Ethic, if I subordinate the individual's estimate of the comparative value of his states of consciousness to the fact, that he is one conscious being among others, or even that he is a conscious being at all, I put the idea of a conscious being, which in physiological psychology is an organism, into the place of the ultimate End, τελειότατον τέλος, of all conscious action, and thereby vitiate beforehand the results of my ethical analysis of consciousness, by carelessly assuming a foregone conclusion. The law of self-preservation in organisms may be an ultimate law of nature, as the expression of a tendency physically essential to every organic structure. But from this it by no means follows, that the precept of self-preservation is an ultimate law in morals.

It seems, then, that, by pursuing any method but that of metaphysical analysis, the results both of Ethical and Logical theory are dictated beforehand, and those sciences consequently rendered futile, since they cannot possibly avoid reproducing in their conclusions the same conceptions which have been tacitly involved in their premisses. On the other hand, in pursuing the method of metaphysical analysis, it will, I think, become evident, both that logical laws have deeper roots in experience than the conception of substance, or even of a thinking agency, conceptions which, on the contrary, their presence is requisite to attain, and that the ethical estimate of values has roots deeper than the conception of conscious beings, or organisms, for the attainment of which conception the presence of those deeper roots is similarly a pre-requisite. We think logically before we form the conception of things or agents; we think ethically before we form the conception of persons.

The outlines of the task before us in Book III. are thus in a measure traced for us. We have to analyse, compare, and marshal the states and processes of consciousness belonging to the whole domain of Redintegration, until they disclose to us the nature and method of conscious action, and thereby enable us to establish the fundamental conceptions and principles of Ethic and of Logic, which together cover its entire field. As the positive sciences were in some sort the goal of the analysis in Book I., so the practical sciences will be in some sort the goal of our present analysis. And as there we found that it was not necessary to take stock of every kind of sensation, but could without detriment to our general purpose omit the examination of several, as, for instance, of the whole class of internal, systemic, or bodily sensations, and consider them as covered by the reasoning applied to selected instances of sensations which were not definitely presented as extended, or which in other words were perceived as having only duration, change, and succession, and so as occupying time without themselves occupying space, so a similar freedom will be permissible here. It will not be necessary to pass in review the whole catalogue of images, conceptions, emotions, and passions, which are the phenomena, or rather the content, peculiar to redintegrative processes both spontaneous and voluntary, or to attempt to define emotions and passions in detail by reference to the particular representations, images, or conceptions, with which they are normally combined. The laws, not the full content, of redintegrations are here our primary object, and these will emerge with sufficient clearness from an analysis of processes which, though always experienced in some particular content or material, are yet unaffected by the particular content or material which from time to time is their embodiment or vehicle. In selecting particular emotions or imagery, therefore, for analysis, our choice must be guided by the light they may seem capable of throwing upon the principles and methods of the redintegrative process.

§ 1. General scope of Book III.

By this method we shall, I think, be enabled to form some definite idea of the range and power of human capacities, as well as of the nature and limits of the knowledge which is within their reach; and we shall moreover thereby be laying the analytical foundations for an answer to the questions which will meet us in the fourth and last Book, devoted to what may be called the Constructive Branch of philosophy. We shall at the same time be completing, on the same lines and principles of method, the analytical enquiry on which we entered at the outset of Book I. There it was found, that conscious experience was given only in form of a process, the process of reflective perception. But at first we had no other clue to guide us in our attempt to analyse the content or tissue of which that process was composed, than to begin with the simplest, and go on to examine more and more complex moments of it. Again, we had at first starting no reason to give, why consciousness was experienced only as a process. There was nothing before us but the simple fact that it was so. But when the examination had led us to perceive that certain of the phenomena formed groups of objective thought, corresponding to and representing objects more or less permanent, which together composed a world of material things, and interacted one with another in what we called an order of real conditioning, distinct from the process of objective thought or consciousness simply, we thenceforward had a clue to explain the fact of process in consciousness simply.

That is to say, we had a repetition of the phenomenon in a modified form, we had the fact of another process disclosed by the analysis itself, with which we could bring the originally observed fact of process in consciousness into connection, and exhibit the two together as a constantly exemplified harmony between different parts, and different kinds of facts, included in our total experience. And the real conditioning of the process of consciousness being thus discovered, consciousness itself assumed a second character. To its former character of a process in time, which was continually objectifying itself in acts or moments of reflective perception, there was added the new character of being a real existent, conditioned upon material processes, taking place partly beyond and partly within the organism of a conscious being.

Now, of these material processes, those which are within the neural system are constantly going on, and it is upon one great class of them that redintegration depends. For redintegration, as we have seen, is the name for all states and processes of consciousness, which are supported by those among the neural processes which are not directly and solely set up by the action of stimuli coming from beyond the neural system. In fact, the only phenomena of consciousness excluded from redintegration are sense-perceptions in actual presentation. From the moment when any of these cease to be actually presented, their reproduction is a fact of redintegration, and depends on the processes which support it. But these processes, like the organs in which they take place, are functionally continuous with the organs and processes which support sense-presentations; so that not only are the latter the original source of the ideas which represent them in redintegration, but also the reproduction of these ideas is liable to be stimulated afresh by new sense-presentations of the same or similar nature. In this way, sense-presentations govern representations or ideas, and to this extent *nihil in intellectu quod non prius in sensu* is true. What is added in redintegration consists (1) of emotions (including desires, sentiments, and passions) arising in combination with the represented imagery, and (2) of spontaneous and voluntary modes of ordering the redintegrative content, the voluntary mode being attended and evidenced by a feeling which must be classed as a feeling of effort or tension; whether this content of redintegration is taken, in given instances, as composed of emotions, or imagery, or both in union. Of these, emotions, passions, spontaneously arising desires, and spontaneous associations, must be included in the *sensus* of the above dictum, if we draw a sharply defined line between its *sensus* and its *intellectus*. But the truth is, that voluntary modes of ordering the redintegrative content, as well as the emotions, passions, and spontaneous desires and associations arising therein, are really conditioned upon the nature and working of the neuro-cerebral mechanism, or rather of those parts and processes of it which immediately support redintegrations. And these parts and processes are not only open to modification by stimuli subserving presentations from without the body, but are also in connection with the extra-neural tissues of the organism, to many of which they can also convey stimuli by efferent neural action.

In thus defining the nature and range of the enquiry which lies before us, I wish to leave entirely apart the question, whether the redintegrative neural organism is not also susceptible of impressions coming directly from without, but not through the nerve channels which normally subserve sensation either systemic or special. Its being so susceptible would mean, that it would be like a sense-organ in receiving original presentations, but that, unlike a sense-organ, the presentations which it received might have either the quality of what we now call representations as distinguished from sense-presentations, or that of sense-presentations, in case the central terminations of sense-organs were affected. It would, in short, be immediately perceptive, or, as some would call it, *intuitive*, of images or ideas conveyed to it from without, not fashioned by its own reproduction of sense-presentations. Such a susceptibility would supply a ready hypothesis, on which to build an explanation of the real or supposed phenomena of thought-transference and clairvoyance. A physical medium for such perceptions and communications is already at hand in the all-pervading ether, which is commonly assumed as the vehicle of light, radiant heat, electricity, and magnetism.

I confess I see no inconceivability or inherent impossibility in the hypothesis of there being such a susceptibility in the redintegrative neural organism, or such a vehicle of perceptions, and medium of communication between one brain and another. If the ether-vibrations are rightly assumed to act on nerve, it must be held on physical grounds, that nerve matter is capable of re-acting on the ether. And if such a re-action takes place in one specially constituted nerve organ, the eye for instance, an analogous re-action may conceivably take place, under other special conditions, in other nerve organs. Moreover, it seems to be generally admitted, that physical influences are transmissible, without immediate contact, from one organism to another, by which the states and processes of the recipient organism are powerfully affected. The question, then, relates not to the transmission of a physical influence, but to the possibility of definite states or processes of consciousness accompanying the influence. Can the redintegrative nerve organism receive impressions attended with consciousness, either from similar organisms (which is the case of thought-transference), or from objects and events generally (which is the case of clairvoyance), independently of the ordinary channels of sense-presentation? Supposing the reality of thought-transference established, and its principal laws and processes ascertained, it is readily conceivable that it would offer a means of explaining many cases, not only of apparent clairvoyance, but also of apparent prevision and prediction of future events.

At the same time it must be remarked, that the whole question of the susceptibility of the redintegrative organism to impressions coming immediately from without, upon which so many minor questions depend, is one which awaits solution on purely scientific grounds, and by purely scientific methods. None of them are questions which can be settled by the subjective analysis of metaphysical philosophy. It is for science in the first place to ascertain the facts experimentally, and then to frame hypotheses and theories accounting for whatever facts may be so ascertained. The task indeed has been already undertaken by many members of the medical profession who have facility of access to large numbers of cases of abnormal mental working, more especially in France, and who have added the new domain of Hypnotism to the previously recognised departments of medical science. These men are of necessity dealing directly with the fundamental question, the susceptibilities of the redintegrative mechanism. But the subject has also been approached, on the side of phenomena apparently belonging to it, which are more popularly striking, as well as open to all investigators, both by individuals and by Societies formed, like the Society for Psychical Research in this country, for the express purpose of investigating all such phenomena. Whatever may be the results finally arrived at, by either class of investigators, some definite conclusions will certainly be reached; success in one direction or in another will assuredly crown the patient and zealous labours of their scientifically prosecuted task. It may be that a new and definite tract will be added to the dominion of psychology, of which the metaphysician of the future will have to take detailed account in attempting his *rationale* of experience.

§ 2. We return, then, to our analysis of the stream of consciousness, the process of objective thought as distinguished from objects thought of as material or as real conditions, at the same time taking the term *thought* in a wide sense, to cover spontaneous as well as volitional elements. And this stream of objective thought we must again suppose ourselves to experience in successively present moments of reflective perception, which is in fact the case, as was sufficiently shown by the analysis given in Book I., where the whole process of reflective perception, including sense-presentations and representations together, was repeatedly described, and instances of it examined.

We have yet another restriction to make in order to bring our special *analysandum* distinctly before us; we must abstract from its sense-presentations. We have to analyse the stream of objective thought *minus* its sense-presentations, though *not minus* the ideas or images which represent them, and also, as already said, *plus* the emotions, desires, sentiments, and passions, which accompany the representation. In other words, our *analysandum* is the whole panorama of objective thought, its meaning, and its value, compared and connected with the two things which we exclude from it for the purpose of analysis, sense-presentations on the one side, and material objects thought of on the other, by both of which in fact it is, in different ways, created and controlled.

A. The field being so wide, we must necessarily begin our analysis by general considerations. And in the first place, where do we draw the line between sense-presentation and redintegration or representation? The line is clear enough in theory, though often difficult to apply in practice. We do not say that a sense-presentation has become a representation or belongs to a redintegrative

BOOK III. CH. I.
§ 2.
Some leading characteristics of redintegration.
A. Line of demarcation between presentation and representation.

process, until it has once at least actually faded from consciousness and has been revived in consciousness again. Its revival is its representation or redintegration. So much is clear in theory. But now take a simple case. Suppose we hear some one recite the couplet:

"Achilles' wrath, to Greece the direful spring
Of woes unnumber'd, heavenly Goddess, sing!"

By the time we hear the word *sing* at the end of the second line, has or has not the word *spring* at the end of the first ceased to be presented, and is or is not the perception of the rhyme due to a redintegration of it? *Spring* has certainly faded from its first vividness, but can it be said to have sunk completely below the threshold of consciousness, when *sing* strikes upon the ear? Different people will perhaps decide this question differently. I bring forward the instance to show (1) that in the simplest cases, when tested by minute experiences, the difference between presentation and representation is a difference of degree not of kind, and (2) that the transition from one to the other is continuous, the same, or parts of the same, neural organ being employed in both cases, and retaining an impression from the presentation which is revivable by means of a similar impression in a slightly altered context.

The phenomenon thus brought before us is the same which we met with when analysing the process of reflective perception in Book I. A presented sensation begins to recede into the past of memory from the very moment of its rising into consciousness, or appearing above the threshold. I do not say merely from the moment of its attaining its maximum of vividness as a presentation, but from that of its rising into consciousness at all, prior, it may be, to its greatest vividness being reached. This is saying in other words, that representation is included as an inseparable element, or ingredient, in all presentation. The nerve process which subserves presentation preserves the impress of the stimulus which originates it; and the consciousness which attends it, being likewise a process, preserves the likeness of its first presented moment. In this sense all perception whatever is redintegration, simply because it is a process; and in this sense representation is one undivided half or aspect of presentative perception; and it was with this sense of the terms that we were chiefly concerned in the analysis of Book I.—It must be noted that redintegration or representation as here described is not the same phenomenon as that which is well known under the name of "after images." These are a particular case of redintegration, the case in which the representation is confined to that part of the whole organ which is immediately exposed to the action of an external stimulus. These after images and their sequences are also represented in redintegration, just as if they were original presentations.

But it is clear that this is not the sense in which the distinction between presentation on the one hand, redintegration and representation on the other, can now be taken, if it is to be of service to us in the present Book. What we want is a distinction which shall serve also as a division between the phenomena under discussion, so as to enable us to isolate one of them for analysis.

Book III. Ch. I.

§ 2. Some leading characteristics of redintegration.

A. Line of demarcation between presentation and representation.

§ 2. Some leading characteristics of redintegration.

A. Line of demarcation between presentation and representation.

We want to include one without the other in our *analysandum*, while at the same time keeping in view the connection between them. I shall therefore adopt the clear theoretical distinction above stated, and apply the terms *redintegration* and *representation* to those cases only where a presentative sense-perception has, or is assumed to have, previously faded away below the threshold of consciousness, and then to have been subsequently revived or recalled into consciousness again. For the intermediate state interposing between the fading and the renewal, the terms *retention, retentiveness*, and (if the coinage may be permitted) *retent*, may be used. It is of course implied that this intermediate state is not one of consciousness.[1] The nerve mechanism belonging to it is functioning, so to speak, below the threshold. Retentiveness, retention, and retents belong to it; but the retents are no part of consciousness, though the names by which alone we can speak of them are terms of consciousness, terms which describe them either as presentations or as representations, that is, as concomitants of nerve processes above the threshold. By these distinctions we shall at any rate know precisely what phenomena it is intended to speak of, and shall be able to hold sense-presentations and retents apart from the special object of our analysis, which is to include representations and redintegrations only.

Perhaps to avoid misconception the fact should again be noticed, that neither a presentation nor

---

[1] Very different from the "memory as mere retentiveness," and from the "retained presentation," of the earlier Chapters of Book I. See more particularly, on the present subject, Book I. Chap. III. § 3, *Memory Proper*, including its *Digression to Real Conditioning.*

a representation is ever strictly speaking recalled or reproduced; but that, when these or similar terms are employed, their meaning is that, in a new context, a content of consciousness is called up, which more or less exactly resembles another content in a different context, both of these resembling contents, with their contexts, being recognised by the Subject as former and latter parts of his own single chain or panorama of experience.

§ 2. Some leading characteristics of redintegration.

B. In the next place let us see what we are doing, and why, in excluding sense-presentations from our special *analysandum*. To many it may seem an arbitrary mutilation of the phenomena as actually experienced. On the one hand we never have waking experience, and perhaps not even the experience of dreams, without the constant presence and immixture of sense-presentations. And on the other, to abstract from sense-presentations in experience is to leave the remainder fragmentary, inexplicable, and incapable of coherence. This is quite true. But the answer is, that it is not with the fabric of existing knowledge and ideas as a whole, including its inferred objects, that we are now concerned, but with the processes of consciousness which are employed partly in building it up, and partly in realising ideal purposes of our own, on the basis partly of sense-perceptions, and partly of needs and feelings originating in the Subject. It is not an analysis, nor a history, nor any sort of theory, of the structure and progress of already existing knowledge that we have in view. It is an analysis of what are called the Subject's powers of

B. The blanks in pure redintegration.

Thinking, Willing, and Feeling, which we want to arrive at. Knowledge is one thing, Thought is another. The confusion between these two things has ruined more than one ambitious system of philosophy. Thought includes both Being and Not-being, in virtue of its own principle of movement, while Knowledge is of Being alone; for all knowledge of Not-being is a knowledge of it only as a determination within thought objective to itself in reflection, and not as an existent object thought of, contradistinguished from thought in its entirety as a mode of consciousness. If a theory of knowledge as it now exists were our aim, or if we were pursuing any of the positive or of the practical sciences as at present constituted, or even if we were occupied with Epistemology or the Theory of Knowledge in its widest sense, supposing it to start, as in fact it does, by assuming the distinction between Subject and Object as an originally known fact, the case would be different. But since we are occupied with Philosophy, that is, with the knowledge of experience or consciousness in its whole extent, and start by analysing it without assumptions of any kind,—a knowledge which doubtless will include Epistemology or the Theory of Knowledge in its proper place, that is, when the true distinction between Subject and Object has been determined by analysis,—our course must proceed on different lines. Accordingly, since a knowledge of consciousness in its whole extent,—which, as the first steps in analysis have shown, is knowledge of it as the subjective aspect of Being in its entirety, —is the aim and purpose of the whole present work; since we are therefore concerned with the possibilities, conceivabilities, and inconceivabilities, of existence generally; and since we have in Book I. analysed sense-presentations so far as to see how they contribute to our knowledge of external realities, and among them of Subjects themselves as real conditions; it seems consonant to reason, that we should now abstract from sense-presentations and from their real conditions, in the analysis which is the basis of the remaining portion of the enquiry, that is, in analysing the processes of thinking, feeling, and willing, dependent on real powers and capacities in the Subject, which our analysis has already disclosed to us. For by so doing we bring before ourselves that remaining portion of experience in the very form and shape in which it is actually experienced, notwithstanding that, in order to do so, we take it out of the context of an already constructed system of knowledge, admitted to be a knowledge of reality, whether that system takes the shape of science, or is the ordinary common-sense view of persons and things.

In thus abstracting from sense-presentations, material objects, and real conditions, we are by no means dismissing them from our purview altogether; on the contrary it is intended always to indicate their place and connection in the whole panorama of objective thought, the redintegrative parts of which are our special object of analysis. The whole panorama of objective thought, as experienced in the series of successively present moments of reflective perception, is what we have before us, with the intention of analysing those

BOOK III.
CH. I.

§ 2.
Some leading characteristics of redintegration.

B.
The blanks in pure redintegration.

parts of it which consist of redintegrations, marking as blanks, not now to be analysed, those parts which are occupied either by sense-presentations, or by the inferred presence of real objects thought of, so far as they are founded on sense-presentations, or by nerve processes which we here and now have reason to know of, but which are not included in the consciousness which they are actually conditioning. Nerve processes, in fact, are excluded from our *analysandum* simply as real conditions, whether they are attended by consciousness or not, but include only what I have now called retents.

At the same time the connection between the blanks and the *analysanda* so defined is to be studiously kept in view. As already said, it is the real existence of what we now call blanks which alone renders intelligible the existence of the *analysanda*, and preserves their coherence as parts of the Subject's total panorama. Objective thought, as we have seen, contains the whole of the evidence we have for the nature and existence of any reality whatever. Those parts in it which I have now called blanks, taken together, constitute what is commonly called the real world; those which I have singled out as *analysanda* constitute that moving picture which sometimes goes under the name of subjective thought and imagination. And of these two halves of the total process-panorama of experience, the blanks and the *analysanda*, the real world and the subjective picture, the latter is plainly, as a whole, representative of the former as a whole; it is the process of consciousness in and by which the whole of the real world, considered as an existent reality, whatever it may contain in detail, is brought into immediate connection, not as before with presentative, but with representative and intellectual knowledge. The blanks do not cease to be our object by our selecting for analysis the process by which they are passed and repassed before us in review. Only it is with the process as a process that we are now concerned, and with its content as belonging to the process, instead of to the objects which the process represents.

C. Coming, then, to the process which has now been definitely brought before us as our immediate object, the first thing to be noted is its relation to its content. Since this content is representative of reality, it is plain that the process is a panoramic picture as well as a process. It is a panoramic picture, which has duration in time, while its parts are subject to perpetual change; so that the successive moments of its duration may be marked by means of the successive configurations of its parts. Regarded from any present moment, or moment of actual experience, the process seems to be ever being left behind, or receding into the past of memory, carrying with it successive planes or transverse sections of its content, distinguished by means of their respective configurations. At the same time it seems also to be advancing into the unknown future, the content of which is given only in whatever imaginations may be projected from the receding past. The content again, seen from any of the same successive present moments, appears to extend without limit in all directions of space, the directions being measured from a common centre, which we may define as that point of space within the content itself, from which the remainder of it appears to be viewed at any given present moment of time. Normally, of course, this central point will appear to be located in the body of the Subject, which will normally be represented as the central object of the panorama. The content always has duration, which is its existence in time; and the process always has spatial extension, at least for beings endowed with sight and touch, which is its existence in space. Time and Space are thus the two fundamental forms in which all our conscious experience is cast; and of these Time is the most indispensable, since no perception can be imagined without duration, and none is experienced which is not a process. Time is the ultimate nexus of all phenomena whatever, first of those which have duration or duration and succession only, and secondly between these and those which are the special content of the spatial panorama.

The words *at least for beings endowed with sight and touch* may serve to show the dependence of the process-content of redintegration upon sense-presentation. From the point of view of Thought we can imagine beings without these senses, and then should find it difficult to conceive their having experience of anything spatially extended. At the same time, for beings who have them, the reason becomes evident, why their redintegrations normally tend to assume a pictorial shape, and consequently why we throw whatever we try to think of accurately into forms borrowed from space; as for instance when we represent time, and the phenomena which occupy time alone, under the image of a line or stream having direction in space. The reason is two-fold; first, because the form of space as given in visual sense-perception enables us to relate an indefinitely great number of different phenomena to each other in a single moment of consciousness, and secondly, because, owing to the close combination of sight with touch, in the perception of those real existents which are also real conditions, all the phenomena, whatever they may be, which we relate to one another under the form of space, are thereby brought also into a thought-relation to the world of reality.

In this way we construct for ourselves a *mundus intelligibilis*, or thought-world, out of the phenomena of objective thought, phenomena which have passed into objective thought from sense-presentation, sense-presentations being one of the two kinds of *blanks* above spoken of in our immediate object of analysis. And again, through and out of this thought-world have passed, after verification by means of sense-presentation, all those real objects thought of, which by inference have taken their place for us in the world of reality, as at once real existents and real conditions, which were our *blanks* of the second kind. That is to say, we thenceforward think of these inferred and verified objects as having an existence independent of the process of thought, by which our knowledge of them has been acquired.

Moreover we can keep our hold on these objects, so as to reason about them as realities, by associating them either with general names and defini-

BOOK III.
CH. I.

§ 2.
Some leading characteristics of redintegration.

C.
Time and Space the fundamental forms of the world of objective thought.

tions, or with mathematical symbols, the latter of which enable us to deal with them as individual existents, individualised by their time and space relations both *ad intra* and *ad extra*, with infinitesimal minuteness, yet without employing any figurative imagination in the reasoning process; since we have in the names or in the symbols, attached to them by association, the sure means of recalling them into figurative thought again, and as it were retranslating the symbols into the things which by association they were made to symbolise. It is a *sine qua non* condition of the truth of any conclusion reached by either of these symbolic methods, logical and mathematical, that the phrase or symbol expressing that conclusion should be retranslateable into figurative imagery, or in other words, construable to thought. If not so construable, it is said to have become *imaginary*, and its meaning *unreal*. This connection of names and symbols with the imagery or content of redintegration is the link between the reasoning of formal logic on the one hand, and mathematical reasoning, which is calculation, in its whole extent, on the other, with the figurative reasoning of ordinary life, which is the originally inseparable attendant on redintegrative processes. I am, of course, far from intending to suggest, that it is only to verified realities that this use of names and symbols is applicable. On the contrary, since it is their character of being objects thought of which makes it applicable to them, it is plain that it may be applied to any object thought of, whether real or only imaginary, which we may think it worth while, or may be compelled by the process itself, to express by name, definition, or symbol. The whole ground of redintegration, its whole content, both real and unreal, is thus covered alike by logical and by mathematical processes.

The *mundus intelligibilis* or thought-world, on the other hand, which we build out of the phenomena of objective thought, taking it apart from these systems of symbolism, logical and mathematical, and containing the unfilled *blanks* which we have spoken of, is thus a world of provisional images, conceptions, and hypotheses, framed on the lines of sense-presentations and their forms of time and space, and awaiting, in some cases the verification afforded by sense-presentations, in others the concrete filling up of its abstract skeletons by either presented or represented details, in others the *fiat* of decisive volitions. It is a world within, or perhaps I should say beyond, the world of reality; a world of possibilities and conceivabilities, which are actual as thoughts, but not yet known to be actual as things. Yet this same world it is, which is the only world immediately present to, immediately experienced by, man considered as a rational, that is, an active, thinking, and emotional being; the only world which in consciousness is immediate to thought and will; the world through which alone he has coherent *knowledge*, in the complete sense, of any reality whatever.

The proof that the world to which this coherent knowledge relates is indeed a reality, in the full sense of the term, consists in the fact, that representations may be called up in the Subject, which are not strictly speaking memories, that is, simple reproductions of any part of his own prior experience, but yet are of a nature to be verified by sense-presentations, and refer to objects, the non-existence of which would be incompatible with the previously verified and ascertained facts of his own simply rememberable experience. Such representations, which are most properly to be called verifiable imaginations, constitute a domain additional to that of memory proper, a domain which completes the whole panorama of real existence, so far as it is positively known or knowable. These imaginations may be called up in various ways, for instance by way of testimony, as when we accept the narratives of travellers, or the evidence of historical documents, or by way of reasoning or calculation, as when an astronomer imagines the real existence of a planet till then unobserved, in consequence of observed perturbations in other bodies which are not otherwise to be accounted for. The late Professor Tyndall's name should ever be held in honour, for his clear and repeated recognition of the place occupied by the imagination in science, and the indispensable function which it performs therein.

The fact of verifiability is alone sufficient to warrant the unhesitating acceptance of the reality of the world to which the objects of such representations belong, and in philosophical, as well as in ordinary thinking, has usually been held to be so. I say *verifiability* not verification, because the verification of one clearly conceived object implies the verifiability of all objects similarly conceived, the verification of which has not been shown to be impossible, and therefore of a world, be its other objects what they may, to which that single verified object belongs. But the final link which completes, or rather the final circumstance which rivets, the proof of that reality is given, for the Subject, by the scientific discovery of the physiological organs and processes, on which those imaginations are proximately conditioned, I mean the neuro-cerebral mechanism supporting redintegration or association of ideas. For, on the one hand, this knowledge of the proximate real conditions of his consciousness places the Subject's verifiable imaginations on the same footing, for him, as memories proper, and memories proper on the same footing, for him, as memories in the sense of simply retained presentations, by exhibiting all alike as cases of redintegration, with or without association of sensations of different kinds; and on the other, it is knowledge of an object, the non-existence of which would be incompatible with his originally ascertained knowledge of the real existence of his own organism, which, with all which it may be found to include, has become known to him simultaneously with the real material world, of which it is (to him) the constant central object,—the knowledge of both objects alike having been originally acquired by experiences which lie within the limits of memory in the sense of simple retention of presentations, though presentations disparate in point of kind, as was duly set forth in the analysis of our perception of an external world, in Book I. In short, the fact of the co-existence of immediate visual and tactual perceptions, which, when attended to, constitutes an individual's experience of his own body in contact with other real bodies, is now explained by the further knowledge, derived from that experience,

Book III. Ch. I.

§ 2. Some leading characteristics of redintegration.

C. Time and Space the fundamental forms of the world of objective thought.

§ 2.
Some leading characteristics of redintegration.

D. The emotional content of objective thought.

of the relations of real conditioning in which these bodies, and their parts, stand and have stood to one another, prior to the arising of the immediate perceptions which they condition, in which immediate perceptions his whole knowledge originates.

D. Coming yet nearer to the content of the redintegrative process of objective thought, another general characteristic strikes us, I mean its emotional character. As a rule, sense-presentations are more vivid than their representations; the pain or the pleasure of them more keen; the contrasts more trenchant; the forms more distinct; the outlines more clear. On the other hand their representations acquire or develop in redintegration quite new characteristics. Pain and pleasure of sense are exchanged respectively in representation for grief and joy, aversion and fondness, fear and hope, repugnance and desire; while their character as pain or pleasure of sense becomes part of the imagery, as distinguished from the emotional element, of the representations. The representations lose their sensational pain or pleasure, and acquire pain or pleasure of an emotional character. The emotional feeling pervades and colours the representational image, of which a representation of sensational pain or pleasure has now become a part. The image becomes, as it were, the framework of an emotion, and the whole formed by the two elements, imagery and emotion together, may be spoken of by either name; just as we found in earlier Chapters, that one and the same state of consciousness might be called both a sensation and a perception, according to the context in which we happened to be considering it.

Emotions and passions, including the pain or pleasure peculiar to them, are in fact the material element in redintegration, and an element inseparable from the representations or imagery of the redintegration; just as the qualities of sensations, including their peculiar pains and pleasures of sense, were the inseparable material element of sense-presentations, as set forth in the analysis of Book I.

§ 2. Some leading characteristics of redintegration.

D. The emotional content of objective thought.

Pain and pleasure of sensation and pain and pleasure of emotion are two very different kinds of pain and pleasure, notwithstanding that the latter has one of its roots in the former. We must, however, distinguish those cases of pain and pleasure, in which they seem to hold an intermediate position, and to belong wholly to redintegration, though not being pains or pleasures of emotion. I mean cases of the simple redintegration of pains or pleasures of sense, spoken of above, in which they make part of the imagery only of the representation, leaving it for the moment wholly free from any emotional colouring derived directly from sense, and in which they are experienced simply as facts which are indifferent to the percipient, while the representation which images them takes its own emotional content from the connection in which it stands to other representations or imagery contained in the redintegration. The conditions of having such a detached or indifferent experience as the bare representation of pain or pleasure of sense we need not now consider. It is sufficient here to have shown the place which it occupies in the redintegrative content.

Returning to the contrast between pleasures and pains of sense and those of emotion, it is plain that both kinds are general classes, each of which includes a great number of species. The species of those of sense are at least as numerous as the different bodily organs in which they have their origin; and the varieties under each species as numerous as the several distinct modes in which those organs can be affected. The varieties of distinguishable pains are far more numerous, and the intensity of which some of them are capable is far greater, than those of distinguishable pleasures. In attempting a classification of pleasures and pains of sense, there is no other ultimate standard to which our classification must conform, than the specific characters of the individual sensations themselves.

But the case is different, when we pass to the emotions which in redintegration pervade and colour the representations of them. Here the specific characters of the sensations represented are weakened, and their general characters, in which they resemble one another, become consequently more prominent. In representation attended by emotion we no longer distinguish the specific sensational character of pains and pleasures of sense. We have, for instance, no name appropriated to the emotional pain arising from the representation of a toothache, or for the emotional pleasure arising from the representation of satisfying hunger. In redintegration the two ultimate genera of pain and pleasure alone remain. These in redintegration are the two fundamental emotions of grief and joy; and the species and varieties of feeling which those great genera contain under them are distinguished by quite other characteristics than these belonging to the primary specific sensations out of which they arose.

The reason is, that they are now governed by the fact that they belong to a redintegrative process, that is, depend on nerve functions which are only indirectly dependent on external stimuli, and which, in their re-actions upon impressions from without, exercise a partially collective and independent power. Moreover the fact, that redintegration is a process, is a fact of primary importance in grouping the emotional content of its representations or imagery. Putting aside for the present the emotions, if any, which may under certain conditions be developed out of what I have called above the detached or indifferent representations of pleasures and pains of sense, all other emotions seem to pre-suppose, and to be more or less remote modifications of, the two fundamental and primary emotions of joy and grief. The contrasted nerve processes, which we must conceive as respectively supporting and conditioning these two fundamental modes of emotion, date back to a very early period of evolution, both in individuals and in the race; a period co-eval with the evolution of the redintegrative process itself. The evolution of the emotions must therefore be conceived as proceeding *pari passu* with that of the representational imagery which they pervade, and both together as dependent on the evolution and development, in mass and complexity, of the nerve mechanism, the functioning of which supports redintegration as a process of consciousness.

Grief and joy in their most general and undeveloped state are by no means mere abstractions;

BOOK III.
CH. I.

§ 2.
Some leading characteristics of redintegration.

D.
The emotional content of objective thought.

they are the concrete but rudimentary emotions out of which more specialised emotions have been developed, and which have had an actual existence as rudimentary emotions at the historical commencement of the life of redintegration. At that period they must themselves have been developed out of the earliest pains and pleasures of sense, as these passed into the representational state. True, we now distinguish them only by going through a process of abstraction. This, however, does not preclude but leaves open the possibility, that they may have had an actual historical existence as undeveloped feelings; and their origin from sense-presentations shows that this must have been the case. They are not like such abstractions as triangle in general, neither equilateral, nor isosceles, nor scalene, of which no historical origin can be shown, and which is an abstraction and nothing more. They mark a stage in the historical development of conscious beings, and are the material element, to use this word again as a term of consciousness, out of which later emotional states are composed with modifications.

The first and simplest modifications which they undergo are due to the fact, that redintegration is a process, that is, a change in time from present to future in order of action, and from present to past in order of knowledge. Imagery pervaded by the emotion of grief, and represented as past or present, becomes an object of aversion, that is, the imagery is thenceforward pervaded by the emotion of aversion, a modification of grief. Imagery pervaded by the emotion of joy, and referred to the past or present, similarly becomes an object of fondness. In the same way, imagery pervaded by grief and referred to an uncertain future, that is, imagined as possibly occurring in the future, becomes an object of fear and repugnance; pervaded by joy, an object of hope and desire. To define these modified emotions, aversion, fondness, fear, repugnance, hope, desire, we do not need anything but the fundamental feelings of grief and joy, with their imagery, and the time-relations in which the object of that imagery is represented as standing to the present moment of consciousness. We have their essence as emotions expressed in definitions so framed. It is not requisite that the imagery should be imagery of any particular kind of object rather than another. It suffices that it is imagery which is grievous or joyous simply. Imagery of any or all kinds is covered by the definition, so long as this condition is satisfied. Its more specific character is indifferent to the essence of the emotion. All these emotions, in short, are such as we can conceive arising spontaneously in the very lowliest organisms, without pre-supposing any effort of conscious thought on the part of the percipient, still less any conscious contradistinction, on its part, of itself from surrounding agents.

§ 3. To complete this preliminary outline of the phenomena of redintegration two general characteristics still remain to be noticed, as well as some of the results which spring from them in determining the stages of its historical evolution. The first is the distinction between the two modes of redintegration, spontaneous and volitional; the second is the distinction between the redintegration

§ 3.
Spontaneous and volitional modes of redintegration.—Representation of primary and of complex objects.

of primary perceptions and that of complex and coherent groups of them, every such group being the representation of a concrete object thought of, whether real or imaginary. Both distinctions are common to the whole range of redintegration, as we know it at the present day. States of spontaneous and of volitional redintegration are found perpetually alternating with each other in every kind of experience; and the same is true of the two kinds of representations which fall under our second distinction, namely, representations of primary and of complex objects.

Nevertheless it is evident on consideration, that the former member of each distinction is in every case the condition of the second, in a way in which it is not in turn conditioned upon it. There is a sense in which spontaneous redintegration conditions volitional, and representation of primary objects conditions that of complex, and never *vice versa*. Unless primary percepts had first been represented, representations of complex objects could never have taken place, since there would have been nothing to combine; and similarly, without the existence of spontaneous redintegrations, volitional would have been impossible, since there would have been nothing to alter or select from.

The phenomena analysed in Book I., when considered in reference to their historical order of occurrence, afford evidence, that the redintegration of primary percepts initiates and therefore precedes their redintegrative combination into complex objects, that is, complex percepts having more or less permanence, or similarity in their recurrences;

and also that spontaneous redintegration initiates and therefore precedes volitional in the same way, though the length of time occupied by the preceding and separate existence of the primary and spontaneous processes severally is not thereby determined. For unless this was the original and continuing order, or rather more strictly the order of *nature*, in the two pairs of phenomena, (taking *nature* in the metaphysical sense of the term already familiar to us in Book I.), it would be necessary to assume that the conditioning agency in redintegration was that of an immaterial agent capable of giving itself specific primary percepts, for the purpose of realising general ideas, of which it was conscious solely by an effort of its own will. This would be necessary because physiological psychology plainly shows, that sense-presentations retained in representation precede pure representations, and that pure representations precede the actions of purposively attending to them and comparing them ; an order which cannot be reversed without breaking entirely with physiological psychology, and having recourse to an *a priori* psychology, which places the initiation of all sequences of consciousness in some faculty of thinking and willing, imagined to be fully formed *ab initio*.

The question of the order of occurrence of process-contents of consciousness, in all cases where its members are conceived as separable one from another, which is the case in the present instance, are questions which concern the order of real conditioning ; and it is through a consideration of that order that we must pass, if we would ascertain the order of nature (in the metaphysical sense of the

§ 3. Spontaneous and volitional modes of redintegration.—Representation of primary and of complex objects.

term) which holds good in process-contents of that kind. When, accordingly, we put the question of real conditioning to the facts of redintegrative perception, with the view of ascertaining the order in which different classes of them occur; that is, when we bring together such phenomena as were analysed in Book I. and the conclusions as to real conditioning which were reached in Book II.; we find that the only hypothesis which could justify a reversal of the order here maintained, between spontaneous and volitional redintegration and between primary and complex objects, is one which is directly negatived by scientific or physiological psychology, as wholly unthinkable and fictitious.

We are therefore warranted in taking it as proved, that in the original order of occurrence, and consequently throughout the whole history of redintegration, so as to constitute a characteristic of its nature in the metaphysical sense of the term, spontaneous redintegration is the antecedent *sine qua non* condition of volitional, and primary percepts the similar condition of complex percepts or complex objects, in a way in which the two latter members of each distinction are not the antecedent conditions of the two former, notwithstanding that, in the stream of actual experience, we find them constantly alternating with each other. The general result is, that the earliest and conditioning stage in the process and development of redintegration, at all periods in the history of the race, as well as of the individual, is the stage of spontaneous redintegration of primary percepts: and it is in processes of this kind that the foundation for the analysis of redintegration as a whole, and as we now experience it, must be laid.

In speaking as above of spontaneous redintegration as the condition of volitional, and primary as the condition of complex percepts, I mean it, of course, to be understood, that the real conditioning involved belongs to the nerve organism supporting those processes, which are only to be described by terms importing consciousness. The terms *spontaneous* and *volitional*, if they could be taken apart from the implication of consciousness, would then be strictly applicable to neural processes taken alone, supposing that we could know them *per se*, or without having recourse to their conditionate consciousness. My use of them, however, may appear strange to many, though I do not now take them in this sense for the first time. The ordinary usage is, I think, to identify spontaneity with volition. This arises from the prevalence of the traditional notion of an immaterial agency in consciousness; for this agency (being really a fiction) is supposed to act spontaneously, *proprio motu*, or out of its own free-will. Spontaneity and volition, being thus identified, are then alike opposed, both to a supposed passive receptivity on the part of the immaterial Subject, and to those of its actions which are supposed to be determined *ab extra*, that is, by physical and mechanically acting forces. In my use of the terms, on the contrary, which I think is justified by the analysis of Matter given in Book II., they are not identified but opposed; and any process of the nerve organism subserving redintegration, prior to its modification by volition (which is also an action of the nerve organism), is

§ 3. Spontaneous and volitional modes of redintegration.—Representation of primary and complex objects.

spoken of as spontaneous, notwithstanding that its character is chiefly determined by previous impressions which have subserved sense-presentations.

The next point to notice is, that, starting from the foundation of spontaneous redintegration of primary percepts, the supervening of volition, in the shape of attention including desire of new experiences throwing light on present ones, is necessary as the condition of modifying the series of pure representations spontaneously occurring into a series of systematically connected concepts, or of percepts which have passed through and out of a conceptual process; that is, into a train of Thought, in the strict and proper sense of the term, a train into which are taken up, first those primary representations upon which the attention is fixed in the first instance, and secondly those complex objects, or groups of primary representations, whatever they may be, which are formed in consequence of such acts of attention to primary representations. The supervening of this kind of attention, which is volition, upon trains of spontaneous redintegration and the representations of which they consist, is the birth-place of Thought or Thinking in the strict sense. Any representation, simple or complex, in such a train of spontaneous redintegration, upon which volitional attention is so fixed, is thereby modified from a percept into a concept, that is, a percept expectant of new experiences being joined to it; and since these must either be similar to it or dissimilar, it becomes, in respect of those that may be similar, a general or covering percept, expressible by a general name, term, or symbol.

Conception and Thought have at once their nature and their origin in the supervening of volitional attention upon the spontaneous redintegration of percepts.

We have already seen this volitional factor at work in the concrete, that is, in experiences consisting of sense-presentations and redintegrative representations together, in Book I, where it was shown, that without attention to primary percepts for the purpose (as it was there expressed) of knowing more about them, which results in ascertaining their place among, and relations to, the primary percepts which are their original context, we could not arrive at that grouping of them which is known as the perception of material objects, a grouping which furnishes the type on which our conceptions of all real complex objects are constructed. Furthermore it was seen what kind of attention was there required. We saw that attention for the purpose of knowing something more about a given primary percept than is involved in the mere fixation of it, (which, though a re-action, may yet be involuntary),—attention roused by something strange or unexpected in it, attention involving desire of better acquaintance with it, and therefore directed upon it in relation to its context present or expected,—in short, attention of the kind called *selective* in a former Chapter (Book I, Chap. III, § 5), was requisite in order to break up the stream of primary perceptions as it originally occurs, and to group its members, or some of them, into sets corresponding, in objective thought, to real objects thought of, as existing in Nature.

§ 3. Spontaneous and volitional modes of redintegration.—Representation of primary and complex objects.

It is in this way, as we saw in Book I, that our knowledge of ordinary material objects, such as a box or a bell, as well as of our own bodies, is originally acquired. The sense-presentations, and consequently the representations, of the visual and tactual perceptions which constitute our knowledge of any such material object, thought of as the common object of both kinds of perceptions, do not come to us already grouped together and separated from other sense perceptions simultaneously given. We must first attend to them, with reference to their context, before we find out that their grouping together, separately from others, corresponds to a permanent grouping together, in Nature, of the real conditions on which as existent perceptions they depend. At the same time, be it noted, we do not group some of the perceptions together, or separate them from others, for any *a priori* reason of our own, or by means of any clue supplied by a grouping or synthetic faculty. What we do is simply to attend to the simultaneous and closely corresponding changes which take place in the two series of perceptions, visual and tactual, and to the fact that the perceptions occupy one and the same portion of spatial extension at the same time, each new visual perception as it occurs being recognised as similar in kind to the previous visual perceptions, and each new tactual perception the same. The grouping which results, that is, the resulting representation of the remote[1] material object, is nothing more than the perception of a more recondite order in the original series of primary perceptions, repeated

---

[1] *Remote* is the term which I have employed in former works to characterise such concrete material objects as are here spoken of, the real objects of common-sense thought.

in representation, than was evident in it on a first inspection, that is to say, when it existed as a series of spontaneously redintegrated perceptions. It is an order recognised as one which we might have perceived, though we did not, at the very time that we were experiencing the original series of primary perceptions. The act of volitional attention, therefore, in cases like these, results immediately in nothing more than the discovery of facts till then unobserved; but it is an act which is indispensable to the discovery.

Instances taken, like the above, from the process by which knowledge of an external world is originally acquired, are of course instances in which spontaneous representation is not exhibited in isolation, in order to be contrasted with volitional. It is an essential ingredient, but not the whole process. Sense-presentations are going on, as the other ingredient, the whole time. One sense-perception is being represented while another of exactly similar kind is being presented; and sense-presentations are both the foundation of the rest of the process, and the test of truth in the resulting representations. But the relation now exhibited between spontaneous and volitional redintegration is just the same, whether new sense-presentations intervene or not, thus showing that, even in cases where sense-presentations are implicated, the attention, which is volition, has its origin in the redintegrative and not in the presentative part of the process as a whole. So it is, for instance, when I try to recall in thought the precise nature and order of the incidents in an occurrence of yesterday; or when I endeavour to

§ 3. *Spontaneous and volitional modes of redintegration.— Representation of primary and of complex objects.*

bring a particular object or event under a general conception not hitherto applied to it, which is a process involving comparison; or when I try to work out a consistent train of pure thought, to recall adverse instances, frame hypotheses for their explanation or removal, or compare the claims of rival theories. Spontaneous redintegrations here supply the whole material out of which, by means of selective attention, that is, volition for the purpose of knowing something more about that material, my conclusion springs, and of which it is a modification. And the supervening attention is always marked, both in its origin and in its sustentation as a process of volitional redintegration, by a certain feeling of effort, tension, difficulty, or embarrassment, however faint or unnoticed it may be, which is especially the case whenever the interest of the pursuit in hand is great.

It is next to be noticed, that representations thus formed by the aid of volition, whether they are representations of single objects or events, or general conceptions embracing an indefinite plurality of objects, do not necessarily remain volitional, but tend to fall back into the mechanism of spontaneous redintegration, and to recur in consequence as spontaneously reproduced representations, though of a higher degree of complexity than the primaries out of which they were constructed. The stream of spontaneous representations is thus constantly having some of its constituent perceptions modified into volitional representations, and constantly receiving back again into itself volitional representations, of which it was originally the parent. Whenever either a general conception or a complex volitionally formed image becomes practically indissoluble and habitual, it no longer requires an act of attention to discover or to recall. Its structure, place, and times of occurrence, in consciousness, are thenceforth assured by the mechanism of simply spontaneous redintegration. What was once volitional has now become spontaneous, and the stream of consciousness is enriched by the acquisition of a permanent content, as a result of experience.

We see, too, that the distinction between the spontaneous and volitional modes of redintegration is exhaustive. Every redintegration is either the one or the other, or, if its length or its complexity is considerable, contains both, without containing anything which belongs to neither. And this applies to redintegration in its whole history, both in the race and in individuals, including even the commencement of the whole, which as we have seen consists of spontaneous redintegrations only. In other words, the distinction is applicable to every successive stage of evolution, from the simplest and earliest to the latest and most complex. The whole stream of redintegration is composed, as it were, of two currents flowing together and interfused with one another, the spontaneous and the volitional. Of these the spontaneous is the continuation and development of sense-bearing stimuli in the redintegrative organs, and the volitional of the re-actions of these organs upon those processes of continuation and development. The former has its origin in sense-impressions, the latter in certain re-actions on the part of the organism.

BOOK III.
CH. I.

§ 3.
Spontaneous and volitional modes of redintegration.— Representation of primary and of complex objects.

It will be observed that I have used the term *volitional* in place of the more familiar *voluntary* in analysing redintegration. I do so because it best expresses the distinctive character which I wish to bring out, its origin in acts of volition. It is the more restricted term of the two. The term *voluntary* applies to trains of redintegration or of action, which as wholes are initiated or governed by volition, but do not consist of volitions exclusively. *Volitional* applies only to the element of volition which they contain.

Turning now to the other distinction which depends upon this in the way we have just seen, I mean the distinction between representations of primary percepts and representations of remote objects, or of any complex object thought of as real, the case here is somewhat different. Representations of the latter kind, when once they are introduced by means of volitional action into objective thought, tend to become permanent features of its mechanism; and on becoming so, they mark definite and successive stages in its historical development. It is thus that the perception of a real external world, of what we have called real conditions, among which the percipient Subject's own body is his central and permanent reality, is marked as an epoch of prime importance in the evolution of experience, at whatever point in the experience either of mankind or of individuals we suppose the perception to be acquired. The perception once gained is never afterwards lost, and not only colours and dominates the whole subsequent period of experience, but becomes indispensable to such a degree, that many persons seem incapable of thinking at all without assuming it as part and parcel of their thinking process. We have in fact seen, in Book II., that this same perception of material objects, as real in that fullest sense of the term which led us to conceive and characterise them as real conditions, was the foundation of all positive science, including psychology; the material Subject being the special material object upon which psychology is based, bearing as it does the character of being the constant proximate real condition of consciousness.

§ 4. But important as this conception is, and especially that particular instance of it, the conception of the Subject, in the history and evolution of man's scientific knowledge, they are far from possessing, at least directly, an equal importance in the analysis of redintegration as a process of consciousness, or of objective thought which is, as it were, the panoramic outspreading of that process, the analysis of which in the first instance is necessarily philosophical. Just as redintegration and objective thought, as we have defined them for examination in the present Chapter, begin, not with sense-presentations involving pleasure and pain of sense, but with representations pervaded by the emotions of joy and grief, so the chief epoch in their historical development is marked by the conception, not of anything which, like the Subject, is inferred as the proximate real condition of consciousness, but of something which is first of all perceived as part and parcel of the train of representation itself, then inferred to have been a necessary ingredient in sense-presentation also, and lastly found to be perceivable in all consciousness when we attend to it analytically, with the idea of its presence already suggested to us. The perception I speak of is that Unity in all consciousness, which we objectify in contradistinction from all the varying content which from time to time is unified in consciousness, and call the Ego or the Self. I mean, that the Ego or Self belongs from first to last to the order of objective thought, even when it is the object thought of thereby (since all thoughts are real objects to reflective perception), and not to the order of real conditioning, except as a conditionate in that order. In other words, the Ego or Self is not an object thought of as a real condition, unless it is fallaciously hypostasised.

The Ego holds in the world of consciousness or experience generally, which is the *analysandum* of philosophy, a parallel position to that held by the Subject in the world of psychology; both being central objects of the worlds to which they respectively belong, that is, objects to which all others, in their respective worlds, are referred for systematic co-ordination. But the sense in which this is true is not the sense in which it would be understood or accepted either by common-sense philosophers, or by the greater number of psychologists at the present day. The view which is most commonly taken of the Ego is one which is incompatible with the conception of the Subject as the sole proximate real condition of consciousness. For on that view the Subject is degraded from ranking as the proximate real condition or agent of consciousness, and is conceived as an intermediary or instrumental condition only, that is, as the Body, or material system of means whereby the material world is brought into communication with the real agent, the real man and his consciousness, this real man being called the Ego. The Ego is thus thought of as an inner or immaterial man, within the body, or nerve organism, which is the Subject of scientific psychology, an inner man who first receives sense-presentations through the bodily organs, and then, in redintegration, compares, decomposes, re-combines, and otherwise deals with them, as members of his own inner or subjective kingdom of thought, emotion, imagination, and volition. The Ego is thus commonly held to be the single central proximate real condition, or agent, of consciousness generally, while the Subject becomes the mere medium through which it communicates with the material world beyond the organism, and the mere instrument or organon which it is restricted to employ, or rather, as a rule employs, in its inner redintegrative actions or dealings with its subjective kingdom; to say nothing of the suggestion which inevitably accompanies conceptions like these, that the material world itself, the Subject included, may in reality be nothing more than an immaterial product of the Ego's own powers of feeling, volition, thought, and imagination.

Now in this, which I take to be the commonly accepted view of the Ego, there is contained one great and fundamental error, the error of assigning to it the function of being a real condition or agent at all. It has been shown in previous Chapters of the present work, that the Subject, in the sense of the nerve organism of scientific psychology, is the only known proximate real condition, or agent, of consciousness as an existent. And since the Ego is a part or mode of consciousness as an existent (as well as a knowing), it follows that it is conditioned upon the Subject, and is not itself a real condition of consciousness or any of its modes, or of the so-called subjective kingdom of objective thought, in both of which it is itself included as a part. Nevertheless this does not deprive that Unity of consciousnsss, which is hypostasised as the Ego, of that central position in the thought-world, that is, in consciousness considered as a knowing, or in the total panorama of objective thought, which makes the perception of it epochal in knowledge, and by which its analogy to the Subject is sufficiently justified. Our world of objective thought would be very different from what it is, if the perception of its unity, as the object of the most fundamental function of the Subject, namely, reflective perception, the same in every successive moment of consciousness, had never been attained.

The meaning and the truth of these statements will be evident when we consider what the Ego really is, what that which we call by the name of *Self* or *Ego* is really perceived as being. There is but one possibility here open to us, if the previous analysis of reflective perception is taken as correct. That analysis determines what the Ego, which is its completing member, must be conceived as being. I refer more particularly to Book I., Chap. II., §§ 5 and 6, and again, for further determination, to Book I., Chap. VII., §§ 1, 2, and 4. In the two former of these passages, the moment of reflective perception, the moment of every actual experience, was found to consist of two aspects or sub-moments, one subjective the other objective, the subjective being the whole moment of experiencing *as a perceiving*, the objective being the whole moment of experiencing *as a percept*. It is one set of these sub-moments, the subjective sub-moments, or subjective aspects, in every empirical or concrete perception or experience, which are now gathered up into unity and themselves objectified as the Ego or Perceiver; though in reality the facts warrant us in objectifying them as nothing more than the Perceiving on the part of the real agent, the Subject.

The sameness in kind of these sub-moments, as a perceiving or being conscious, warrants us in unifying them as the fact of unity in consciousness, notwithstanding all their differences in other respects, and the fact of their being essential to all experience warrants us in assigning to them, in that single character, a range co-extensive with all possible experience. But there is no warrant for attributing real agency either to these sub-moments severally, or to the unity of consciousness in a lifetime, which is generalised from them, any more than there is for attributing it to the several wholes of which they are the subjective aspects, the concrete or empirical moments of reflective perception, which are successively the moments of all actual experience. Time-duration, which is an element in all perception or consciousness, simple or complex, is the unifying, because continuous, element in it. In this no real agency is discoverable. It is this element of time-duration which would be the Subject to which the real agency (if there were any) in perceiving would belong; and what is real in the Ego belongs to the consciousness of the Subject only so far as it is bound up with that element in perceiving. The Ego, in short, is *the being conscious* (not *the conscious being*) perceived as an abstract fact, common to and repeated in all present moments of consciousness, and constituting what I have called the subjective sub-moments in all of them.

We can now see in what sense the Ego is the central fact in all consciouness, redintegration, and objective thought, in which its position is analogous to that of the Subject in the real material world. From and after the moment of our recognising the identity in kind of all the sub-moments of consciousness or reflective perception, as a single unified stream, in whatever shape we may clothe our recognition of it, reflective perception is recognised as the essential circumstance giving unity to our whole panorama of objective thought, including all partial presentments of it, inasmuch as the moment of perceiving is thought of as essential to the perception of every content which contributes or has contributed to compose it. We are then said to be self-conscious, or to perceive our consciousness as ours;—*ours* meaning, in the first instance, that it is distinguished from all its objects save that central object, the Subject, in which it is perceived as located.

But besides this there is an additional perception of this unifying moment, a perception of it which leads directly to hypostasising it as an agent, a perception which we do not recognise until we have recognised the one just mentioned. This is the perception of its existent aspect or character, that is to say, the recognition of the subjective sub-moments of our actual consciousness as existents, these being the moments in which consciousness perpetually arises above the threshold, in dependence on the neural processes in the Subject, which are its proximate real conditions, determining the occurrence of its various modes as processes of consciousness. The real agency of these modes lies in the neural processes of the Subject which condition them, and though these are described in terms of consciousness, they are necessarily thought of as so many distinct functions of the Subject, (or activities of the Ego, if the Ego is hypostasised); whereby the conscious being, whether conceived rightly as Subject, or wrongly as Ego, becomes the object-matter of psychology in respect of his consciousness, which, in being taken as an existent, is *eo ipso* taken as consisting of a certain number of really existent processes or functions.

Now the Subject must, and can without contradiction, be taken as the real condition of consciousness in all its modes and processes. It is not itself consciousness, and therefore can serve as its real condition. But it is not so with the Ego. For the Ego is abstract consciousness, the fact of being conscious abstracted, and made into a single abstract fact, the source of unity in consciousness as a whole, unity being essential both to the whole and every part of it; and from this the step is easy (though wholly unwarranted) to hypostasising it as an Unit, or consciousness as a single existent unit. And when once so hypostasised, it must be conceived as having in itself, potentially, all the successive moments of consciousness from which it is abstracted, and which, under suitable conditions external to itself, it unfolds or develops out of itself, or which, in more technical language, it successively *becomes*. In this respect the falsely hypostasised Ego is its own real condition, *causa sui*, which involves a contradiction. The relation between condition and conditionate is a relation between separables; that between an abstraction and the phenomena from which it is abstracted is a relation between inseparables. The phenomena cannot be the real condition of the abstraction, nor can the abstraction be the real condition of the phenomena. The root of this fatal confusion lies, not in taking consciousness as the abstract fact of unity in perceiving, but in hypostasising that abstraction as an entity; for instance, as the *source* of unity in consciousness. But it is evident that this criticism leaves the unique position of the Ego, taken avowedly as an abstraction, and understood to mean the fact of Unity in consciousness, entirely unaffected, and also allows of the parallelism of that position, in the world of consciousness, to that of the Subject, in the world of real conditions, as the proximate real condition of consciousness. Every moment of consciousness as it occurs is determined and supported by a real condition, but this real condition lies, not in the Ego, but in the Subject.

Psychologists commonly distribute the functions of the Ego under the three main heads of Feeling, Thinking, and Willing, which is excellent as a common-sense classification, although the three functions overlap, and are not mutually exclusive. For scientific and philosophical purposes, a more useful classification would be that which has here been brought forward, namely into the processes or functions of sense-presentation, spontaneous and volitional redintegration, taking each of the three divisions as including its own special kinds of feeling. But the important point to notice is, that both classifications are classifications of processes, that is, are primarily based upon differences, not in the content of the percepts or objects experienced, but in the processes of perceiving or experiencing, as functions of an agent. These, as we have seen, are really functions or processes in the nerve-system or Subject, and as such would fall under divisions physiologically determined, divisions probably quite different from those of their conscious conditionates, which we now use to describe them. To discover these physiologically different functions, and fit them to the divisions discerned, or to be discerned, by simple analysis of consciousness, is the task most urgently pressing for accomplishment by the physiological psychology of the future. Hence it follows, that we cannot fully understand what the Ego, or consciousness simply as existing, is, until we approach it from the side of the Subject, and make it an object of physiological psychology in addition to metaphysic. There seems to be no single seat exclusively appropriated to being conscious in the neuro-cerebral system, but the various functions of the system as a whole have various modes of being conscious dependent upon them, which we may call various modes of the unity of that consciousness. And the chief divisions of these, which have just been signalised, may again be sub-divided into minuter modes of conscious process, on the same principles.

§ 4. The Ego and Personality.

While, therefore, we must avoid hypostasising the Ego as an agent, we may still continue to objectify the unity of the Subject's consciousness, and, seeing that a single term is a practical necessity, continue to express it by the same familiar name. Though no longer hypostasised, the Self or Ego will still have a perfectly unique nature and position. To take it first on the side of *knowing*. Alone among objects it is the objectification of the subjective aspect of consciousness as such, or rather as distinguished from its objective aspect. *Perceiving* is not an object, until it is itself perceived as the perceiving in some given perception or perceptions. It is then a perceiving of perceiving itself, and is generalisable as the subjective aspect in all perception. A later sub-moment of perception is the perceiving of prior sub-moments of perception. Perceiving then becomes objective and subjective aspect of perception at once, without changing its character of being the subjective aspect. For this very subjective aspect is what is then and in that character the object perceived. There is no contradiction in this, because the process of perceiving is always a process, not only in time, but of reflection or retrospection in time, and this process taking place at any given present moment is perceived in subsequent moments of the same process. No relation of real conditioning is introduced between the antecedent and the subsequent perceptions. The relation between the perceiving and the perceived, taken as parts of a *knowing*, is not a relation between separables, not a relation of real conditioning.

Nor is it only moments of perceiving prior to a given present moment, but moments subsequent to it also, which, if the idea is generalised, must be conceived as making part of the Ego ; inasmuch as they also will be subject to the same law, and partake of the same nature, of perception, supposing they come into existence at all. This perceiving of perceiving is what in strictness is meant by Self-consciousness, the Self-consciousness of the Ego. Not that the Ego is the perceiver;—the Subject, not the Ego, is the perceiving agent;—but simply that the perceiving, which we mean when we speak of the Ego, is a perceiving of a perceiving in the sense explained. The Ego *has not*, but *is* Self-consciousness. The fact of being conscious, not the conscious being, is the Self perceived in it.

Then again on the existent side. The perception of the Ego is not the same thing as the perception of feelings and ideas as distinct from material objects, or of objective thought as distinct from objects thought of. The content of consciousness as such is not the Ego. Nor again is the Ego consciousness simply, taken as an existent, yet distinct from its objects or from its content, which would reduce it to a completely empty or colourless abstraction, in fact to *nil*. It is the process of being conscious, when perceived as the same (in point of kind) in all cases; the fact of change in consciousness, which constitutes it a process; the fact that any one moment is a looking back on one content while being filled with another, every content beginning to recede into memory from the very instant in which it arises above the threshold; perceiving perceived as an existent process, or as change, instead of being defined by the contents as distinguished from the process; in short (to say it once more) the reflective character of all perception;—this it is which we perceive, when we are said to be self-conscious, or to perceive our Ego or our Self. To perceive our perceiving is to perceive it as a process which has a nature, or content of its own as a process, namely, change in continuous time; a process which is always the same, and always distinguishable by abstraction from the special contents between which it changes, that is, from the special changes which it includes. When we recall what at any time we were, we remember the fact of our being conscious of this or that, and this fact we attribute to ourselves, as constituting what we were, excluding from ourselves the this or that of which we were conscious, as unessential accidents.

The main argument upon which those most rely, who would hypostasise the Ego, is one which is contradicted by the whole analysis of experience set forth in Book I. It is true that reflective perception is historically prior to the perception of the Subject. It may also be true, that our distinct perception of it as a knowing is historically prior to the existence in us of that perception. But this does not show, either that it is perceived as a real agency, or even that it could be imagined as a real agency, without previous perception of the Subject, from which alone, as we have seen, the idea of real agents and agency is derived. Prior to that perception, no Self or Ego as an agent is perceived, or can be imagined. The priority even of doubly reflective perception to the perception of the

Subject is therefore a priority solely in the genesis of the idea or conception of the Self or Ego as an agent; and it is a fallacy to convert this priority into a priority of the object of that idea, or conception, as a real agent in the order of real conditioning, unless it can be shown that, when reflective perception is originally perceived, it is perceived as a real agency. Now this is negatived by the foregoing analysis, both in the present Book and in Book I.

But even supposing that it were not so,—what then? The result would only be to hypostasise reflective perception itself as an agency, and render the Ego, as hypostasised agent of the process, entirely superfluous. This is why Hegel, who clung to the fallacy of hypostasising Thought as agency, was enabled to dismiss Kant's transcendental Ego (and with it Fichte's absolute Ego) as a fiction. He rightly saw that it was but the Scholastic Soul or Mind over again, only avowing its unknowability. Now it is not this fallacy only, but it is the primary fallacy on which it is based, the primary fallacy of converting a priority in the genesis of an idea or conception into a priority of the object thought of by that idea or conception as a real agent in the order of real conditioning, without distinct proof of its reality in that character,— a fallacy which is at the root of all so-called Idealistic philosophies,—which is exposed, and it may be hoped precluded, by the analysis of Book I., to which I appeal. No mode of consciousness, not even Thought or Will, is or can be immediately perceived as agency; the fact of agency, unlike the fact of process, is a derivative and inferred fact.

The failure or refusal to distinguish what is immediately perceived from what is derivative and inferred, in the experiences commonly known as self-consciousness, suffices of itself to stamp all Idealistic theories as Empiricism.

There are two reasons for treating of the Ego, as I have now been doing, under the head of Redintegration, and in the Chapter devoted to it. The first is, that it cannot be understood unless we have previously seen what the Subject is, or at any rate what is meant by the real genesis and conditioning of consciousness, and are thus enabled to combine psychological conceptions with metaphysical analysis. The second is, that, as a special object, it is originally perceived in redintegration, by attention to trains of perception, and moreover that the perception of it as a special object presupposes, or at any rate involves, the perception of some central material object, as the seat of consciousness distinguished from matter.

The perception of the Ego supervenes upon spontaneous redintegration in consequence of attention, in a manner somewhat analogous to that in which the perception of remote material objects supervenes upon the same process by the same means. Like those objects also it takes its place in subsequent spontaneous redintegrations, as a conception dominating their entire course and content. Thenceforward the perceiving act or moment of perceiving, as distinguished from the contents or objects perceived by the act, is regarded as an object and spoken of as *I*, that is, as self-consciousness, which either is, or makes the agent to which it belongs, a Self or Person. The term *I* is the term by which a self-conscious being denotes and describes himself *qua* self-conscious.

The perception of the Ego has thus, like the perception of the Subject, a history behind it in objective thought, and its object, the Ego, as a part of consciousness, has real existence as an object thought of; it is part of consciousness as a real existent. But the Ego has not also, what the Subject has, the real existence of an inferred real condition. Seen in the light of this distinction, the Ego belongs to objective thought alone, while the Subject belongs to the world of real and material agents. The Ego is the experiential centre of the thought-world, the Subject the experiential centre of the material world thought of. The Ego is seated in and conditioned upon the Subject, and is normally perceived, and ought always to be thought of, as being so.

Looking to the history of the perception of the Ego in redintegrative consciousness, it is plain that the steps which lead up to its attainment, as well as those which enable its precise determination and full development, must have been and will be gradual. The perception of consciousness, or feeling as distinguished from material objects, was no doubt the rudimentary form of the perception of the Ego, whether real or imaginary. And that former perception, we have seen in Book I., was co-eval with the perception of the Body, which may be called the rudimentary form of the Subject, as the central object of the material world. Consciousness was then perceived as seated in the body, and at the same time as possessing a distinct unity, character, and history, of its own. Accordingly it came to be thought of either as depending on an immaterial agency seated in the body, or as being such an agency itself. The true conception of it, as I have tried to show, is that of the Unity of the philosophically subjective aspect of consciousness, not distinctly perceived except by attentive and analytical consideration of the concrete consciousness to which it belongs.

Whenever it comes to be admitted, that the material Subject contains, in its nerve system and nerve processes, all the proximate real conditions of the processes of consciousness in all their detail, we shall get rid not only of all the more ancient hypotheses concerning the real conditioning of consciousness, but of what is perhaps the last and most modern of them, the ill-considered conception, that nerve process and consciousness, or, as it is sometimes expressed, brain and mind, are two aspects of one and the same thing, or are one and the same thing seen from opposite points of view. At the same time we shall have, in the conception of nerve process as the real condition of consciousness, the only adequate means of accounting for and tracking those bye ways of consciousness, which have recently become the most prominent object of physiological psychology; foremost among which may perhaps be reckoned the striking phenomena of multiple personality. The Ego or Self-consciousness rests mainly upon redintegrative, as distinguished from presentative processes, that is, upon processes involving memory and imagination, which are conditioned upon nerve processes. It follows that whenever two or more nerve tracts, or sets of nerve processes, the activities of which would normally give rise to consciousness together, are so dissociated that, whenever the activity of one is stimulated into consciousness, the activity of another remains working, if at all, below the threshold, then each of those dissociated tracts or sets of processes, when its consciousness rises above the threshold, will also be attended by a personality dissociated from those of the rest. In order to restore, in such cases of dissociation, the normal unity and comprehensiveness of the Subject's personality, it is necessary to restore the unity between the several tracts or sets of processes, in respect of the point at which their activities are attended with consciousness, or in figurative language to bring their several thresholds of consciousness to the same level.

The existence of the Ego, that is, of some real feature in consciousness which is expressed by our using the terms *I* and *We*, is an indisputable fact. The question is, what is the nature of that reality, what is really and exclusively implied when we use those terms. It will be obvious that, though I speak of the Ego in this sense as a reality, I do not put forward the conception which I have given of it, which is the result of metaphysical analysis, as identical with the conception formed by common sense, any more than with any of the conceptions current, so far as I know, among psychologists at present. I put it forward as the true conception of the Ego, based on analysis of the facts, on which, unanalysed, both the common-sense and the current psychological conceptions are founded; the analysis being explanatory of the genesis and errors of those conceptions, and the resulting conception being therefore that which I would substitute for them. Some true and philosophical conception is required, of what that is, which we really mean when we say *I* and *We*. The object really present to us when we use those terms is what is technically called the Ego. This it is for which a definition based on analysis is required. Two things must be carefully distinguished, one the perception known as self-consciousness in the actual experience of every individual, the other the true conception or interpretation of that perception given by philosophically directed attention and analysis. It is the current interpretation of the Ego as an agent, knowable or unknowable, which I have tried to show has no warrant in the facts which yield the perception of self-consciousness as actually experienced. An abstract unity, even when it is an unity of consciousness, cannot without gross fallacy be hypostasised as a real agent or agency.

Common-sense thinking is concretive, not analytic, in its action. Just as, in its conception of a material object, common sense places its secondary qualities, as they are called, that is, *e.g.* its colour, heat, sweetness, odour, sonority, on the same footing with its so-called primary qualities, which are those which constitute it matter and a real condition, and considers the material object to be *at once and in the same sense* a compound of all these qualities, so, in the case of the Ego, common sense identifies the consciousness with the agent or activity, real or supposed, which possesses or exerts it, holding the Ego to be both agent and consciousness at once and in the same sense. Now this common-sense conception of the Ego is the root, out of which spring the various current psychological conceptions, some few of which have been noted above, and all of which are modifications of it containing the same fallacy. And that fallacy consists in conceiving the Ego as being Thought, Emotional Feeling, and Volition, and also as their agent or active principle, at once and in the same sense. The truth resulting from a true analysis is, that the Ego is the essential subjective strain or element in all consciousness, and therefore in all these various kinds or modes of it, so far as they are kinds or modes of consciousness, but that, for the agency concerned in them, it is dependent upon the activities of the material Subject. It is conditioned upon those activities of the Subject, but is not identical with it or them. The Ego is a mode or aspect of consciousness as an existent, conditioned upon the Subject as a material existent. And the whole concrete conscious being is double or twofold, not in the sense that its materiality and its consciousness are opposite aspects of each other, or of the same thing, but in the sense of their being immediately related and connected as condition and conditionate.

So long as the common-sense conception is confined to common sense and the purposes of daily life, it is perfectly just, harmless, and indispensable. But when it is carried over into science or into philosophy, and maintained as a scientific or philosophical conception, then and in that character it is, that its inaccuracies become

§ 4. The Ego and Personality.

operative, by substituting a false analysis and interpretation of the admitted twofold nature of the conscious being for the true ones; the truth being, that consciousness and the Ego are related to the nerve processes of the Subject as conditionates to their conditions, and not either as their subjective aspect, or as their animating intelligence.

The mischief of the conception does not lie in its combining consciousness and Subject into a single Conscious Being, for this is a true and patent fact of experience, but in its combining them under false colours, due to a false analysis of that fact of experience, a false distinction between its constituent parts. Hence it is that the mischief in science and philosophy arises, and not in common-sense experience, so long as that keeps to its own province. The Ego may practically be thought of as a new character taken on by the Subject, just as common sense conceives it. And that character in Subjects we express when we call them Persons. An agent which can say *I*, in consequence of reflection on on its own consciousess, is a Person; and Personality is the general term for that characteristic.

§ 5. The Personal Emotions.

§ 5. We have still to consider more particularly how and in what sense the perception of personality is epochal, that is, constitutes an epoch or turning point in the history and development of redintegrative consciousness. Its operation must, I think, be conceived as follows. The perception of the Subject's own personality, or of that of the Body, which is the rudimentary and pre-scientific form of the Subject, is necessarily accompanied by the inference of personality in the other Subjects by whom he is more immediately surrounded. His perception of his own and his inference of theirs begin and develop together, passing through various stages of increasing distinctness and clearness, from those exemplified in infants and in the lower animals, to those exemplified in the adult man of civilised culture. But throughout all these stages, and at whatever point in the evolution we choose to look, we shall find that the personality which the Subject perceives in himself and (by reflection from himself) in others, differentiates the emotions and passions of the Subject, by the new character thus imported into the representations or imagery in which they arise, and gives them an entirely new tone and colour. The emotions (including here and elsewhere certain desires, sentiments, and passions) are thus distinguished into two classes, which exhaust their whole field,—(1) emotions which have not, (2) emotions which have, the redintegrative consciousness of conscious beings, whether Self or others, as their represented object. Emotions of the latter class are more usually called moral or social,[1] but personal is a better title for them, inasmuch as it points more distinctly

---

[1] In my *Theory of Practice*, Vol. I., pp. 181, sqq, I gave them the name of Reflective Emotions. But this name is misleading, inasmuch as, all feelings being strictly reflective, it gives no indication of the special mode of reflection which the emotions in question involve. By this, however, I by no means intend to retract the analysis and classification of the emotions given in that work, or in any way to imply that I consider it superseded by the present brief treatment of the same subject. Dr. Charles Mercier, in his very valuable and interesting work, *The Nervous System and the Mind*, pp. 279 and 286, has mentioned this analysis and classification of mine among others which he has found unsatisfactory. The chief reason I take to be, that the method by which it is obtained is based upon a conception, very different from his own, of the dependence of psychological on metaphysical analysis.

to their mode of origin; although in the earlier stages of their evolution they are rudimentary and ill-defined, like the corresponding ideas of personality, which serve as their representational object or framework.

These emotions, which we feel towards the personality of conscious beings, naturally vary with our representation of that personality. But they are broadly distinguished from those which we feel towards beings which we represent as simply sentient, without redintegration, and still more towards beings which we represent as unconscious. Their *differentia* consists in thoughts, feelings, and volitions, being represented as consciously entertained by the Subjects of them, whose personality is consequently represented as the object of our own. In feeling these emotions, moreover, our own personality stands, as object, on precisely the same footing as the personality of others, in the sense that all alike are the immediate objects of the emotions we experience in representing them. There is however this difference, that the personalities of others have come to occupy that position in our representations by means of inferences drawn from the actions, speech, gesture, glance, and so on, of their respective Subjects, while our own personality is the object of an idea formed by simple redintegration of our own experience. But in all cases alike the personality as represented is the immediate object of the emotion which it is said to inspire, and the representation of it is the imagery or framework of that emotion, in the person who feels it.

Yet the personal emotions do not spring up as entirely new feelings, on the representation of personality; they have a history behind them. Just as the representation of a personality is based on the representation of some Subject, distinguishable from it, and to which it belongs, so the personal emotion is based on some emotion or emotions felt towards beings not represented as persons. These emotions are some mode or modes of grief, aversion, fear, repugnance, or of joy, fondness, hope, desire. These are, so to speak, the undeveloped states of feelings which will become personal emotions, that is to say, modes of personal disliking or liking, antipathy or sympathy, hate or love, anger or passionate attachment, so soon as the personality of another becomes an object represented by the percipient Subject, and is brought face to face with his own represented personality, so as to form with it a complementary portion of his whole represented object. The peculiarity which gives the new and special colour to personal emotion is, not simply that its object is represented as a person, but that we represent to ourselves that this person has a perception, feeling, or knowledge of what we are thinking or feeling towards him, just as we are representing his thoughts and feelings towards ourselves. It is the mutuality of the feeling or knowledge, the fact that we represent it as common knowledge to both persons, or, so to speak, its conscious repercussion from one to the other, which gives to the personal emotions their peculiar tone and character. From this point onwards we live in a wholly different world from before, and conceive ourselves as members of an intelligent society.

There is no further development of a new kind of emotion at all comparable to this. The personal emotions are the basis and foundation of all later modifications and ramifications of moral, social, imaginative, and religious life. The great groups of (1) the æsthetic and poetic emotions; (2) the sense of justice and injustice, of right and wrong, and of the moral approval and disapproval of choice and conduct; and (3) the hopes and fears which attach to the unseen world and connect us with the Divine; all alike have, not indeed their ultimate roots, but their final elaborations and developments, within the sphere which is described, as it were, from the personal emotions as a centre, and occupied by what we conceive as an intelligent society. The whole life and experience of the redintegrative powers are bounded by grief and joy at the lower, and by the imaginative developments of antipathy and sympathy, at the upper end of their history and evolution. But it is the feelings belonging to the second main division spoken of above, I mean those belonging to the personal emotions and their imaginative developments, together with the actions which they seem to prompt, or with which they seem to be bound up, which are more particularly, or at the least, intended, whenever human nature is spoken of. It is these which contain the differentiations which are specifically characteristic of humanity, by rising above the level of the feelings and actions which are common to man with the higher animals. It is but a crude notion which finds the *differentia* of human nature solely in the possession of Reason, without adding that it is reason informing and informed by the higher modes of imaginative emotion.

§ 5. The Personal Emotions.

I therefore do not, and obviously cannot, mean to imply, that these emotions and their developments are ever found operating in that isolation, in which we have now been considering them for the purposes of analysis. Redintegration is not a process which goes on in isolation from the other organic processes of the bodily system, but is always in dependence upon, and re-action with, the processes which spring from bodily needs and tendencies, which are manifested in consciousness by felt appetites and wants, as, *e.g.*, for food, warmth, sexual intercourse, and activity of organs generally, as well as with processes of the special sense organs which bring us presentations from external objects. Nevertheless it is in redintegration or brain-life that the specifically human experience takes its rise; and it is to the peculiar kinds of some of the feelings which have their seat in the brain, and to the intra-cerebral re-actions upon which the play of those feelings depends, that the specific nature of that experience is owing. We can no more get behind the specific nature, either of the ultimate feelings, or of the resulting experience, taken apart from the brain-processes upon which their existence and their combinations depend, than we can get behind the specific nature of sense-presentations. Both are ultimate facts, or bases, of experience. We can no more tell why such specific emotions as love or anger are what they are, than we can tell why there are such specific sensations as light or sound. We can assign the real conditions of their occurring; but no reason can be given for their specific nature. And here once more it is, that we see the immense importance of that profound distinction between nature and genesis, which was first brought out into clear consciousness by the genius of Plato, and which I have adopted, as one of the cardinal principles of philosophical method, in the present as well as in all my former works.

From the brief sketch of the emotional life now given it is evident, that throughout both the divisions of which it consists, the pre-personal and the personal, there runs a great antithesis, analogous to that between pleasures and pains in sensations, on which latter indeed it is originally founded. Through the pre-personal emotions there runs the antithesis between the various modes of joy and grief, and this antithesis is continued, in the personal emotions, into that between the various modes of sympathy and antipathy. As pleasure and pain of sense are the foundation of joy and grief simply, and are then dropped, as sense pleasure and pain, in their further developments, so joy and grief, in their turn, are the foundation of the sympathetic and antipathetic groups, and in their further developments are likewise dropped in their specific character as joy and grief. The emotions, each in its specific nature, become what are called motives or springs of action, and are felt as desires which require satisfaction. Whether an emotion springs originally from joy or from grief, it is a gratification to satisfy the desire to which it gives rise, and the reverse of gratification, that is to say, a pain of emotion, to deny or prevent its satisfaction. There is, for instance, a real and often an intense gratification in satisfying revenge, and inflicting pain on persons whom we hate, just as there is a real and keen gratification in heaping benefits on those we love, or ministering to the wants of those for whom we feel pity. Yet hate has its roots in the grief attaching to the representation of a personality consciously jarring with our own, just as love and pity are founded in the joy of recognising the conscious concord with our own of another's personality, notwithstanding that, in the case of pity, the consciousness represented as common to the two personalities is one which is emotionally painful.

The present analysis of personality and the personal emotions seems to offer a better rationale of what is now the generally admitted fact of the natural innateness or originality of the altruistic emotions, than can be given on the common-sense or empirical basis, on which we begin by assuming a perception of separateness between different persons. This we do, whenever we consider the question as merely a question of psychology, in which individual conscious beings are taken as ultimate facts, whose individuality is something *per se notum*, our conception of which cannot be affected by metaphysical analysis. On such a basis, a special theory is required to account for our feeling altruistic emotions with the same spontaneity and originality as we feel malevolent emotions; a theory which shall be adequate to surmount the perception of separateness of interests between self and others, with which we are supposed to begin, and exhibit fellow-feeling for others as naturally arising from our feeling for self, though it may not be equally powerful. Dr. Bain, for instance, resorts to the hypothesis of seeing, in acts of genuinely disinterested benevolence and sympathy for others, "a remarkable and crowning instance of the Fixed Idea," an idea in this instance acquired and developed by the gregarious nature and habits of the human species, among others, during the long course of its evolution.[2]

But the moment we see what is involved in the perception of another's personality, namely, that it requires a representation of our own and another's personality together, as two complementary parts of one and the same experience, it is evident that the jarring or the concordance between these two parts of our total idea becomes what is called an immediate motive or spring of action, as much in the one case as in the other. Sympathetic or benevolent and antipathetic or malevolent action spring alike spontaneously and alike originally from our own redintegrative experience, and have no difficulties to surmount arising from the perception of the separateness of the personalities, which comes in by inferential processes at a later stage in the development of our knowledge. For it is not enough to say that this development has had a long history, unless we add, that its beginning is co-eval with the redintegrative activities themselves, which, as we have seen in Book I., are pre-requisites of the perception of a world of material objects,

---

[2] *The Emotions and the Will,* p. 121. Third Edition, 1875.

of which the body of the Subject is one. In this history, accordingly, the conception, that the consciousness of every Subject is something entirely separate from that of every other, that is, the psychological conception of entirely separate Persons, is comparatively late in being acquired. Originally we represent the feelings of other Subjects, just as we do material objects, as part and parcel of our own experience, and from these representations we act, long before we arrive, either at the perception, that every real Subject has a totally unique and unshared experience, impenetrable by others, or at the true discrimination of material objects which are real Subjects, possessing personality in the full sense, from those which are not so endowed.

It is a great mistake to transfer this fully developed perception of the separateness of personalities to the beginning of the evolution of the personal emotions, so as to make the conception of it the basis or condition explanatory of their nature or origin. The mischief of this is, that, by thus falsely antedating the full conception of personality, we falsify the relation between emotions and the ideas or imagery to which they correspond, a relation which is really one of simultaneity, and conceive the emotions, either as feelings entertained for some ulterior purpose, as when

> "The dog, to gain his private ends,
> Went mad and bit the man,"

or as logical consequences of ideas previously entertained concerning the objects of them. True, I may justify or explain my anger or my gratitude, for instance, by saying that I know that the object of it intends me an injury, or has done me a kindness, but this is not the real order in which my anger or my gratitude arises. They arise spontaneously along with the first idea of the injury or of the kindness, and are an element in the total state of consciousness, which may be designated either as an idea or as an emotion, according to the purpose we may have in view. The justification or explanation, which is here supposed, proceeds on the common-sense view of the relation between persons, and this again is built upon the perception of separateness between them, which cannot be read back into the analysis of the emotions in question at their origin, or in their simplicity.

There is another pair of emotions, the originality and spontaneity of which are set in a clear light by this analysis, emotions which are closely allied to those we have just instanced, and make part with them of the sympathetic and antipathetic antithesis. I mean the feelings which arise on the perception of justice and of injustice, or, in common phrase, the sense of justice and injustice. These are personal emotions, when the terms *justice* and *injustice* are used in their proper sense, that is, when the relation which is the special object or framework of the emotion is taken as subsisting, either between persons, or between a man's own actions and their consequences as judged by himself. I have, for instance, the sense of justice, when, in a transaction between myself and another person, in respect to which both parties are free agents and of equal power, I can represent my performance as exactly congruent with my promise, and can also think of the other person as representing it in the same way. The exact congruence of expectation and fulfilment, represented as perceived by both persons alike, in matters where both are free and equal agents, is the essence of the relation of justice; incongruity between them, in the same circumstances, of injustice.

So also it is in matters which are self-regarding; as for instance, if I knowingly do a foolish action, under pressure of some present pleasure, and the anticipated consequence follows, I feel the congruity between my action and its consequence, and acknowledge the justice of the retribution. If by some accident I escape the consequence, I set it down to good-luck, which I should call unjust partiality, if I could regard the agency as personal. But in cases of this sort it is I myself who occupy the position of the other person in transactions between two; and *my* justice or injustice consists in condemning or acquitting myself of folly in the action which is mine, when I look back upon it in retrospect. I am unjust if I fail to recognise and regret the folly I have committed.

But although the sense of justice and injustice in their proper sense is applicable only to relations between persons, yet the relation itself, which is the framework of the feeling, has its roots in imagery which is not strictly personal, but precedes the perception of persons in the full sense. This relation consists in a perceived equality, sameness, or equilibrium, between any two objects or events whatever. It is this circumstance and the emotional satisfaction attaching to it which give the relation, wherever found, and therefore when it is carried up into personal relations, its character of being a final standard, not capable of being appealed against, and therefore secure to it the position of being one of the fundamental forms taken by our perception of what is morally right in actions, thereby assuring to it the approval of Conscience, as there will be occasion to draw out more fully in a later Chapter. The ascertainment of justice between man and man consists in harmonising the views which each of them entertains concerning it, in a transaction which is matter of common knowledge to both. It may be that this ascertainment is effected with difficulty, or cannot be effected at all. But this in no way alters the nature of justice, or the emotion of joyful acquiescence with which we perceive it, or what we sincerely imagine to be its real presence. When both parties agree in the same view, both are alike satisfied, equality, sameness, equilibrium of claims are secured, and there is room for no further cavilling on either side.

Emotions, it has been already said, are the peculiar modes of feeling belonging to redintegrative consciousness, analogous to the various modes of sensation; and of these latter, some are ultimate and others are modifications of, or derivations from them. So also it is with the emotions, taken apart from whatever roots they may have in the pleasures and pains of sense, and considered solely as feelings of the redintegrative organs. In this sense some of the emotions are ultimate and irresolvable, while others are derivative and resolvable, but only from and into emotions again. All alike spring up in the course of representation, pervading and colouring the imagery of which it consists. At the same time, although some images or ideas are requisite as the framework or object, as it is called, of the various emotions, yet the emotions are to a considerable extent indifferent to the particular imagery, which from time to time serves as their framework. As feelings, they have one source in the pleasures and pains of sense-presentations; but the source of the imagery, which is their framework, lies in sense-presentations simply. The imagery is thus part and parcel of knowledge, and is subject to its changes, growth, abandonment, and development. The emotions are part and parcel of feeling, and their changes, growth, abandonment, and development, follow a somewhat different law. They are something far more fixed and stable than the imagery, which changes with increasing knowledge. Their changes, so far as they are intrinsic, are changes in intensity, in refinement, in development of subtil shades of sentiment, in complexity of intermixture, counterpoise, and so on. The development of the æsthetic feeling for the beauties and grandeurs of natural scenery is a well-known instance. In redintegration the two elements of imagery and emotion sit somewhat loose to one another, varying at different rates of change, and sliding as it were on parallel grooves. As our imagery changes with our knowledge, we transfer our emotions, with certain changes of its own, to new images, and withdraw it from old ones, which have become antiquated and untrue.

At the outset of the human stage of his evolution, man, it is commonly held, personified almost all natural objects that had, or seemed to have, a separate existence, such as mountains and rivers, the sky, the heavenly bodies, the earth, the ocean, the winds, storms, rocks, and trees. That is, he falsely imagined them to be Subjects possessing feelings and ideas analogous to his own, by which he supposed their actions to be guided, however crude his ideas of personality may have been. There was no *poetry* in this; it was the earliest hypothesis of *science*. And as a matter of fact, one of the first separate material objects with which an infant comes into contact, and the one with which he is the most closely and constantly connected, is a person, namely his mother, from whose breast he draws his nourishment. He has this among other instances, in addition to his own feelings, which lead him to frame his first rude conception of the nature of all separate material objects, namely, as beings endowed with personality. When poets took up the idea, their doing so was evidence, that its truth had been at least partially abandoned; for not until then could it be regarded with sufficient detachment and indifference, to allow of its being played with as a source of purely imaginative gratification.

As the partial divergence between emotion and imagery is a point of some importance, a few more words will perhaps be advisable in elucidation of it. There was found in sense-presentation, in Book I., a clear distinction between the formal and material elements of percepts, that is to say, between the duration and place in time, figure and location in space, (which are the formal element), occupied by any sensation, including its pleasure or pain, and the sensation which occupies that time and space area (the sensation being the material element). Corresponding to this in redintegration we have the distinction between the imagery which consists of representations of sense-presentations in their entirety, which is analogous to the formal element, and the emotions which fill or pervade those representations, and are analogous to the material element in sense-presentations. It has also been noted, in a previous Section of the present Chapter, that we may redintegrate sensations, including their pleasures and pains of sense, solely as part of the imagery of representation, without experiencing pleasure or pain of emotion due to the pleasures or pains of sense so included in the imagery. In redintegration the imagery will be accompanied by emotions of its own, arising from the new context in which it will appear.

Accordingly, with this change to redintegration and its analogous distinction between imagery and emotion, there also comes in a certain degree of independence between the material and the formal elements in redintegration, compared to the relation between the corresponding elements as they appear in sense-presentation. Elements of both kinds, it is true, are equally necessary as before, to constitute any and every moment of concrete consciousness. But there occurs a shifting, so to speak, of the particular elements constituting moments of consciousness, when we pass from processes including presentations to processes of pure redintegration, in which latter processes also the same phenomenon is continued. The reason of this seems to be as follows. Emotions are due to an elaboration, effected by the redintegrative organs, of the pleasure and pain inherent in the material element of sense-presentations. The special qualities of emotion are produced directly and immediately by the activity of the redintegrating organs, and only indirectly and remotely by the imagery which represents sense-presentations in their entirety. The emotions are thus the immediate modes of feeling of the brain, arising indeed on representations of imagery, but not necessarily or exclusively attached to one image or set of images only. The imagery contains of itself both a formal and a material element, derived from sense-presentations, but the emotion is a material element only, and cannot stand alone. It is a material element of a new kind, added in redintegration, on the imagery of which it leans, as it were, for support. There is, therefore, always some imagery to which an emotion is attached, but this imagery is not always the same.

Neither is the rate of change of the two elements, imagery and emotion, the same, when taken on the large scale of their historical development. The former element changes much more rapidly than the latter, being immediately dependent on the growth of our acquired knowledge; the latter changes slowly, being dependent on the elaboration and modification of the ultimate modes of feeling proper to the brain substance itself. A permanent change in the character of the emotions, or the development of a new kind or variety of emotion, would require a correspondingly permanent change in the structure, or mode of functioning, of the cerebral organs. This is in perfect agreement with, and may serve as a partial explanation of, what has long been recognised as a fact, the rapid growth of man's intellectual acquirements, and his scientific command over nature, compared to the slow progress which he makes, and the frequent retrogressions to which he falls a prey, in respect of moral disposition, and strength of moral character. The late H. T. Buckle's insistence upon this fact, in his memorable *History of Civilization in England*, will doubtless present itself to several of my readers.

A word must be said in conclusion of what I fear has been a somewhat tedious Chapter, with regard to the character commonly attributed to the emotions, of being motives, ends, or springs of action. The truth must once again be recalled, that the emotions are not themselves motives, or ends, or springs of action, but are evidence of the motive agency which is really at work. They are dependent concomitants of the nerve actions or processes which issue in the actions, to which they themselves are commonly said to give rise. The emotions seem to bear this motor character, because we are accustomed to look and think and speak from the point of view of the Ego assumed as a real agent. And this again is the natural and spontaneously adopted view of common sense, because in redintegration we are not immediately and simultaneously conscious of the really operative nerve mechanism, and yet at the same time the actions which are performed seem to be immediately prompted by something within the Subject, and not by the objects upon which they are directed; that is, are not prompted by presentative perceptions of those objects, but are imagined and executed in consequence of representing or imagining them. They thus seem to common sense to flow directly from ourselves, that is, either from our feelings or from our volitions, as the only motives of which we are immediately conscious. As already said, there is no mischief in this way of speaking, so long as it is carefully restricted to the sphere of common sense, and not mistaken for a truth of philosophy or science.

CHAPTER II.

THE LAWS OF ASSOCIATION.

§ 1. The task now before us, marked out by the preliminary analysis given in the foregoing Chapter, is to analyse trains of purely spontaneous redintegration, with a view to discover the general laws which they follow in their composition, or in other words, the general uniformities which are observable in different instances of them. Since these trains are all of them parts included in the one great stream or moving panorama of a Subject's consciousness, as it retreats into the past of memory from any given present moment, which as already said is always the moment then occupied by the conscious Subject himself, we may say that this whole moving panorama is itself indirectly our object. But we are at present directly concerned with the analysis of one kind only of its components, namely, its trains of spontaneous redintegration. The connection of these with the other two, sense-presentations and volitions, which are, as it were, their points of departure and of arrival, as well as the connection of them with the neuro-cerebral processes which are their real conditions, must always be kept in view; but our analysis will be directed only upon the uniformities displayed by the processes of spontaneous redintegration themselves, these uniformities being that which is properly intended by the term *Laws of Association*.[1]

This method of treating the phenomena of redintegration differs in three important points from those commonly followed, notwithstanding that these may differ in many comparatively minor points from one another. It differs (1) in keeping trains of consciousness which are the *analysanda* distinct from their proximate real conditions, while at the same time appealing to their dependence upon them, when any hypothesis concerning the laws which trains of consciousness follow has to be either supported or impugned; (2) in isolating for immediate analysis redintegrative processes from their foundations in sense-presentations, and from their results in transeunt action, though reserving here again the right of appeal to these, in support or attack of hypotheses; and (3) in beginning with the separate examination of spontaneous redintegration, as the simplest of its divisions, simpler, that is, than voluntary redintegration, in respect of the absence of selective and purposive attention from its content. Without spontaneous redintegration as a basis, volitional could not come into being, since there would be no content for volition either to insist upon or to reject. That the laws of association, properly so called, are laws only of

---

[1] The introduction of the term *Redintegration* into English psychology, and its formulation as a general law under which all the other laws of association might be brought, are due to Sir William Hamilton. This I have expressly and fully recognised on the first occasion of my treating the subject, in my *Time and Space*, Chapter V., pp. 256 sqq.

spontaneous not of volitional redintegration, will presently be made evident.

These points are commonly if not universally disregarded as rules and safeguards of analysis, in treating of the subject of redintegration. Their adoption is precluded partly by the empiricist tendency to look at the conscious being as a whole in his relations to things and persons around him, and partly by the practical tendency to consider the redintegrative processes, not for themselves, but as means of explaining the building up the fabric of knowledge on the one hand, and the mediating and directing overt actions, speech, and conduct, on the other. There is also another reason, which, if less deeply seated than these, is at the same time one which it is less easy to avow. This consists in the dislike, on the part both of transcendentalists and of psychologists who follow traditional methods, to face the question, Whether there is such a thing at all as Mind or Psychical Energy; and who consequently shrink from any attempt to distinguish either of them from consciousness.

This reluctance they usually hide from observation by the pretext, that while the *reality* of mind and psychical energy is admitted on all hands, their *ultimate nature* is a question for metaphysicians, and in no way concerns themselves as psychologists. But in this pretext two things are forgotten, first, that the reality of mind and psychical energy is not an universally admitted fact, but is impugned by physiological psychologists of the strict school; and secondly, that what is required of them as psychologists is not to assign the ultimate nature of mind or psychical energy, but to give an intelligible conception of them, showing at least their possibility as real agents, some conception of them which shall stand on a similar scientific and phenomenal footing as the intelligible conception which physicists furnish of Matter. So long as such an intelligible conception of mind and psychical energy remains a desideratum, those who speak of them as realities can be considered as standing only on the ground of pre-scientific common sense, and not in any degree on that of psychological science, the essential purpose of which is to discover the real conditions of consciousness as an existent, and the laws under which they operate in conditioning it. The latter is impossible without the former. The pretext in question, therefore, is hollow. But it is also contemptible, as an endeavour to put off one's own proper work upon other shoulders. It is also mischievous, since it serves to foster that false conception of the nature and scope of Metaphysic, on which it relies for its plausibility. It is vain, and worse than vain, to enquire into the essential nature and laws of entities, for the very possibility of which there is no evidence. The case is quite different with body, and with matter generally. That objects corresponding to these names are not only possible but real, is shown by evidence of the clearest kind. Let psychologists show the same, if they can, of psychical energy or mind.

§ 2. The first question, then, for us is, What is a train of spontaneous redintegration? Let us take a simple instance by way of steadying our notions of the phenomena intended.[1] Suppose, then, that while walking homewards one afternoon I hear a news-boy shout "Terrible railway collision in Northumberland. Twenty lives lost"; and suppose farther, that in the old coaching days I had myself nearly lost my life, by being upset at night in a long journey by mail coach; moreover, that I was not thinking of this at the time when I heard the news-boy's shout, but that it rose into my recollection on hearing it. We have here an instance of redintegration which seems to involve the two chief laws to which its phenomena are usually, and in some sort correctly, referred by psychologists, namely, association by similarity, and association by contiguity. Let us consider the real nature of this instance.

In the first place it is to be noted, that the mere hearing of the words shouted is the sense-presentation which sets on foot the whole sequence in redintegration, but is not by itself a redintegration at all, as redintegration has been defined for our present purpose in § 1 of the foregoing Chapter. On the other hand, the fact that the meaning of the words, the idea of a fatal railway collision, is connected with the hearing of the words, is a fact of redintegration, and this fact seems to depend on contiguity, namely, on the long established connections between those representations of sense-presentations, belonging to different senses, which make up the complex idea of a fatal railway collision, and the sounds which recall them, each of which

---

[1] The analysis contained in this and the following Section was incorporated in an Address delivered before the Aristotelian Society, Nov. 1890, on *The Laws of Association*. See the Proceedings of the Society, Vol. I. No. IV. Part I. London. Williams and Norgate. 1891.

§ 2.
Association in Imagery.

is connected with a separate image or representation.

Secondly, the recalling of the mail coach accident seems to depend upon the similarity of the two accidents, the railway collision represented first on the hearing of the words, and the upsetting of the mail coach, which it is said to recall into consciousness and redintegrate in memory. But here it may possibly be objected, that, supposing similarity to be the law governing the redintegration of the recalled idea, in that case the idea to be recalled should be that which had the greatest degree of similarity to the idea recalling it, and consequently that some other fatal railway collision, and not an accident to a mail coach, would be the first idea to be redintegrated. Let us then assume, since our instance is only selected hypothetically, that this is the case, and that the idea redintegrated is that of some other terrible railway collision which I have witnessed or read of, and not the idea of a mail coach accident.

The case of redintegration under the two great laws of contiguity and similarity, as they are commonly reckoned, is thus opened up for examination. The question is, Are these the really operative laws of the redintegrative train? We see plainly, that they afford a good description of the phenomena as they apparently occur, that is to say, are a good common-sense account of it as an *explicandum*, rendering it intelligible by bringing it into line with a vast number of instances which are matter of familiar experience. But the question is, Are contiguity and similarity in the process-content of consciousness really operative circumstances; are they real conditions governing the redintegration, as well as being circumstances which characterise it as an otherwise conditioned phenomenon? This is the first question we have to face.

Now, bearing in mind that it is the nature of the moving panorama of objective thought or consciousness, to be experienced only in a succession of present moments, it is evident that no portion of it is ever strictly repeated, but retreats into the past of memory, or of oblivion, irrevocably. What we mean by the *repetition* or *recall* of any portion is the occurrence of another moment more or less like it, perhaps even indiscernibly like it, in point of content; in which case we call it identical or the same; the two being distinguished only by means of the different contexts in which they occur. This can easily take place, since both contexts are brought partially into consciousness together at the moment of repetition, just as the two contents are.

For instance, to show what is meant, take a simple case of memory. Suppose I visit a strange town, and on walking out at a certain hour on the second day after my arrival, see a blind beggar seated at a street corner. Suppose that this sight is attended with the awareness of having seen the same beggar, seated at the same corner, the day before, at the same hour. This is a case of simple memory. The sight of the beggar of the day before has become a thing of the past beyond recall. What then is meant by saying, that I recall it in memory, or am aware of having had the sight? Clearly, at the moment of memory, on the second day, I have in consciousness two images at once, the image of the beggar in the context of to-day, and the image of the beggar in the context of yesterday, the two images, each with its context, being identical in respect of their main feature the beggar, and the former, or recalling, image being continuous or co-incident with the actual presentation of the beggar on the second day. This double image is the only evidence which I have, at that moment, for the fact of my having really seen the beggar on the first occasion.

Similarity of content, then, which, if reaching indiscernibility by the absence of any perceivable intrinsic difference, we call identity, or more briefly, sameness of content in difference of context, is the real fact designated by the term *repetition* or *recall* of an idea in redintegration. An idea recalled is thus really two ideas in point of number, though, if these are indiscernible in intrinsic content, they are unified or clumped together as one, by our ordinary way of speaking, and treated as if they were one idea occurring at different times. It is against this clumping or unifying of ideas that we have to guard, when hearing or using the ordinary language about their recall, redintegration, or repetition.

Let us apply this first to those cases of apparent redintegration by similarity, in which both the idea recalling and the idea recalled are pure representations, as, in the instance supposed, the idea of the railway collision in Northumberland, which is the recalling idea, itself suggested by the news-boy's shout, which we will call A, and the idea of the railway collision witnessed or read of previously, which is the recalled idea, and which we will call B. In such cases it is now evident, that, until B has been actually recalled into consciousness, neither its similarity nor its identity with A is recalled. When it re-enters consciousness, then, but not till then, its similarity or identity (as the case may be) enters with it. And the same is true of any other relation which may happen to hold between them, as for instance, if A is a general or provisional image of a railway accident, and B a special or particularised case of one. Until B has actually entered consciousness, the fact of its being a particular case of A is not perceivable.

Or again, if the relation between them is one of contrast, or of antithesis of any kind, as *e.g.*, black and white, presence and absence, cause and effect, substance and attribute, father and son, and so on, the same reasoning holds good; and would still hold good, if we classed any of these instances under the head of contiguity, instead of similarity. The relation cannot be the link in consciousness, because it does not rise into consciousness unless and until the second member of the relation, the idea recalled, is itself present. The only way in which it could be a connecting link between them would be by the intervention of a volitional act of thought or reasoning; as for instance, if I were to fix my attention on A for the purpose of knowing something more about it, thus bringing the idea, either of its intrinsic content, or of its relation to other ideas, into consciousness, and thereby going, as it were, through those ideas to some particular ideas falling under one or other of them.

But this would at once, and of itself, take the case out of the number of spontaneous or non-voluntary redintegrations, and consequently out of the phenomena which are subject simply to Laws of Association. It would not be a case of association between ideas simply, but a case of Thought setting up an association between them. The laws of thought, including their origin from ideas, would then be our first object of investigation, contrary to what has already been shown to be the true order of enquiry. Putting all such laws aside, the result is, that no relation in consciousness between the ideas recalling and recalled, such as A and B stand for,—whether of similarity, identity, generality and speciality, contrast, causation, antithesis, or any other,—is the real link or nexus between them. For these are not ideas which intervene between the two occurrences, but ideas which supervene upon the occurrence of the later of the two. And the supervening relation is part of the total phenomenon of the redintegration, but is not an operative condition of its being the redintegration which it is. It is part of the *explicandum*, but not of its *explicatio*.

The phenomenon is, that, a certain railway collision having been once witnessed or read of by me, and then forgotten, a duplicate image of it, B, enters into my consciousness, (duplicate because represented in a different context from its present one), on occasion of a similar image, A, being brought into my consciousness by my hearing a news-boy's shout. We have seen that no immediately perceivable relation between A and B, or between A and the original of B, can be brought in to explain why B occurs on the occurrence of A. What, then, is the conclusion? Indisputably this;

that the really operative condition lies outside the phenomena immediately present in consciousness, that is, in some power or process working below the threshold of consciousness. And we are forced to suppose real conditions which are not states or processes of consciousness, because a state or process of consciousness cannot be conceived to have, as such, any operation, when it has fallen, and so long as it continues, below the threshold, that is, has ceased to be a state or process of consciousness at all. It cannot continue to act, when it has ceased to exist. *Non entis nulla operatio.* There is, then, some agency at work below the threshold. And those of my readers, who share my inability to form any positive or definite conception of an immaterial agent, will have no hesitation in identifying the agency really operative in these cases with that of the cerebral mechanism. We cannot possibly avoid having recourse to some real condition or conditions acting below the threshold of consciousness. The only question is, whether we are to imagine them as belonging to an immaterial or to a material agent.

Not that it is wholly indifferent what form of further error we embrace, supposing us to have answered wrongly on this fundamental point, and imagine the really operative conditions to be of an immaterial nature. If for instance we hold, that similarity in consciousness expresses the law of the condition which is really operative below consciousness, then we simply imagine the mind, soul, Ego, or thought-agency, whatever it may be, acting unconsciously in the same way as the concrete conscious being is imagined to act consciously, in common-sense descriptions of it. If on the other hand we see the true expression of the really operative link in the identity which obtains between an universal and the singulars which it covers, then our theory must be, that logical ideas or forms of thinking operate unconsciously as real conditions in psychology, which is to reduce psychology to the rank of a branch or derivative of logic. In the present state of psychological and Idealistic controversy, this remark may perhaps be not unimportant. Still, as already said, the main question is, whether the conditions really operative in redintegration are material or immaterial.

Let us, then, see in the next place, whether the hypothesis of cerebral or neuro-cerebral agency is applicable to the case before us. We may conceive its operation somewhat as follows. B, the idea of the railway collision once witnessed or read of, may be called, in its latent state before being recalled to consciousness, a *retent*; it is a *retent* at the time of my hearing the news-boy's shout, which gives me the idea A, the fatal railway collision in Northumberland. Now B's original entrance into consciousness was conditioned upon a part or parts of the redintegrative organism being set in motion, by propagation of sense-impressions into some central parts of the brain. These parts acquired thereby a certain readiness or facility for being again set in motion in the same or a similar way, in case of the same or a similar stimulus being imparted to them; that is, they are retentive of the original B, below the threshold of consciousness. The new stimulus required is given them when A occurs, for the occurrence of A in consciousness is conditioned upon motions being set up in parts of the organism, which are to a greater or less extent the same as those, whose motions subserved the original B. The fact that A is similar to B shows that it is subserved by similar motions in the same parts of the organism. Hence it is, that the motions subserving A set up motions which subserve a duplicate or second edition (so to speak) of B, a duplicate, be it observed, both of the original B and of its representation in its original context; so that there are *three* Bs in all, two simultaneously present at the moment of recall, and one original, which, at the moment of recall, is inferred to have existed in the past, from the two then present in duplicate. The real link or nexus between A and the two simultaneously present Bs, between these two themselves, and between them and the original B, for the past existence of which they are the evidence, lies in the permanent nerve or brain organism, which retains the tendency to vibrate twice as it has vibrated once, to vibrate thrice as it has vibrated twice, and so on with strengthened tendency for every additional vibration. Unity of organ and similarity of motions in it are thus the real conditions of the redintegration of similar ideas. What precisely these motions are, whether they are to be figured as mechanical or chemical, as vibrations or as partial disintegrations and integrations of neural structure, is a question for neural physiology, not here to be entered on.

Turning in the next place to the remaining part of our supposed instance, that in which the association apparently depends upon contiguity, we shall find that it admits of a similar interpretation. Here we can afford to be much more brief. The connection between the hearing of spoken sounds and the ideas or meaning which they convey to us is allowed on all hands to be matter of convention, instruction, and habit. Its ultimate foundation, which is the ultimate foundation of language itself, lies in the utterance, not in the hearing of sounds. Now the utterance of sound is a reflex action consequent upon stimulus externally or internally received. The sound and the stimulus are therefore connected by contiguity, being originally disparates; and the adoption of the sound to express the stimulus, or the object from which the stimulus is received, or to convey a knowledge of it to others, is a volitional action, supervening upon the association between the two. It is true, that, in one class of cases, volition may have adopted imitative sounds as names of the objects imitated, and so, to that extent, may have based language on association by similarity, not contiguity. But whatever motives may have originally determined the volitional adoption of particular sounds to express and convey particular meanings, it is in this adoption, and not in its motives, that the reason for particular sounds having particular meanings, in the case of all fully formed and established languages, must be found. In other words, the act of volitional adoption, which alone makes sounds into language, also makes the association between sounds and their meanings into an association by contiguity. The establishment of the connection between them, in the experience of individuals, is part of their history and education.

THE LAWS OF ASSOCIATION.

We have learnt the meaning, say, of *terrible*, of *railway*, of *collision*, of *Northumberland*, by having had the meaning called up through other channels and then brought into juxtaposition with the sound of the word for it, by being told the sound for each at the same time.

Thus contiguity in the sources of redintegration consists in simultaneity or close sequence, either between presentations, or between presentations and representations. But upon what does this simultaneity or close sequence itself depend, since nothing within the content of its states, as states of consciousness, can be shown capable of accounting for it? There can be but one answer. It depends upon the connection or functional continuity of the intra-cerebral terminations of nerves coming from the disparate organs upon which the disparate sense-impressions are in the first instance made. And the connection, say, between a sound and its meaning, subsequently comes, in time, to be easy and habitual, because the channel or other mode of communication between the organs subserving each comes, in time, to be easily and almost instantaneously facile or permeable. That is to say, contiguity in redintegration depends upon features in the structure and functioning of the neuro-cerebral organism, closely resembling those upon which similarity in redintegration depends.

Similarity and contiguity in redintegration are thus dependent concomitants of brain structure and brain processes, and so far as they go are evidence of their nature and mode of operation. These latter are the real conditions governing the course of redintegrative trains of consciousness, at least so far as they consist of ideas or imagery, as in the case just examined. It is in them that we must look for the really operative mechanism, and in similarity and contiguity only so far as they are evidence for what these are and do. Apparent association by similarity is evidence of similarity in brain processes in one and the same part of the brain; and apparent association by contiguity is evidence of an established continuity or permeability of channel between different parts of it. Similarity and continuity in brain processes are the real conditions, being also what are called *veræ causæ*, of similarity and contiguity in the states and processes of consciousness in trains of redintegration.

Depth or strength of impression, of which vividness is one mark, at the time when an idea or image is originally received, will thus be one circumstance favourable to its recall by another stimulus similar to the first. For its depth or strength will render it readier to be stimulated; and the readier the original impression is to be stimulated, the slighter will be the stimulus needed to set it on foot again. This will also hold good, if the depth or strength of impression has been acquired, not from a single powerful stimulus, but by habit arising from frequent repetition.

Again, the number of connections, which a particular brain process has with processes in other parts of the cerebral organism, is an important circumstance; a high number must be favourable to its recall, inasmuch as each additional connection opens up a fresh channel by which a stimulus can be conveyed to it. And here again the facility or permeability of the connecting channels may be increased by frequency of repetition.

Strength of original impression, number of connections with other impressions, and the increase by habit either of a particular impression or of any of its connections with others, seem thus to be the chief circumstances favourable to the redintegration of any given idea or imagery, under the two main laws of similarity and continuity of brain processes. It is, however, evident, that this carries us but a very little way towards being able to predict the course which, in any given individual, a redintegration, starting from a given idea, will take in actual occurrence; and still more towards formulating a law enabling the prediction of the course of redintegration in a number of individuals, that is, a general law of the course which given ideas will take in spontaneous redintegrations, in the case of mankind at large. For this to be possible, we should require much more than even a perfect knowledge of the laws governing spontaneous redintegration; we must also know the particular history and circumstances of the individuals, in whose concrete lives trains of spontaneous redintegration are but a single strain or factor, a strain not isolated from the rest in reality, as it is in thought for purposes of analysis.

§ 3. One branch of the enquiry suggested by our supposed instance of redintegration still remains to be followed up. It will be remembered that we rejected the supposition, that the idea recalled by the news-boy's shout was that of a mail coach accident, which had nearly proved fatal to the Subject of the redintegration. We rejected it in order to follow another supposed recollection, in which the similarity between the recalled and the recalling imagery was greater. But it will be admitted, that the rejected recollection might very easily have been the actual one in the case supposed. Let us, then, go back to this our original supposition, and see whether it throws any additional light on the question of association.

It cannot be said, that the recall of the mail coach accident is due to the depth or strength of the original idea or image of the accident, in its character of idea or image; but, if we so speak of it, we must admit that this greater depth or strength, which facilitates its recall, is itself due to the individual interest attaching to it, from the fact that the accident had nearly proved fatal to the Subject of the redintegration, or from the peril in which he found himself. The greater impressiveness of the idea or image of the accident consists in the alarm or other emotional element which it contains, its emotional interest for the Subject individually. Not that the emotional interest is itself the condition of the readier recall; but here again the same general law applies, and compels us to regard the emotion as evidence of some peculiar brain process subserving it, and included in the total brain process subserving the redintegration as a whole. And this peculiar brain process, subserving the emotion, will then plainly be the really operative condition determining the recall of the mail coach accident by the idea of the railway collision, in preference to that of another railway collision.

Moreover it must be noted, that this brain process, in subserving emotion, subserves and is part of the proximate real condition of the moral Character of the Subject. For it is in those feelings or states of consciousness which spring directly and immediately from differences in the nature of the redintegrative organism, and only indirectly from the workings imparted to it through channels of sense-impression, that the ultimate grounds lie, by which we judge of Character. The emotion, say, of alarm in a dangerous accident is a very different thing from the sense-perception of the circumstances constituting the accident. Different persons may feel such emotions in very different ways; some may feel no alarm at all, others may be overcome by it; the sense-perceptions being alike for the consciousness of all. The working of the redintegrative organism adds of itself the emotional accompaniment to the sense-perception, and makes that its special contribution to the total impression constituting the Subject's experience of the event. In ordinary phrase we should say, that the image or idea comes *from without*, and the emotion which is combined with it *from within*. There is, therefore, a wide and essential difference between the factor in redintegration evidenced by emotional interest, which I have now pointed out, and the factor or factors evidenced by similarity and contiguity in imagery or ideas.

It is matter of actual experience, that emotional interests of every kind, painful as well as pleasurable, and arising from our relations with persons as well as things, do apparently determine the course of trains of redintegration, just as similarity and contiguity of imagery or ideas appear to determine it. More than twenty-five years ago, in my *Time and Space*, I endeavoured to draw attention to this fact, and to indicate in what way the emotional element struck in, so as to modify the course of the spontaneous redintegration as a whole.[1] Nor, except so far as the real conditioning of the process is concerned, have I seen any reason to alter my opinion. The supposed case just considered stands for multitudes of similar ones in real experience. And from these it may, I think, fairly be inferred, that there are brain processes specially subserving emotions, closely bound up with those which subserve imagery, and entering with them into many of the parts, if not all, of the whole redintegrative organism, and into the connections between them.

If this inference is admitted, we shall have added another distinct source or mode of real condition, contributing with those already recognised to determine the course of redintegrative trains ; but we shall still be nearly as far as ever from the desired end, indicated above as ideally or conceivably possible, namely that of predicting the actual course which will be taken by the spontaneous redintegrations of any individual or number of individuals. The hope of approximating thereto must lie in the continued investigations of physiological and experimental psychology, at least in the first instance. At the same time it seems most probable, that the cerebral organs and processes which subserve emotions, and those which subserve

---

[1] *Time and Space*. Part I., Chap. V., pp. 264 sqq., where previous authorities for the fact are quoted or referred to.

ideas or imagery, are alike subject to the laws which have just been pointed out in the case of the latter. I mean, that the redintegration both of imagery and of emotion depends upon (1) depth or strength of the original impressions which are afterwards liable to recall; (2) number and permeability of the connections between different cerebral organs and processes; and (3) increase of what belongs to both the first and second of these heads by frequency of repetition and consequent habituation. The whole ground of spontaneous redintegration is thus in some sort covered by these laws, since the distinction of its content into imagery and emotion is exhaustive.

The result of our enquiry, then, so far as it has hitherto gone, is this, that we can no longer speak of contiguity and similarity as real Laws of Association. They, together with the third feature which I have now pointed out in the dependent process-contents of consciousness in redintegration, I mean emotional interest, are evidence of the working of the cerebral mechanism, in which the real laws, or general facts, of its working are inherent; which general facts or laws are always fulfilled or exemplified in it, whatever particular course the redintegrations included under them may take. And for these laws we have, in consciousness, some evidence at least, in the shape of the three features named, that is to say, contiguity, similarity, and emotional interest.

But when we come to ask, what we know of the actual course followed by particular trains of spontaneous redintegration, in individuals, at particular times, say for instance, the evolution of

§ 3.
Association
in Emotion.

particular reveries or dreams, we are launched on a very different enquiry, and one which carries us beyond the region of spontaneous redintegration taken alone. This may perhaps be called the individually predictive part of the whole question. Here it would be necessary, not only to know beforehand the general character of the individual who was the Subject of the dream or reverie, but also to know which of the cerebral processes evidenced by similarity, contiguity, and emotional interest, was likely to prove the strongest, both at the beginning of the redintegration, and at every new turn, or newly represented incident, which occurred in the course of it. Even the description of such cases has hitherto been left to artists in imagination, such as novelists and poets; and it is in this sub-division of psychology that Browning has won his deservedly great fame as a specially psychological poet. Not that he keeps strictly within its theoretical limits. Like all poets he treats man as a whole, or in the concrete; and therefore always depicts the action of his spontaneous redintegrations in inter-connection and alternation with the volitional action of reasoning, adoption of ends, formation and criticism of plans and projects; only that, in so treating his characters, he is careful to let his readers see the play of spontaneous redintegration which supplies the material or pabulum for their reasonings and volitions.

§ 4.
Trains of imagery apparently new.

§ 4. Nevertheless there is another domain comprised in spontaneous redintegration, to which it is equally necessary to advert. Hitherto we have been occupied only or mainly with cases of simple repetition or reminiscence, cases where the state or process called up into consciousness is recognised as being so closely similar to one which has been in consciousness before, that we call it a repetition or memory of the very same image. What we have now to notice is the occurrence of imagery, ideas, and emotions, in redintegration, which are apparently produced therein for the first time, and seem to be in no way reproductions of anything that has preceded them. At the same time they are clearly of the nature of representations, not of sense-presentations, though in respect of their newness they are presentations in redintegrative processes, and must be referred to the action of the redintegrative organism. These trains of redintegration take a course which seems entirely their own, consisting of quite new imagery and its corresponding emotions. And they are as completely spontaneous or non-volitional as the former reproductive trains. The sole difference seems to lie in the one kind being productive of what is new, the other reproductive of what is old.

Reverie and dreaming afford instances of this kind of productive redintegration, though most commonly with some intermixture, be it more or less, of reproduction; as when remembered or familiar scenes and persons are represented in the course of a dream, which is otherwise entirely new. But for an instance of the most purely productive trains, reference may be made to a well-known phenomenon which many persons can observe in themselves, during the transition from waking to sleeping, and which has been well described by

§ 4.
Trains of imagery apparently new.

Locke in his short Essay *On the Conduct of the Understanding.* I mean those trains of successive images, most commonly human faces, which change one into another, each in turn persisting for a few seconds and then giving place to a different successor, the change beginning perhaps in some particular feature, but none of which we can identify with any face which we have had presented or represented previously.

There is another kind of apparently productive redintegration, which is most frequently to be noticed during the transition state from sleeping to waking, as the kind just noticed in that from waking to sleeping. Instances of this kind are when we have been much occupied, before falling asleep, with some question or problem which has interested but baffled us, and to which our thoughts recur, as it were, of themselves, so soon as we begin to be half-awake. Ideas which throw the whole problem into a new shape, or which even contain its solution, are then frequently observed to present themselves; suggesting that the redintegrative organs have been really operative during sleep, below the threshold of consciousness, have made advances towards harmonising or adjusting those of their processes which were before in conflict, and now present us with the result of that harmonising action in the shape of an apparently new and it may be luminous idea, or with a simpler view and arrangement of the facts.

We may, I believe, assume, that the nerve state in sleep is one of relaxed tension and sensitiveness, not only to sense-presentations from without, but also to stimuli transmitted from part to part within the redintegrative organism. It may also be, that this relaxation of tension affects some sets of nerve processes only, or the strata (so to speak) of the nerve organism in which they take place, and not others; a supposition which would accord with the difference which is easily verifiable between the imagery which immediately precedes falling asleep, as for instance the trains of faces just spoken of, and the redintegrative imagery of ordinary waking experience. On the first, or on both, of these suppositions, the imagery which occurs towards the end of the transition to sleep may be expected to bear but small relation to that which occupies our waking moments; and that which occurs just before we are well awake, in the reverse transition, will be more closely related to the imagery of waking life, or rather will already belong to it, the brain having already begun to resume its normal state of tension.

We need not hesitate, then, to explain cases of apparently pure production of new imagery and ideas, with their accompanying emotions, as being in reality cases of reproduction, in which some of the contributory elements are suppressed, while others are reproduced separately from their original context, and in new combinations with other reproduced elements, owing to the nerve processes which subserve them acting partly below, partly above, the threshold of consciousness, while continuing to enter into new relations with other nerve processes. On this hypothesis productive redintegration will be subject to the same laws as those we have noted in reproductive; but there will be a still greater difficulty, than in the former case, of actually verifying

§ 4.
Trains of imagery apparently new.

and demonstrating the associations which take place under them.

The variations in the play of the molecular changes and inter-actions within each organ, cell, or fibre, of the redintegrative organism, and between these different organs or parts of organs themselves, may be compared to the variations in structure, property, and action, which present themselves in all members of the vegetable and animal kingdoms, and which are the basis upon which the Darwinian theory of natural selection in the struggle for existence is founded. Some account is no doubt to be given of all these variations, as well in the one case as in the other; that is to say, they are not conceivable as being beyond the range of some general law or laws of nature. And every variation must, in both cases alike, arise from a double origin or source, one within the structure itself, the other in its relation to the environment with which it is connected. It is no denial of the necessity of a source of variation within every particle of variable structure, to refer, as now suggested in the case of redintegration, the apparently productive instances of it to the reproductive, as the more general class under which the apparently productive are an included species. For the same necessity of having one source of variation within the organs concerned holds good as well of the reproductive, as of the productive process. In taking this course we are doing nothing more than proceeding from instances of a process which are more, to those which are less, open to observation and analysis. And then the former supply us with hypotheses, which it would be in vain to expect the latter to furnish.

THE LAWS OF ASSOCIATION.

§ 5. The foregoing brief survey of the whole field of spontaneous redintegration, from the simplest cases of mere reminiscence to the most complex of apparently new production, includes cases in which representations of what I have called 'remote' objects spontaneously recall each other. The instance analysed in § 2, so far as it depended on similarity, the recall of the idea of one railway collision by that of another, was a case of this kind, both ideas being representations of 'remote' objects. It has indeed been noted as an admitted fact, that any complex idea or objective thought, when once it has been formed, may be reproduced spontaneously, without the intervention of any purpose or volition on the part of the Subject. But whether complex ideas, and especially those which are the objective thoughts of 'remote' objects, can be originally formed without such intervention, is a very different question.

Now the idea or objective thought of a 'remote' object is not an ultimate datum of experience. It is built up of simpler elements, and this very building up is the work of redintegration, founded on sense-presentations, which may and, in cases of familiar experience, do come in, over and over again, with the apparent result of testing, correcting, and guiding the construction of the idea which we form of the object in question during the whole process of our forming it. Representations of simple sense-presentations, with their accompanying emotions, if any, are thus the ultimate facts of which trains of redintegration are composed. And these may either recall other simple representations and emotions, or they may recall the complex representations of 'remote' objects, into which they have entered as constituents, or conversely any such complex representation may recall any one or more of its own constituents, with its accompanying emotion.

The spontaneous redintegration of immediate and elementary perceptions, therefore, is plainly one indispensable ingredient in the formation of our complex ideas of 'remote' objects. And since the redintegration of these, when formed, is an important part of spontaneous redintegration, the question is necessarily suggested, whether their formation also, in the first instance, is due wholly to spontaneous redintegration, or in other words, whether redintegrations of this kind, including the sense-presentations which are from time to time taken up into them, are sufficient as well as indispensable to account for those complex, but in many cases practically indissoluble combinations, which we call perceptions of 'remote' objects. Among these objects those are of most fundamental importance and significance for knowledge, which compose the visible and tangible, external and material, world of science and common sense. The epoch in the history of experience which is marked by the acquisition of these perceptions has been already shown, in Book I., to be of pre-eminent importance.

Now here it must be remarked in the first place, that the action of attending to a content of consciousness cannot (except by abstraction) be excluded from trains of spontaneous redintegration, any more than it can be excluded from a series of sense-presentations. Attention is a re-action called forth or determined by new, prominent, or comparatively vivid feelings, or changes in feeling, and is the note we take of them as features in the current of consciousness as it occurs. It is more than the re-action by which we simply perceive; it is a heightened re-action which is forced upon us by certain perceptions, which we then perceive either in contrast with, or to the exclusion of, others; and the attention and content together may accordingly be described as, in fact, a selection of one content and a dismissal of another, though the selection is determined by the content, and not by the attention, and therefore goes no farther than to note or register a content already prominent in perception. It is not determined by any purpose, nor does it include a consciousness or recognition of itself as a selection of one content in preference to another. It plays a part in the course of sense-presentation and spontaneous redintegration, and enters into both of them alike as an element in their actual and concrete current. But it does not alter their non-volitional or spontaneous character. It is simply the note taken of the perceived differences and similarities, of which both alike are composed. (The attention here intended and described includes the two main divisions of it treated of in Book I., Chap. III. § 5, as distinguished from the "conceptual attention" treated of in § 6). We have, then, to consider, whether spontaneous redintegration, allowing for this element in it, as well as for the sense-presentations which may be taken up into its course, is adequate to give us the perception of 'remote' objects.

Let us take an instance. Suppose a man has an orange before him, and that it is the first instance of his becoming acquainted with any material object, not excepting his own body, but that he is now making acquaintance with the material world for the first time. Of course this supposition is a mere artifice, for the purpose of eliminating prior or extraneous knowledge from our *analysandum*. It is not pretended that it is historically possible.

An orange is an object of at least three senses simultaneously, sight, touch, and smell, by the exercise of which we become acquainted with it in respect of colour, shape, markings and indentations of surface, a certain hardness, elasticity, and odour. We commonly speak of it as if we knew it, in these respects, by sensation alone, which is only strictly true if we include representation of sense-presentations in the term *sense*. The part played by representation as distinguished from sense, in acquiring the knowledge, is equally essential with that played by sense as distinguished from representation. Of these the part played by representation depends plainly upon conditions coming under two heads:

First there must be connection or functional continuity between the cerebral terminations of the three disparate senses, which are the origin of our knowledge, so as to bring the sensations belonging to them into simultaneous or closely sequent connection, and thus unify them into a single complex percept, partly presented partly represented. The association here is association by what is called contiguity, which, as we have already seen, is really association by continuity or connection of nerve organs.

THE LAWS OF ASSOCIATION.

Secondly there must be, within the central termination or terminations of each several organ of the three disparate senses, redintegration of each several impression of the sense-presentations belonging to the same general kind. For instance, we do not see the orange all at once, or once for all, as round and coloured, but we have in the course of even a short observation, say two minutes, a succession of alternating sense-presentations and representations of coloured shape, or shape and colour together, which depend upon repetitions of the same or closely similar molecular nerve movements, which on their part hang together and form a group such that any one of them, when set up again, will proceed to set up the others, unless inhibited by some other agency. Redintegrations of this kind fall under the head of associations by similarity, which, as we saw above, really depend upon continuity and similarity in the nerve processes in one and the same organ. The same is true also of the knowledge acquired through touch and smell severally.

Two preliminary combinations have thus to be effected, (1) between the representations of the three kinds which originate in three disparate sense organs, and (2) between the representations of each of these sense organs severally taken. And then, thirdly, the further combination of these two operations with each other gives the whole idea of the orange, as a single object of the three senses of sight, touch, and smell.

But in order to effect this latter combination, so as to attain the idea of the orange, attention both to the content and the context of representations

BOOK III.
CH. II.

§ 5.
Association of elementary perceptions.

§ 5.
Association of elementary perceptions.

is requisite; since it is necessary to observe and register in the nervous system, not only the changes of the representations, but the exact synchronism of particular changes of representations coming from one sense with particular changes of representations coming from another; as for instance, minute changes in roughness, hardness, elasticity, and shape, given by touch, with minute changes in light and shade, colour, and shape, given by sight. Only by this being done can we register the whole group of changes as constituting the orange a single complex percept.

The question, then, is, Whether, among the acts of attention required for building up this complex percept, are to be found only acts which note and register the phenomena as they occur, or whether any of them are acts which involve a purpose or desire of knowing the phenomena better, that is to say, acts of conscious comparison and reasoning. I think it almost certain that the truth lies in the latter alternative, or in other words, that volition is involved in the formation of all such complex percepts as those which are the ideas or objective thoughts of 'remote' material objects.

But since the further discussion of this question does not now concern us, I pass on to another feature in the case, in which volition is unquestionably involved, and which will set the distinction which I wish to bring out in the clearest light. I ask, then, Is this complex idea all that we mean by the orange as a 'remote' object? The answer must be, that it is not. The orange as a 'remote' object is conceived as something real in the full sense of the term, namely, as a real condition; it is not merely a complex percept, but a complex percept conceived as having in it or behind it a real nexus, which is one condition of its unity as a percept, or of the percepts which compose it hanging together and forming a single object. It is only a percept-orange, not a real orange in the sense of being a source of perceptions, which could possibly be accounted for solely by the spontaneous redintegration of sense-presentations, including simple attention to their similarities and dissimilarities, their changes and synchronism of changes. All this is indeed indispensable or pre-requisite to our perceiving the orange as a 'remote' object, but it is not that perception itself. For this something else is required. What is that something?

The answer has been given implicitly or by anticipation in the Chapter of Book I. where the perception of the world of real conditions was analysed. It is the putting the question *Why*, or *How*, to the perceptions which spontaneously or involuntarily present themselves. In other words, it is the development of simple attention into attention guided by the desire of knowing something more of the percepts attended to than is contained in the percepts as they actually occur. It is only in consequence of putting this question, in some shape or other, that we arrive at the perception of realities as distinguished from percepts. But the putting this question, the change from attending simply to attending with a purpose consciously in view, is a matter of volition, a change whereby we pass beyond the limits of spontaneous, and enter upon the region of voluntary redintegration.

On referring to the Conspectus of Acts of Attention which was given in Book I., Chap. III., § 6, at the conclusion of that Section, it will be seen that what I have now called simple attention comes under head I. of that Conspectus, and that what I have now called attending with a purpose in view comes under head II., including its two subdivisions A and B, and therefore including also acts falling under heads III. and IV., which are purposive modifications of those subdivisions. That is to say, processes falling under the heads II. III. and IV. of that Conspectus are strictly volitional. The enquiry into them must therefore be reserved for another Chapter.

Without the entrance of this further element of questioning, and its consequences, into processes of spontaneous redintegration, the whole of experience would be nothing but a more or less consistent dream, although it would also be one which we should have neither means, nor occasion, for contrasting with reality in the full sense. For, the idea of reality in the full sense being unknown there would be nothing to suggest that this dream experience was unreal. Simple attention, therefore, as distinguished from purposive or consciously selective attention, belongs to, and is the limit of, spontaneous redintegration on the side of higher and more complex modes of experience, as representation, in contrast with immediate sense presentation, is its limit on the side of lower and less complex modes. And without attempting to decide in doubtful cases, at what precise point consciously selective attention comes in, we may, I think, take it as established, that, at whatever point it comes in, there, and to the extent of its operation, the redintegration in question loses its purely spontaneous character and becomes volitional, that is to say, becomes a spontaneous redintegration modified by volition.

§ 6. A most important point is disclosed by the relation which, as we have just seen, simple attention bears to trains of redintegration. Although it is indispensable to the formation of certain most important groups of percepts, yet it does not alter either the perceptions composing them, or the order of sequence or simultaneity in which they occur; nor does it in any way constitute a nexus between them. The simultaneities and sequences of their components are perceived but not produced by means of it. The sense of effort, or of interest, attaching to the percepts to which simple attention is said to be paid, is not perceived as in any way altering those percepts or their order. We can, in fact, in many cases watch trains of redintegration, in which we can observe simple attention alternating with acts of volitional and modifying attention. I mean cases of dream when the slumber is light, or of reverie, or of those phantasms which sometimes occur just before we fall asleep; in which we may often be aware of the precise moment when we exert a modifying influence on the course taken by the imagery of the redintegration. We seem to say, 'No, I can't have that,—I must have something else.' In brief, acts of simple attention are included in trains of spontaneous redintegration, as part of their content and their course, and not as an interference with them.

The first clear indication which we have of trains of spontaneous redintegration being interfered with, modified, and their course changed, by a re-action on the Subject's part, is given by the consciousness, arising within the redintegrations themselves, which is known as the experience of attention being, not only awakened, but of a purpose or desire being involved in that awakened attention. In moments of this kind we dwell on one part of the content offered, and reject, that is, refuse to attend to, any contents offered by spontaneous redintegration, unless they are perceived as related to that part, or to the desire or purpose which it involves. This, I take it, is the first or lowest shape in which that re-action which we call Volition makes its appearance in consciousness; I mean volition proper, as distinguished from instinct, appetite, or impulse of any kind, whether these are or are not accompanied by consciousness. It is the lowest and simplest shape of volition, as the conscious choice between alternatives.

Trains of spontaneous redintegration, including simple attention only, are clearly pre-supposed by such re-actions as those now described; for these can be understood only as modifications of them. And the laws obeyed by trains so modified will plainly be very different from the laws obeyed by the purely spontaneous or unmodified trains, which latter are known as Laws of Association. Those obeyed by trains modified by volition will be laws, not of association simply, but laws of Action and aws of Thought.

THE LAWS OF ASSOCIATION.

§ 6. The Limits of Spontaneous Redintegration.

Hence it is, that we can draw the line sharply between spontaneous and voluntary redintegration, not as if they were two stages, former and latter, in the historical evolution of the race, or of individuals, but as two different kinds of processes practically co-eval, and modifying each other from the beginning to the end of life's history. They are processes different but closely connected *ab initio*, or nearly so, in all conscious beings of a certain rank in the scale of organisation. Spontaneous redintegration as a process takes its rise from two re-actions, first, a re-action which is receptive of impressions on the nerve organism, evidenced by simple or elementary perception, just as in the case of sense-presentations, and secondly, a re-action which subserves simple attention to the redintegrated content, but does not extend to change the course of the impressions which it receives and registers. The process of voluntary redintegration begins at a higher power of this latter re-action, namely, at that point of it where it becomes consciously selective, or is accompanied by a conscious purpose or desire, and therefore extends to change the course which spontaneous redintegration would have taken without its intervention.

In the actual course of concrete redintegrations, into which all these elements of perception and re-action enter as constituents, and which we may also imagine as taking up new ingredients from sense-presentations of every kind, we are continually moving on lines of spontaneous redintegration, modifying these by consciously selective attention, and starting again with the train so modified, on lines determined by its connection with states or processes spontaneously offered, and belonging to the spontaneous train of ideas. In deciding whether any state or process of consciousness in the whole train is spontaneous or volitional, we must look at it as a present moment. Are we simply perceiving and attending to something offered, or are we selecting, with conscious purpose, what we shall attend to, and what we shall dismiss? If we are simply perceiving, it is a moment of spontaneous redintegration. If we are simply attending, it is one of what has been called, first I believe by the late Dr. W. B. Carpenter, "consensual" re-action, which does not modify the course of the redintegration. If we are purposively selecting, it is a moment of volitional redintegration, modifying the course of spontaneous. The two kinds of redintegration, the spontaneous and the volitional, thus go on together, alternately modifying each other, and forming, with sense-presentations, one complex stream of consciousness, of which, analytically speaking, spontaneous redintegration is the main body or central member, perpetually fed by sense-presentation at its lower, and perpetually feeding volitional redintegration at its upper limit.

Moreover it should again be noted in this place, that the results of volitional or purposively selective redintegrations, as well as the perceptions into which simple attention alone enters, may be themselves incorporated into the body of ideas which form subsequent trains of spontaneous redintegration, notwithstanding their origin in volition. No sooner is any complex idea formed, than it becomes liable to be reproduced spontaneously, under the laws of association, without requiring a new volition to form it afresh. Not only the ideas of real material objects, but any ideas whatever, are liable to spontaneous reproduction; as for instance, the ideas of force, of law, of substance, of beauty, of negation, of Utopia, and in short of any term, general or particular. But obviously, the less familiar or habitual any idea is; the less interesting to the Subject; the less vivid at the time of its origination; or the fewer its connections with other ideas; the less liable it is to be so reproduced.

To understand this we must consider, that the connection between ideas in spontaneous redintegration may be either direct or indirect. It is direct in cases like that of the orange, where either the mere visual impression, or the mere odour, or the mere touching in the dark, or finally the mere name, will call up the whole complex idea of an orange, when once this complex idea has become familiar. It is indirect in cases where any one of these elementary perceptions calls up, through the idea of the orange, say the idea of Andalusia, or of Nell Gwyn, or of Goethe's Mignon, or of Turner's picture of orange boats in a squall at sea. By such indirect transitions as these, the simplest and commonest elementary perception may rouse again into consciousness any part of its acquired garniture, with all its attendant imagery and emotional accompaniments, notwithstanding that the ideas so roused may have originally cost much volitional effort to acquire.

Thus, wherever volition strikes into the train of redintegration, it always finds something to modify, and when it has done so, the resulting modification becomes liable to be reproduced spontaneously, and play its part in trains of spontaneous redintegration. The bizarre juxtapositions of familiar and unfamiliar objects in dreams, and even the forcible though unreasoned impression of knowledge, which in dreams we often seem to possess, as to what and who the places or the persons are, and even what and who we ourselves are, in the dream scenery, are instances of redintegrations which for the time have become purely spontaneous, though containing and dealing with ideas once acquired, at any rate by attention, and perhaps for the most part by consciously selective attention of volition.

Finally it may be remarked, that the stimuli coming from without the redintegrative organism, which may set all its machinery in motion, need not be themselves accompanied by sense-presentations. Consciousness is in all cases a dependent concomitant of nerve action of a certain degree of intensity, not a real condition, or a real link in the chain of its own states and processes. Nerve processes which themselves go on below the threshold, having no consciousness attached to them, may yet act as stimuli to other parts of the nerve organism, and there give rise to processes which are accompanied by consciousness. Nor does this apply only to nerves of special sense. It applies also, if not to the sympathetic nerve system, at any rate to nerves which to a great extent follow the same course, and which may thus transmit stimuli to the brain from all parts of the body, including internal glands, tissues, and viscera, even at times when their own action is not attended by any sense-presentation. The whole nature and complexion of the cerebral redintegrations, that is to say, the trains of their imagery and their emotional character as gloomy or cheerful, may thus be influenced by the temporary state of the internal bodily organs, though the stimuli which are the bearers of the influence are not bearers of sensation either pleasurable or painful.

CHAPTER III.

VOLUNTARY REDINTEGRATION.

§ 1. I begin this Chapter by recalling the three very different classes of nerve re-actions, distinguished, not on physiological grounds though fully in harmony with them, but merely by reference to the modes of consciousness which they subserve, which were arrived at in the foregoing Chapter. The first is that which subserves simple elementary sense-presentations and spontaneous redintegrations, many of which are nothing but the propagation, repetition, and combination of sense-presentations without the interference of any other kind of re-action. The second class is that which subserves simple non-purposive attention, either to sense-presentations or to some content of spontaneous redintegration. The third is that which subserves volitions proper, which are always selective of some feeling or idea, presented or represented, for purposes of one kind or another, all of which may be classed ultimately under the two main heads, knowledge and conduct.

I. Some sense of effort is an invariable ingredient in the consciousness immediately dependent on re-actions of the two latter kinds. It is in fact the mark in consciousness by which we distinguish

VOLUNTARY REDINTEGRATION. 139

them. Not so with the consciousness dependent on re-actions of the first kind; for which reason we commonly hear them spoken of as a passive receptivity, either to sense impressions from without, or to needs, appetites, desires, and impulses from within. In reality, however, a mere passivity is impossible. Some re-action on the part of the recipient is necessary even to his receiving an impression; just as the wax which should make literally no resistance to the seal would not be wax but a vacuum. So it is also with the nerve organs which receive and propagate the impacts of stimuli, whatever be the kind of physical operation concerned, all possible kinds of which, coming under the physiological term *metabolism*, I would be understood everywhere to include by expressions importing any particular kind, such as impact, vibration, chemical change or explosion, electric or magnetic change, integration, disintegration, and so on. The impact, then, of a stimulus, let us say, calls forth a re-action within the organ, the resultant of which action and re-action, within the organ, is immediately attended with consciousness. But of this resultant and its components we are never aware, except by inference. Its immediate effect, or more strictly conditionate, is the sense-presentation, or the redintegration, which accompanies it. There is no separate representative of the re-action in the state of consciousness which depends upon it.

II. The case is very different with re-actions of the second class, those which subserve simple attention. Here we are conscious of a feeling, named sense of strain or effort, in the dependent

Book III.
Ch. III.

§ 1.
Volition.

and accompanying states of consciousness, over and above the increase of clearness or vividness, in the differences, or of distinctness between the parts, of the percept said to be attended to. In momentarily attending to the image, say, of a tree or a stone, though without any consciousness of purpose in doing so, I am or may be distinctly aware of effort. And in the case of sense-presentations it can be pointed out, upon what this sense of effort depends. It depends upon some considerable excess in the momentary strength of the stimulus over the strength, either of the normal or of the momentary phase of action in the organ upon which it impinges, supposing the organ to possess a store of energy sufficient to re-act with the stimulus upon fairly equal terms.[1] In that case the feeling due to the meeting of stimulus by re-action may be distinguished in the total sensation. There is, as it were, a hitch in the smooth sensation-current, a feeling which we call a sense of obstacle or difficulty, if taken prior to the completion of the sensation, and which we call sense of strain or effort in attending, if we look back upon it after the difficulty is overcome, and the total sensation has been experienced. In other words, the difference between the strength of the internal and the external factor, when due to an increase in the strength of the latter, is now represented or evidenced, in cases of simple non-purposive attention, by a sense of effort, which is an element in the resulting experience as a whole.

---

[1] See Professor Delbœuf's *Examen Critique de la Loi Psychophysique,* 2me Partie, pp. 29 to 41 ; a work from which a passage was cited in a previous Chapter.

VOLUNTARY REDINTEGRATION. 141

The same feeling of obstacle or effort involved in simple non-purposive attention occurs also in trains of spontaneous redintegration; and here it is most probably to be interpreted in a similar way. The difference is, that here, in place of an external stimulus and an internal re-action, we have two or more portions or organs of the cerebral system in action and re-action with one another. I am attending momentarily to an idea just as much as to a sensation, if the organ which subserves the idea is roused to re-action by a stimulus coming from another cerebral organ along lines subserving associative processes, provided the strength of that stimulus is in a certain considerable excess of the action, which at the moment is the phase of action of the organ stimulated. The following passage from Professor Delbœuf is as much applicable to processes of spontaneous redintegration, allowance being made for the kinds of consciousness which they subserve, as it is to processes of presentative sensation, of which alone it directly speaks: "There always comes, then, a phenomenon of tension to join itself to sensation in a more or less marked degree, and this is why the sensation changes its quality. The sensation of heat as it increases gradually changes into pain. For here the tension is rapidly augmented, and masks the sensation. General sensibility comes to the front and throws special sensibilities into the background."[2]

The feeling of obstacle or effort is the feeling which marks the entry of this "phenomenon of tension" into consciousness, a moment which we describe as one of attention to the particular

---
[2] Work cited, p. 41.

142 VOLUNTARY REDINTEGRATION.

BOOK III.
CH. III.
§ 1.
Volition.

content in which it occurs, irrespective of whether or not it subsequently develops into a feeling of discomfort or pain. In neither of the two cases of attention, I mean those in sensation and spontaneous redintegration, is there any need to suppose an intervention of any other organ or part of the nervous system, beyond those which were already subserving, sensation in the one case, and a train of spontaneous redintegration in the other, previous to the occurrence of what I have called the hitch.

In further elucidation of the re-action subserving simple attention and its immediate consequences in consciousness, I would adduce the following passage from Professor Schäfer's Address, already cited in a previous Chapter : " It has been shown by Gotch and Horsley, [*On the Mammalian Nervous System, its functions and their localisation determined by a new method.* Philos. Trans. Vol. 182. B. 1891], to whom we owe our knowledge of the fact just mentioned," [viz.: the change of *rhythm*, as well as loss of time, in the stimulation of one centre by another, in at once transmitting and modifying impulse] "that nerve-impulses pass very readily from the nerve-centre *down the afferent channels*, although the strongest excitation will not cause them to pass from the efferent channels *up the spinal cord.*"[3] From this we see, that the re-action subserving simple attention to sensations may throw the whole afferent nerve channel concerned, including its peripheral termination, into a state of tension, thereby increasing the vividness and

---

[3] Prof. E. A. Schäfer, F.R.S., on *The Nerve Cell, &c.*, in BRAIN. Parts LXI. and LXII., p. 165. 1893.

distinctness of the sensation subserved by it, an effect due to what may be called the resultant of the stimulus and the re-action.

Not to be confused with these feelings of obstacle or effort in simple attention, whether in sense-presentation or in spontaneous redintegration, which immediately depend upon purely immanent re-actions, are those feelings, also known by the name of feelings of effort, which depend upon transeunt re-actions, that is, in this case, upon reflex actions directed upon muscles or other non-neural tissues; though it is possible that the very same central nerve terminations may be the seat whence the re-actions of both kinds issue. For instance, in adjusting the eye to a bright object which arouses attention, or in responding by a movement to a sharp touch or blow, or in making an involuntary gesture, or uttering a sound, in consequence of an idea suddenly occurring in redintegration, I have in consciousness, over and above the attention with its feeling of effort involved in these sensations, another feeling of effort due to the resistance offered to the reflex nerve action by the muscle or other non-neural tissue upon which it is directed. And this additional feeling of effort is held by many psychologists, notably by Dr. H. Charlton Bastian,[4] Professor William James,[5] and Professor Hugo Münsterberg,[6] to depend proximately, not upon the efferent or reflex nerve action, but upon a nerve current set up by the activity which that

---

[4] In *The Brain as an Organ of Mind*. 1880. Appendix, pp. 691, sqq.
[5] In *The Feeling of Effort;* Anniversary Memoirs of the Boston Society for Natural History, 1880, already cited; and *The Principles of Psychology*, Chap. XXVI. Vol. II. pp. 493, sqq.
[6] In *Die Willenshandlung*, pp. 82—88.

efferent action stimulates in the non-neural tissue, and transmitted to some sensory nerve centre by an afferent channel; so as only mediately to depend upon the reflex, efferent, and transeunt action, previously directed upon the non-neural tissue. It is evident, that this latter feeling of effort is quite distinct from the feeling of effort in simple attention, which was first described. The feeling first described is an ingredient in attention, and depends on a neural re-action which is wholly immanent; the one now described is subsequent to attention of the first kind (supposing it to exist), and depends upon an afferent stimulus being received from a non-neural tissue, upon which an efferent, reflex, and transeunt neural action has previously been directed.

In these two distinct kinds of felt effort, as they appear in connection with the phenomena of simple attention, in sense-presentation and spontaneous redintegration, we have the first appearance or source of the distinction, which will meet us presently, between acts of purposive attention, or volition proper, in immanent voluntary redintegration, and overt or transeunt acts performed in obedience to volitional acts of choice. There is in fact a sense of effort which is not the immediate accompaniment of acts of purposive attention, though it frequently arises in consequence of them; I mean the sense of effort which is caused by bodily actions, whether purposively performed or not. Similarly there is a kind of attention which, although it involves a sense of effort, is yet non-purposive and pre-volitional; the sense of effort which it involves being the evidence of a re-action on the part of the Subject, the resultant of which re-action and of the stimulus which calls it forth is wholly immanent, and is accompanied, in the Subject, by increased vividness, clearness, or distinctness, of the content said to be attended to. In cases of simple attention, the sense of effort is attributable to differences of energy in the re-actions of one nerve centre on another; the increased vividness, clearness, or distinctness of the content, to the resultant or total action of the original stimulus and the re-action together. These acts of simple attention, with the sense of effort which they involve, are as it were the matrix out of which volitions proper take their origin, or of which they may be regarded as a differentiation.

III. Coming at last to re-actions of the third class, or volitions proper, we find them to be of a complex character. They are re-actions which are purposive selections, a consciousness of the selection made being part of the consciousness attending them. In these there is always an alternative actually, though it may be dimly, represented in consciousness, whether this consists in two or more positive contents, or in the idea of a positive content and of its absence, negation, or omission. The re-action is complex or selective because it is directed, not merely to keep or intensify a content of consciousness, but to keep or intensify one, and thereby to reject or lower the intensity of another, the idea of both alternatives being in consciousness at the moment when the selective re-action takes place. The consciously selective character of the re-action as a whole consists in its double content, its retaining one and dropping the other or others of two or more contents present in consciousness, previous to the moment of decisive choice. We must therefore conceive the nerve area subserving the whole process as correspondingly enlarged.

In cases of attention of this kind, unlike those of the non-purposive class, we must suppose that another nerve organ or centre is first affected from, and then re-acts upon, the organs subserving either sensation or spontaneous redintegration, with their simple attention. The affection or stimulation of the second or higher centre is accompanied in that centre by an idea of the perception said to be attended to; and its consequent re-action is accompanied by an intensification of that perception in the organ which stimulates it, and upon which the re-action is directed; which will also involve its being retained longer in consciousness. The higher centre or organ secondarily affected, and then re-acting, must be conceived as forming part of a whole group or mass of centres, the interactions between which subserve those processes of comparison and deliberation, which precede decision in immanent acts of volition, where two or more alternatives are as it were offered for selection. This mass of centres is what is meant by the enlargement of area spoken of above.

Two things follow from this view of volition proper. First, that it is always a redintegrative act, since otherwise it could not involve comparison between alternatives. Secondly it follows, that no volition as such can be disobeyed or ineffective, since one and the same re-action is in itself both command and performance, being a single act. Volitions proper are not so much acts of an agent, as they are the agent himself acting. There is no action distinct from an agent, except by abstraction; just as there is no motion distinct from a moving body in physics. Volition is thus one exemplification among others of the double nature of the conscious being, as made up of real conditions, consisting of nerve substance and processes, and their concomitant conditionates, states and processes of consciousness.

The nature or whatness of any particular volition proper lies in the alternative chosen compared to that or those rejected, and the alternative chosen is always a feeling or an idea, namely, that to which the volitional re-action gives prominence or intensity, in being directed upon the nerve process which subserves it. Suppose, for instance, I am offered the choice between a basket of apples and a basket of pears, and I choose the pears. Now I cannot in the strict sense *will* to have the pears, for that is not wholly in my own power. I desire to have the pears, and I prefer having the pears to having the apples. But what do I *will?* I will the desire and the preference. And this I do by re-acting upon, or giving weight to, the nerve process subserving the idea of pears, and allowing it to stimulate, say, the organ of speech, or the hand, the organ of prehension, which it does by means of efferent neural currents in the functionally continuous neuro-cerebral mechanism. The act of volition consists in the distinct adoption of the desire for pears in preference to the desire for apples. The adoption of an alternative, represented as an alternative, is the essence of volitional action, so far as that action is immediately known in consciousness. Nor is it at all necessary that both alternatives should have a positive content, as they have in the above instance. We may adopt a desire as the alternative to rejecting it, or we may reject it as the alternative to adopting it, and both the adoption and the rejection are volitions. In the latter case, the rejection of a desire, the idea to which I give weight or prominence is the already existing content of consciousness or some part of it, or something which has become a part of it during deliberation, *minus* the idea which I reject, or the previous context with a blank in place of that idea. This is called *inhibiting* the idea.

Turning to another point, we always know when this decisive moment of volition comes, by a certain sense of effort, or more strictly a certain change in the sense of effort, followed by its cessation or rapid decrease, which accompanies the volition. In the instance just given, this change in the sense of effort would attach to the fact of the re-action exerted by the whole neural area or process, in subserving the comparison and deliberation, being directed upon one single part of it, namely, the area or process subserving the idea of pears; which involves the withdrawal of re-action upon that subserving the idea of apples, and so dissolves the previously existing tension between them. We keep one in consciousness and exclude the other. That is to say, we attend to the one, with knowledge that we *eo ipso* withdraw attention from the other. In the last resort, then, volition proper is an exercise of attention, but it is a complex instead of a simple exercise of it. There is first the attention, with its involved sense of effort, in comparing and deliberating, and then there is the attention to the selected idea, evidenced by the change in the sense of effort and its cessation or decrease just spoken of. It is not as if two ideas, or the nerve processes subserving them, were contending for the mastery, and the stronger of the two prevailed at a given moment to repress the other. The volition does not consist in the simple victory of one over the other;—this would make it a case of merely spontaneous redintegration;—but in that re-action of the whole neural area subserving the comparison or deliberation, which gives the victory to one over the other. And it is plain, that a reaction of this kind must move from that nerve process which subserves the representation of the two ideas as alternatives to each other. This nerve process it is which compares, selects, and then re-acts upon the process subserving the selected alternative alone; which selective re-action is volition proper.

This is seen even more clearly in cases where the antagonistic alternatives are not *in pari materia*, that is, in cases where the choice lies, not between desires which cannot be indulged together, but between some strongly felt desire on the one hand, and the idea or thought that its present indulgence is forbidden by prudence, or by a law of conduct to which obedience is due; cases in short, in which pleasure in the specific sense is opposed to reason, abstracting from the fact that there is also a pleasure, of a certain grim kind, in repressing specific pleasures at the command of reason. In these cases it is evident, that the final decision takes place in the nerve area subserving comparison, because one of the alternatives is itself an idea in which comparison is involved. If the pleasure were adopted wholly without comparison, it might indeed be said to have mastered reason, but the action would have been one, not of volition, but simply of appetite or passion; no conscious choice between alternatives would have taken place. It deserves notice, that actions of this kind are not to be conceived as necessarily prior to comparison and selection between alternatives, or in one word as pre-volitional. They may also occur, and occur habitually, as the consequence of a long series of volitional acts, in which the dictates of reason have been rejected in favour of the allurements of pleasure. It is a case precisely analogous to the spontaneous recurrence of complex ideas in redintegration, ideas which it has taken much labour of conscious thought to build up originally.

I turn now to another part of the subject, namely, the transeunt or overt actions which we perform in consequence of an immanent act of choice. These are voluntary acts because, and in so far as, we represent, compare, and choose between them and their alternatives, in an immanent volitional redintegration. The reflex or mechanically performed actions, not distinctly present in consciousness, which lead up to the performance of the one selected, after its selection, may here be left out of account; as, for instance, the taking up hat and umbrella, when I have decided on leaving my fireside and going out in the rain. The actual going out in the rain may be said to involve an effort of will; the firmness of my resolve is put to the test when I find that the rain is just about to come down in torrents. A somewhat disagreeable sense of effort is involved in actually going out, and the representation of this sense of effort, in the comparison and deliberation which preceded my decision, is an element of the volition proper which issued in that decision.

But this represented sense of effort, represented as involved in one of the alternatives between which my choice is made, is quite distinct from the sense of effort involved immediately or as a presentation, in actually attending to the representations of the two or more alternatives, and deciding between them. The last named sense of effort belongs to the process of redintegration as a process, and is a feeling of the same general kind as that which is an ingredient in all attention, only that it here re-appears in a more complex process, namely, that of choosing between alternatives. The represented sense of effort involved in going out in the rain, on the other hand, is a mere incident of the process of choice, due to the special kind of action which presents itself as one of the alternatives for adoption. There was, for instance, nothing corresponding to it in the choice between the apples and the pears. It has of course its own weight as a motive in determining the issue of the volition, but it is not the sense of effort involved in the volitional act itself. The effort represented as belonging to a part is not the same thing as the effort actually, that is, presentatively, felt in attending to the whole. The parentage, so to speak, of the represented sense of effort is in the re-actions, either between the nerve system and non-neural tissues, or between the organism and external things, represented as giving rise to sense of effort; that of the other, the freshly presented sense of effort, is in the re-actions of parts upon parts of the nerve system itself, conditioning sense of effort, without representing it as conditioned.

The closeness with which the two kinds of sense of effort are often combined must therefore not blind us to the fact of their essential distinctness. The difficulty which I feel in coming to a decisive choice between alternatives, either when the reasons *pro* and *con* are of unusual complexity and so appear almost equally balanced, or when motives which suggest the gratification of some strong propensity or desire are waging an almost equal conflict with a sense of what is truly preferable or morally right, is a difficulty which belongs to the play of different parts of the redintegrative nerve system upon one another, a difficulty which attaches solely to the immanent deliberative process, preceding volitional choice, and delays the final moment of decision. This presentatively felt difficulty is the sense of effort just spoken of as immediately conditioned upon the redintegrative nerve process, and is an essential element in our consciousness of volition.

But here comes into view a further complication, another, or, third, sense of effort, different at first sight from either of the two just discriminated. For this very process which immediately conditions sense of effort, without representing it, may also and frequently does produce, with or without our intending it, overt and transeunt action; it may give rise to tensions of muscles

VOLUNTARY REDINTEGRATION.

and integuments, particularly of the head and face, and affecting the respiration, which send back feelings of hard and painful effort to sensory centres, and give the Subject the impression of being engaged in a struggle which taxes all his powers.[7] We have here, in fact, come across a sense of effort, of the very same kind as that which we met with a few pages above, in contrast with the effort involved in acts of simple attention.

Now on this it must be observed, that, closely as this third sense of effort is bound up with the first, it is not immediately but only indirectly or mediately conditioned upon the redintegrative action, to which the first is immediately due. It is not its immediate concomitant, but a secondary effect, an effect conditioned upon the stimulation of a non-neural tissue by that redintegrative action, and the consequent re-action of that non-neural tissue upon the redintegrative system by means of afferent currents. Consequently its connection with the immediately conditioned sense of effort is a connection due to association, an association which in this case is of extreme frequency or even constancy, so as to take place almost instantaneously, and render the two results apparently inseparable, or even indistinguishable. But this being so, it follows, that this third sense of effort is in reality a case falling under sense of effort of the second kind, and not the first. That is, it is a represented and not an immediately conditioned or presented sense of effort. And we have,

---

[7] For the phenomena here indicated see Professor W. James, *Principles of Psychology*, Vol. II., p. 500; Professor H. Münsterberg, *Die Willenshandlung, ubi supra*; and Professor James Sully, *The Human Mind*, Vol. I. pp. 122-124, and 149-150.

after all, not three but only two kinds of sense of effort in volitional attention, (1) that which is immediately conditioned by the redintegrative process in so attending, and (2) that which is represented as attaching to transeunt actions which are performed in consequence of it. That which I called the third kind has now been shown to belong to the second, as a special case of it, due to a spontaneous association of the sense of physical strain or effort with the sense of effort immediately involved in volitional attention, an association so close and constant as to mislead many persons into overlooking the existence of the latter altogether. The present discrimination, and consequent reduction of three to two kinds of sense of effort in volition, must therefore be regarded as of capital importance.

Both the kinds of felt effort and difficulty, as now discriminated, enter into our state of consciousness as a whole, in cases of strenuous deliberation; and it is important to notice, that the second will appear as the most fundamental, if not the sole essential characteristic of volition, so long as we take the conscious being in relation to his environment as our basis, and consequently consider transeunt reflex action, guided and modified by the action of higher cerebral centres, to be what is properly intended by that term. But the relation of the conscious being to his environment can never be the ultimate basis of psychology, whatever may be its value in biology. We might trace the filiation of something that looks like volition in biology, somewhat as follows :[8]

---

[8] For this schema of filiation I am mainly indebted to Professor Höffding's *Psychology*. See English Translation, pp. 308—309, and 322—23—24. See

VOLUNTARY REDINTEGRATION.

Book III.
Ch. III.
§ 1.
Volition

1. Internally initiated movement, as in an amœba.
2. Internally initiated movement, in which a bystander can perceive a definite direction or end;—*Instinct.*
3. Instinctive movement, accompanied by an indistinct consciousness of the direction or end;—*Impulse.*
4. Impulsive movement, in which the concomitant consciousness becomes distinct as a desire;—*Appetition.*
5. Appetition which is accompanied by consciousness of the preferability of the particular end desired;—*Volition.*

But a scala of this kind, though marking its steps by reference to consciousness, is yet a mere schematism, opening up and preparing the way for a psychological examination of the subject. Psychology has to go far more minutely than this into the question of the origin and sequence of states of consciousness, and their connection with specific parts of the organism, their states and processes. A true psychology must be based, as we have already seen, on the relation between consciousness and its real conditions; and it is this distinction alone, which places us at the true point of view for considering all the profounder questions which arise within it. Thus it is, that the relation of volition to the proximate real conditions of its genesis in the organism, not to its remote real conditions in the

---

also in connection with the present subject a remarkable paper by Dr. Charles Mercier, on *Reflex Action, Instinct, and Reason*, (in the form of a book-review), in Brain. Parts LXXVII. and LXXVIII. Spring and Summer 1897 (the latest No. current as I am revising the present Chapter), pp. 201 to 219. The distinction which he establishes is (roughly speaking) a distinction between nerve actions which are (1) wholly determinate, (2) partially determinate, (3) indeterminate.

environment, decides what we must think of it. Approaching in this way, we see at once, that not reflex action *ad extra*, but the mutual re-action of the nerve centres which subserve redintegration, is the true stock out of which the consciously selective re-action of those centres is developed, and that this alone it is, to which the term *Volition* is properly applied.

I therefore cordially concur with the following sentences from Professor William James' *Principles of Psychology*, though with a *caveat* to be mentioned presently : " We have now brought things to a point at which we see that attention with effort is all that any case of volition implies. *The essential achievement of the will, in short, when it is most 'voluntary,' is to* ATTEND *to a difficult object and hold it fast before the mind.* The so-doing is the *fiat;* and it is a mere physiological incident that when the object is thus attended to, immediate motor consequences should ensue."

And again : " *Effort of attention is thus the essential phenomenon of will.*" But " This *volitional* effort pure and simple must be carefully distinguished from the *muscular* effort with which it is usually confounded." [9]

My *caveat* is as follows. It is ambiguous and *pro tanto* misleading, to speak of the *effort* of attention, or the volitional *effort*, as the essential phenomenon, without carefully circumscribing the import of the term. The neural re-action subserving attention, evidenced but not constituted by *sense of effort*, is the essential phenomenon; but

---

[9] In Chapter XXVI. Vol. II. pp. 561 and 562. The italics are in the original.

the sense of effort gives us no real knowledge of the nature of the neural re-action taken alone, which in that very phrase we call effort, and speak of as if its nature was already known *aliunde*, and its presence immediately perceived. We do not know *what* either the Will or the nerve-system really does, when it is said to make an effort, merely because we call those re-actions, which are accompanied by the feeling called sense of effort, volitions. Effort or *nisus* in organisms is the parallel of Energy in inorganic substances. Both are ultimate though complex facts, our conception of which cannot be drawn solely from the consciousness which, however closely, is conditioned upon them.

I call this a *caveat*, because on this point I do not venture to expect that Professor James will agree with me. An "effort of attention" may mean an effort put forth by a supposed immaterial agent, the Will, or the Self. And that this is really Professor James' meaning seems to be shown, when a few pages later (p. 567) he says, that what he wants is "to emphasize the fact, that volition is primarily a relation, not between our Self and extra-mental matter, (as many philosophers still maintain), but between our Self and our own states of mind." These words would hit the mark exactly, if they did not seem to imply, that an immaterial Self was to be taken as the real agent which puts forth effort in volition, instead of being conceived as a special mode of consciousness dependent, equally with sense of effort, upon nerve substance and action. But however this may be, it is at any rate indisputable, that what we call real effort and the feeling known as sense of effort should be carefully kept unconfused, whatever theory we may adopt concerning the real agency in question.

The foregoing analysis has shown that these two things are perfectly distinct. Although the sense of effort is a feeling which arises in neural re-actions, and is the experience in which our idea of activity in consciousness originates, as is shown by the analysis of the various cases of attention, in which alone it comes forward, yet it is by no means the case, that all neural re-action, in which some nisus or real effort (so-called) is necessarily involved, is accompanied by sense of effort, nor, when it is so accompanied, does the intensity of the feeling afford any direct measure of the strength of the re-action.

In cases of simple attention, which belong to the re-actions of our second class, the sense of effort is great in proportion to the increase of energy initially put forth, in response to a stimulus, by a nerve organ, over the normal or the momentary phase of energy existing in the nerve organ at the time, not in proportion to the strength of the re-action which that organ puts forth in responding to the stimulus, as compared to the strength of the stimulus. The action of the stimulus and the re-action of the nerve organ are both factors in a process of adjustment or accommodation of the nerve organ to the stimulus, and on the degree in which this accommodation is effected depends the degree of clearness and distinctness of the concomitant perception. But in this process, the sense of effort, which is initially great, will begin and continue to decrease, notwithstanding that the re-action is maintained, up to the point at which the organ becomes completely accommodated to the stimulus acting on it, which is the point of greatest clearness in the resulting perception. The sense of effort therefore is not proportional to the strength of the re-action, notwithstanding that it depends for its existence upon the energy of the re-acting organ. It depends upon the varying excess of stimulus over the pre-existing re-action, from moment to moment, and is therefore proportional to the varying increase of the re-action put forth in answer to the stimulus, during the whole process which we may take as beginning with the emergence of the sense of effort, and ending with its disappearance at the instant of attaining perfect (though momentary) accommodation of the organ, and maximum clearness of the perception.

Similarly when we come to re-actions subserving volitions proper, which belong to our third class. Here the place of stimulus *ab extra*, or that of the muscle or non-neural tissue which, when itself stimulated by reflex action, transmits a sense of effort by afferent channels to the brain, is taken by some other nerve centre or centres, belonging to the same group of organs as those upon which they act, centres which in turn re-act upon them, the whole group being that which subserves the process of comparison, deliberation, and choice. The action of every centre concerned in a process of this kind is at once stimulus and re-action to the rest; but the origin of the sense of effort is the same as before. That is to say, the sense of effort felt by each centre is proportioned, not directly to the action which it puts forth, but to the momentary resistance which its own action meets with from the re-action of other centres. The sense of effort is not an immediate perception of the effort put forth, but a perception immediately conditioned upon the resistance which that effort meets with from moment to moment. We may therefore say generally, that changes in intensity of the sense of effort vary directly as the changes of resistance offered to the re-action which the sense of effort accompanies. But these changes in the sense of effort are severally known to us, not by comparison with the corresponding changes in the resistance, but by comparison with the previous and subsequent changes in the sense of effort itself, which all follow the same law.

It is the difference in point of strength between the re-actions of every pair of centres actually subserving volitional consciousness, a difference which varies from moment to moment, or which, in other words, is a change in the relation of their activities, which gives rise, in that consciousness, to a sense of effort varying in intensity. So long as the resistance to the re-action of any centre, being in excess of the energy involved in its re-action, calls forth an increase of that energy, that increase will be accompanied by an increasing sense of effort. But this feeling does not inform us whether the store of energy, which the re-acting centre has in reserve, is great or small; it tells us nothing as to the so-called absolute strength of the re-action which the centre is even then putting forth. Still less does it tell us the strength of the resistance which the centre, with which it is re-acting, is capable of offering. Consequently the sense of effort, taken alone, gives no direct intimation of the strength of the resultant state of energy in the total nerve area concerned in a volitional action, that is, of the energy available either for maintaining the resolve or choice in which it results, if an immanent state of feeling, desire, or thought, is the object chosen, or for directing upon efferent nerve channels, if it is overt or transeunt action that has been decided on. Knowledge of this kind is obtainable only by introspectively observing many instances of deliberation and choice, including of course the varying states of sense of effort which they have involved, and by comparing their results with each other in relation to those varying sensations. Indirectly, therefore, the varying sense of effort is a valuable contributory to self-knowledge.

§ 2. Volitional activity, then, is one thing, and the sense of effort accompanying it is another. The consciousness of volition does not consist in sense of effort, but in sense of choice, in which a sense of effort is an ingredient, and one which only indirectly varies with the strength of the re-action, by which the choice is determined. The sense of effort varies with resistance to re-action, between the extreme points of null re-action on the one hand, and null resistance on the other. The Will, meaning by this term the permanent capacity of a Subject for re-actions determining conscious choice, may be strong, where there is little or no sense of effort, owing to the absence or feebleness of the forces which interfere with its deliberations, and oppose its coming to a decision; and again it may be weak where there is a great sense of effort,

VOL. III. L

owing to these opposing forces being present in overwhelming preponderance. The sense of effort is therefore an accident of volition and of the capacity for it; and being so, it must also be considered as an accident of the Ego, whenever the Ego is regarded as the real agent or agency concerned in volition. In other words, the sense of effort is no evidence for, is not the self-consciousness of, an immaterial Will or Active Ego, any more than it is evidence for that agency consisting of nerve and neural processes. The real agency of the latter stands on independent grounds of experience.

It is therefore not with the Ego conceived in this way, not with the hypostasised Self of common-sense philosophies, that I am now concerned; it is not with this Ego that I am concerned to bring the phenomena of volition into relation. My purpose is briefly to indicate how these phenomena, as presented in the foregoing Section, are related to that group of facts which the common-sense philosophers refer immediately to an hypostasised Ego or Self, as their original source and final explanation; I mean the facts included in what is known as the consciousness of personal agency and personal character, self-determination, conscience, and moral responsibility. For my contention is, that the whole of this experience, including the facts which lead us (erroneously) to hypostasise the Ego itself, are as fully maintained and asserted, in their undiminished integrity, by the analysis which I have now given of self-consciousness and volition, as they would be by describing them as actions of an Ego assumed as a real agent, and making that description do duty as a real explanation. It is with the Ego as metaphysical analysis leads us to conceive it, that I am now about to connect the foregoing analysis of volition.

§ 2. Relation of Volition to the Ego.

We have already seen, in Chap. I., § 4, of the present Book, what the true analysis of the Self or Ego is, namely, that it is the unity involved in all perceiving, whatever be the content perceived; that is, the unity involved in every subjective sub-moment of consciousness, or, what is again the same thing, in every successive moment of Reflective Perception. This unity, when once it has been distinguished and objectified in what is called self-consciousness, is the true meaning of the term Self or Ego. We have now to see the connection of the Self so understood with acts of volition, whereby these assume the character of personal and self-conscious acts. Purposively selective attention, that is, volition, must have preceded the first act of self-consciousness, that is, the first objectification of its total subjective aspect. But dating from the moment when this self-consciousness first takes place, and in proportion as it becomes a more and more habitual ingredient in an individual's train of ideas and feelings, from that moment and in that proportion two degrees or kinds of it become distinguishable, one in which it is the ordinary and almost unnoticed accompaniment of all our experience, and is the object of simple attention in spontaneous redintegration, hardly distinguishable from consciousness simply; and the other, in which it comes again into distinct prominence, from being closely bound up with acts of the kind to which it owes its origin, namely, acts of volition, and in which, therefore, volitions are perceived as the specially and distinctively self-conscious acts.

We have already seen the nature of acts of volition. The fact, that the consciousness involved in all attention, not only contains some sense of effort, but is also forward-looking into the future, gives to the real process upon which it depends the character of being an action, instead of being simply a process; and the consciousness, that the action of comparing alternatives with a view to choice is continuous in consciousness with that which selects one alternative to the exclusion of the rest, gives to that whole unified action the character of self-consciousness, that is, in common-sense phrase, of an action performed by an agent who consciously purposes what he is about to do before he does it. These circumstances, the sense of effort, the forward-looking attitude, the anticipation of realising a foreseen alternative, and the unity of action in the anticipation and the realisation, are the essential elements in our conception of self-conscious volition, or the volition of a Person. Hence every volition subsequent to the first perception of self-consciousness is perceived, or may be perceived if reflected on, as a building up of the Character of the conscious Subject, as an act of *being* as well as of *doing* something.

Our perception of ourselves as agents thus takes place in and through complex acts of volition. These are the acts in which we trace the union of the Subject and its consciousness. In these it is, that the subjective sub-moment or aspect of consciousness is perceived as taking on the character of volition, that is, of action, in addition to, or

VOLUNTARY REDINTEGRATION.

rather union with, the character of perceiving. The whole act is now thought of as subjective, just as the perceiving was before. But the consciousness of agency is rendered distinct only in and by the consciousness of a choice between alternatives, which are represented prior to the act which adopts one of them to the exclusion of the rest. These are therefore the acts which (1) actually build up the character, (2) give us the sense of acting or not acting according to our better knowledge, and (3) make us aware of our responsibility to our own judgment as moral beings, or Persons in the full sense of the word. We have still to deal with the two latter points.

Volition we have seen is a process of conscious choice, a process of comparison and deliberation followed by a decision. Volition is thus not a simple act, but a complex process. Now this consideration discloses a great difference between the two stages of which it consists, (1) the comparison of alternatives ending with perception of the preferability of one to the other or others, and (2) the decision adopting one to the exclusion of the others. And the alternative which is perceived as preferable is by no means necessarily or always the alternative actually adopted. The reason is, that the judgment is an intellectual act founded on a more or less complete survey of all the facts, both of imagery and emotion, which enter into the alternatives compared, while the act of adopting one of them may be determined by the momentary strength actually possessed by one or more of the emotional elements, when brought into the survey. Therefore the fact, that comparison and deliberation are essential to volition, does not involve the consequence, that to adopt the preferable alternative is essential to it. Whatever alternative we adopt, after deliberation, we adopt by choice, that is, by volition. Volition and good or right volition are therefore two things and not one; they may but do not necessarily coincide. There is often a conscious effort required to choose right, in the final moment of decision, over and above the conscious effort involved in the preceding deliberation.

It is not of volition simply, but of morally good volition, that Professor W. James speaks in the following admirable sentences :

" If in general we class all springs of action as propensities on one hand and ideals on the other, the sensualist never says of his behaviour that it results from a victory over his ideals, but the moralist always speaks of his as a victory over his propensities."

And again :

" If a brief definition of ideal or moral action were required, none could be given which would better fit the appearances than this : *It is action in the line of the greatest resistance.*" [1]

Now these two facts, the difference between the two stages in a complete though wholly immanent volition, and the difference between volition simply and morally good or right volition, at once disclose to us the nature and function of Conscience, and the source of our distinction between what is *de jure* and what is *de facto*, and also show the correctness of the conception of the Ego, which has been set forth above. We always do as a fact

---

[1] *Principles of Psychology.* Chap. XXVI., Vol. II., pp. 548 and 549.

seek to identify our Self with our knowledge of what is preferable as a result of comparison and deliberation, and not with the act of decision which follows it, in all cases where there is discrepancy between them. We always seek to justify our actual decision, if possible, before the tribunal of our judgment of preferability; if not possible, we seek to excuse it on the ground of its not being strictly and solely our own act, but having its origin in alien motives, which we distinguish from our Self. In either case we appeal to our Self as identified with our self-conscious perception. If the Self or Ego were the single real agent both of our knowledge of preferability in alternatives and of the choice we actually make between them, no such attempt at justification or excuse would be possible. The act of knowledge and the act of choice would then have the same undivided source, the same undivided authority, and that no source of justification at all; or in other words, the distinction which we now draw between act and justification would not arise. Consequently there would either be no discrepancy between our knowledge and our act, which we know is not the case, or the discrepancy would be inexplicable, a standing paradox;—for which, in fact, it was recognised, but no solution given, in Greek philosophy.

What, then, is the explanation? If, as here maintained, the Ego is the moment of self-consciousness, or reflective perception objectified, the reason is plain. For then we identify our Self with our self-consciousness in its widest range, and therefore, in cases of volition, with that form of it which embraces in one view both our judgment of preferability and our decisive act, whether in accordance or disaccordance with it; that is to say, we identify ourselves with our Conscience. This is no separate or peculiar faculty. It is nothing but reflective perception having the consciousness in volitions for its object, and therefore, when these are immediately present, the self-consciousness in volition. We thus necessarily perceive our conscience as our true Self; and any act of choice which is in disaccordance with it is an act of the Subject which divides it against itself, by forming *pro tanto* an actual character in the individual, which is antagonistic to his actual knowledge of what is best for him as he really is. The neural activity which subserves the act and that which subserves the judgment upon it are thus thrown out of harmony with each other; discord is introduced into the system as an organic whole.

The union of self-consciousness with action in acts of volition is in this way the birth-place of our perception of our own moral, as distinct from our merely *de facto*, and even from our merely intellectual nature. Conscience is the ultimate source of the distinction, not only between moral right and wrong, but of that still more general distinction between what is either right or wrong on the one side, and what is merely *de facto* on the other. The *differentia* of conscience, the point which distinguishes it from self-consciousness simply, consists in its originating as selective attention (including therefore volition), for the purpose of better knowledge, to the consciousness in volition, during the volition, and therefore to the steps or elements composing it, as a process actually taking place. We are then aware both of our judgment of preferability, the sincerity or *bona fides* of which we can test by immediate introspection, and which, if so tested and approved, is in fact a judgment passed by conscience itself, and also of the accordance or non-accordance of our act of decision with that judgment. We thus judge our own volitions in and by a moment of reflective perception; and a higher or more authoritative mode of consciousness than this it is not in our power to conceive. It is *experience* in the strictest sense. The very perception, and consequently the idea, of right and wrong in actions has here its origin. Our highest ideals are those which are formed in obedience to the voice of conscience.

Moreover, with that mode of self-consciousness which is conscience, approval or disapproval is necessarily bound up. It is so because all choice is between a better and a worse *for us to do*, that is to choose, a better and a worse desire *for us to adopt;* the comparison being made prior to the decisive act of choice which completes the volition, and thus allowing room for a discrepancy between our genuine judgment of which is the better, and the decisive act which adopts or rejects it. These considerations leave entirely untouched the question, which will meet us in a later Chapter, whether there is any standard or criterion determining the judgment or perception of better and worse in desires, inherent in the perception of them, or any necessary principle of judgment

170 VOLUNTARY REDINTEGRATION.

BOOK III.
CH. III.

§ 2.
Relation of Volition to the Ego.

bound up with the self-consciousness which perceives the choice. What we perceive and perceive inevitably by conscience, so far as we have gone at present, may be summed up under two heads, (1) whether our perception or judgment of preferability in alternatives is *bona fide* and sincere, and (2) whether we actually choose or do not choose the alternative which we actually perceive or sincerely judge to be the preferable one. This complex perception, namely, Conscience, is the ultimate basis of all knowledge of morality, and consequently of all Ethical theory.

§ 3.
The two chief modes of Voluntary Redintegration;— Desire for Knowledge, and Desire for Feeling.

§ 3. Having thus exhibited the nature of volition in its relation to self-consciousness or the Ego, our next step must be to distinguish and classify the modes of voluntary redintegration to which it gives rise, in modifying the trains of spontaneous redintegration, which are its material or pabulum. The highest active, moral, and intellectual functions of humanity are but so many modes of voluntary redintegration thus arising, when we consider them apart from sense-presentations on the one hand, and from the overt or bodily actions of the Subject, and effects thereby produced, which are their more or less immediate consequences, on the other. The different modes of voluntary redintegration, or immanent conscious action, thus springing from volition, are therefore the sole remaining kind of phenomena with which we have to busy ourselves, when considering, as we now are, the various powers and capacities for feeling, knowing, and acting, which are as it were, the high-water mark of human nature. All other powers and capacities of man are either the pre-supposed conditions and constituents, or else the resulting consequences, of these. And then only do we obtain a view of consciousness or experience in its utmost extent and fullness, when we regard it in the shape and form of voluntary redintegrations, distinguishing the different aspects and elements of which they are composed, and thus bringing their several varieties under the headings of an analytically exhaustive classification.

The main or most general distinctions which lie at the basis of the classification must be looked for in the simplest acts of purposive or selective attention to the contents offered by spontaneous redintegration, and the simple attention which, as we have seen, it includes; not in the more complex acts involving self-conscious criticism, the place and function of which can only be ascertained, when the broader lines of classification have previously been determined. Any content of consciousness offered by simple attention, and dwelt on by purposive, though it may be only for a moment, is what is called an operating *Motive;* and thus motives are, as it were, the roots by which volition springs out of and clings to the common ground of physical human nature, its functions and its tendencies. For the feelings or other states of consciousness, however dim, which accompany instincts, tendencies, or impulses of any kind, are all represented in spontaneous redintegration; and thus volition adopts certain desires naturally and inevitably from the content of spontaneous redintegrations, quite independently of the agent's self-consciousness, and prior to any possible criticism of what he is doing, on the agent's own part. These desires, as we have seen in the Chapter on Redintegration, are part and parcel of human consciousness, and are interwoven as inseparable elements in trains of spontaneous redintegration, from which they are carried over, as necessary constituents, into processes governed by volitional action; constituents which the self-conscious being can mould and modify, but of which he can never entirely get rid.

All volitions are, as volitions, forward-looking, all aim at some end, all are modes of the actual being of the agent, all contribute to form the agent's character. These features therefore are common to all the redintegrations which they set up. But over and above these common characteristics of volitions as such, there are others which give a specific character to the voluntary redintegrations in which they predominate, that is, in which they operate as their leading desire, end, or motive; excluding thereby, not indeed the presence of different or opposite characteristics, but their operating as ends or motives determining the nature and course of the redintegrations. It was these leading characteristics which I had mainly in view, when speaking of the part offered by spontaneous redintegration for adoption by voluntary, and so carried over, as it were, from the process-contents of the one into the process-contents of the other.

Now of these main characteristics, those which give the first and most general distinction of our classification are at least two, and not more than two, in number. They are characteristics which arise from the two inseparable elements, formal and material, which we have found to be essential constituents of all process-contents of consciousness, whether presentations or representations. Time and space relations are the formal element in sense-presentations, and the specific sensations, with their pleasures and pains, are the material element. In redintegration, the imagery which is the framework of emotions is the formal, the emotions pervading it, in all their variety, are the material element. There can be no more universal, no more deeply seated, contrast than this in the whole range of experience. And according as interest attaches predominantly, now to the formal, now to the material element, in the processes which constitute objective thought, we find that those processes are governed either by the desire for knowledge of the relationships obtaining between contents of any and every kind, relationships which are part of the imagery or framework of feeling in redintegration, or by the desire for having, that is, experiencing, feelings of some specific kind.

Desires which fall under one or the other of these two most general heads operate as ends or motives in determining the course of redintegrations,—the really motive power lying, of course, in the neural mechanism which subserves them,—and, when they are adopted by volition, imprint quite different characters on the voluntary redintegrations which spring from that adoption, and which for the time they are said to govern. The desire for knowledge is a desire to know what the facts of any given case are, what the real constitution and course of Nature are, without altering them. A better, fuller, and more accurate knowledge of fact is the only new thing aimed at by the voluntary redintegrations so initiated. The desire for feeling, on the other hand, when adopted by volition, is a desire to strike into, modify, and effect a change in the direction of events, in the constitution and course of Nature itself, or in other words, is the desire of producing a new state of things, which shall be a new experience more consonant than the present with the ideals and wishes of the redintegrating agent.

It is clear that these two desires are supplied inevitably by spontaneous redintegration. It is also clear, that neither can knowledge wholly exclude feeling, nor feeling knowledge. At the same time, the predominance of the desire for the one precludes the desire for the other from governing the redintegration which its adoption by volition sets on foot; and thus the redintegrations governed by each are of an essentially different character. Both kinds indeed, as voluntary redintegrations, are governed by desires and aim at future satisfactions, for even the desire for knowledge involves, at least implicitly, the desire of becoming a more completely cognisant being than before, but here their similarity ends. The idea of knowledge implies the existence of the thing known, whether it be past, present, or future, independently of the action directed to know it; the idea of feeling carries with it no corresponding implication of an actually existing objective reality, other than the objective thought which is or will be the vehicle, imagery, or framework, of the feeling itself.

With respect to the Ego, the distinction now drawn between the two great modes of voluntary redintegration confirms the conclusion to which we came above, namely, that, while consciousness in the shape of spontaneous redintegration is a necessary pre-requisite of the volition or re-action which initiates voluntary redintegration, the perception of the Ego, or Self-consciousness in the proper sense, is not necessary as a similar pre-requisite. For the two great modes now distinguished plainly take their origin from the most elementary features in all consciousness, and are therefore, in that respect, essentially independent of Self-consciousness.

Volition is always choice between a better and a worse, or what so appears, or is so felt, at the moment of choosing, and it is also always a looking forward in anticipation, as well as a looking backward upon the content already experienced, and offered at the moment of volition by spontaneous redintegration. And we have no other content to choose from, but one which is offered in this way. In selectively attending to what we choose to dwell upon and so carry forward into the next future moment of consciousness, we modify the train of spontaneous redintegration, because every element, or feature of any kind, belonging to a content of consciousness, has its own kind of associations connected with it, which will be spontaneously brought forward in redintegration, when a feature or element of its own kind is selected by attention, and dwelt on to the exclusion of others. Now just this selective attention is volition. In it we select from the past what we wish to carry forward into the future, there to become the object of a renewed act of attention.

In this way it is, that the initiating volition gives a particular direction to the line which the redintegration initiated by it shall follow. We thereby choose and adopt the line of direction of our voluntary redintegrations.

Here comes in the fundamental and most general distinction, drawn from the two elements of consciousness spoken of above. If the relations of any content in objective thought to others, or of its parts to one another, or of the content itself to the real object thought of by it, are what attracts our interest, what we select to dwell on, and so carry forward into the next future moment, then and thereby we choose the line of Knowledge. If on the other hand some specific feeling or group of feelings, among those which belong to any part of the content, is what interests us, and what we select to carry forward by attending to it, then and thereby we choose the line of Feeling. Some particular modification of consciousness as an existent, not determined by the desire that it should be consistent with other modifications, or faithfully mirror a real object thought of, is then our aim. In the former case, we make simple truth of fact our ultimate criterion of better or worse in the volitional choice; in the latter, we make the continuance or intensification of some specific feeling our criterion of it. In either case we shall be selecting, in the redintegration which we so initiate, a better in preference to a worse; but we shall be selecting it by what we may call a different standard, though the standard is itself made a standard only in and by the fact of the selection which initiates the redintegration.

Observe, I express no opinion as to which of these two selections, or modes of redintegration founded on them, is the better. Nor is any criticism of the original selection, as now described, included in the selection itself. We have, in selective volition as now described, volition in its very lowest terms brought before us. And we see that volition in its lowest terms, that is, in its essential elements alone, is the origin and source of the recognition of comparative worth or value, of a better and a worse, of preferability in any shape, that is to say, of good and evil in their utmost generality. For this mere act of selective attention involves, though without recognising it, what we afterwards call a discrimination or judgment of value, preferability, comparative good and evil. Differences inherent in the percepts constituting trains of spontaneous redintegration are the object-matter which acts of selective attention take the initial step towards ranging in groups or series, and bringing under heads, to which in subsequent acts of comparison and judgment we give the general names of good and evil, and to which we attribute comparative value of various kinds. The origin of our standards for passing all such subsequent judgments is in acts of selective attention or volition, which brings to the task no standard of any sort or kind ready made.

It is clear, then, that the perception of the Ego, or Self-consciousness, is no essential or necessary part either of volition, or of voluntary redintegration, or of the idea of value, or of good and evil in their greatest generality, or of the distinction between the two chief modes of voluntary redintegration, Knowing and Feeling. This conclusion is moreover in perfect harmony with facts established in Book I., I mean the facts, that the perception or knowledge of the Subject as a material object must precede that of the Ego, or Self-consciousness (in any sense of these terms, either popular or analytical), and that the exercise of selective attention is a necessary antecedent of the full perception of the Subject, and indeed of all objects which are perceived as real, in the sense of being real conditions. When, however, the perception of the Ego, or Self-consciousness, has been attained, and when we fuse it, as it were, with volition, in the single but complex perception of our Self as the self-consciousness of the Subject, in the way described in the foregoing Section, then for the first time it is, that we are enabled to perceive and judge our choice while actually making it, approve or disapprove the choice, both as a choice, and as one which we actually make, and in fact become moral and responsible beings in the full sense of the terms, in and through the fact, that Conscience, or the function of being self-conscious of our own volitions, and consequent actions, as ours, has now been added to, or rather developed out of our nature, as the last and highest mode of reflective perception.

The error most frequently committed, as it seems to me, in this matter, is to antedate the arising of Self-consciousness, or perception of the Ego, so as to make Conscience co-eval with Volition. The common-sense use of the terms *I* and *We* makes no distinction between acts of volition simply and acts of self-conscious volition. It speaks of both alike as *mine* or *ours*. At the moment when we use them the self-conscious position has become familiar, and it is a natural illusion to imagine that this position has always and from the first been occupied. Language, in fact, in this instance, and it is a capital one, affords no clue to the analysis of the things intended by its terms, nor even a suggestion that they demand or are capable of analysis. I speak, of course, only of language as commonly used, not of its etymology, which is another matter.

The consequences of this error, natural as it is, are nevertheless serious. For to imagine, that in all acts of volition we necessarily have a consciousness of our Self as an agent, is almost inevitably to imagine, (1) that the distinction between Self and other objects is known to us in all volitions, and (2) that either this distinction or the perception of Self affords some standard or ground of preferability, of which we are bound to take notice in all acts of choice. And this fallacy seems to me the chief source of most of the *a priori* or so called intuitive theories of Ethic, theories which must rest, if the present analysis is correct, on a thoroughly unsound foundation. Moreover, apart from this consideration, the interests of Ethical truth, and indeed of morality itself, so far as Ethic contributes to morality, seem to me far better served by an analysis which, like the present, compels us to resort to subsequent judgments of Conscience for perpetual reformation and renewal of our moral standards, standards originally set up by non-self-conscious, and therefore pre-moral volition, than by a theory which bids us look for some single and intuitively evident standard, inseparable from acts of conscious choice. But this is anticipating. The justification of the view thus briefly stated must be reserved for a future Chapter.

§ 4. Admitting, then, that the chief Modes of voluntary redintegration are two, determined by our adopting either the desire for knowledge, or the desire for feeling; and allowing also, that they may be discriminated from each other by the characteristic difference, that the former aims at altering our knowledge in the future, without altering the things known, while the latter aims at altering in the future the actual course of natural events; the next question concerns the relations which obtain between these two modes in actual experience, or in other words, the way in which they are combined with one another in the concrete; that is to say, in any considerable portions or lengths of conscious living, which may be variously named periods of feeling, cognition, or conation, according to the character which we wish to signalise, or which is most prominent when we think of them.

I begin by recalling the fact noticed above, that volition is never frustrate, or in other words, that whatever we strictly speaking *will*, that we also, and in the very same act, strictly speaking *do* or *are*. Applying this in the first place to redintegrations governed by the desire for knowledge, we see at once, that we cannot will to know; all we can do is to will, or adopt, the desire to know. Knowledge, the result aimed at, depends on other circumstances not included in the volition, and often not in our own power at all. Thus, what we as agents contribute to our own acquisition of knowledge is the effectively adopted desire to know, with its effects in modifying the course of our own spontaneous redintegrations. That is to say, what we, in this sense, contribute is *Thought;* that being the name for our volitional activity in aiming at knowledge. The whole of the content of knowledge, as distinguished from this activity, is contributed by presentations and representations, which come before us in trains of spontaneous redintegration. The distinction between thought and knowledge is thus very plain and deep. Yet there are few philosophical distinctions more often ignored than this, or ignored with more fatal consequences.

We never find Thought *pure;* it is always found as an element in the concrete redintegrations which aim at knowledge, and which always begin and end in concrete perceptions, in the large sense. Pure thought is always an object of abstraction. Yet I need hardly say, it is not the less real on that account, though not as a separable entity or agent. It is another instance, an instance in the domain of voluntary redintegration or action, of an element always distinguishable from the co-element or co-elements, from which it is also always inseparable. What then is it that we do by thought? The answer is plain. Supposing our general direction determined by the desire to know more about some object before us, from coming to some difficulty within, or limit to, our present knowledge of it, what thought does is to select, and dwell on by attention, that feature in its content which puzzles or limits us, and then to watch the trains of spontaneous redintegration, until some content is offered in them which enters into harmonious relations with the feature which we have selected. Thought is thus volition over again, only this time exhibited in the concrete, that is, as starting from a particular given object, as the object concerning which we desire at the outset to acquire new knowledge. In the concrete process of knowing, the agent contributes (1) adoption of the desire to know, (2) selection of the apparent means; both being volitions. The result to which he comes is then determined by the facts as offered by spontaneous redintegration. He is master of the volitions, but he is not master of the conclusions which they contribute to form. The facts to which he attends force conclusions upon him, which he cannot avoid, save by the accession of new facts or further acts of reasoning; or for a time, by acts of volition, founded on some extraneous consideration, as for instance, when we accord our assent to conclusions not fully proved, because they are palatable, or withhold it from fully proved conclusions, because they are unpalatable. But this is in fact allowing desire for specific feeling to interfere with and defeat the desire for knowledge, with which we begin. The art of doing this, without appearing to sacrifice the desire for knowledge of the truth, is the art of which the late Cardinal Newman exhibited the method, in his well-known *Grammar of Assent*.

It is clear that in all such concrete cases, where we start from a given object as the object to

VOLUNTARY REDINTEGRATION.

be better known, the selection of that given object may have been determined by some specific interest of feeling which we take in it; that is to say, our motive for desiring to know it better may have arisen in the second chief mode of redintegration, the desire for feeling, to gratify which we think knowledge a necessary means. The knowledge of the given object is then itself desired as a means to a further end, and its selection is preceded and determined by some specific interest, not by the desire of knowledge simply. Nevertheless, from and after the selection of the object to be known, the redintegration which it sets on foot is governed by the desire for knowledge, and belongs to the first mode of redintegration. And this it continues to do so long as its characteristic purpose is kept in view, namely, the purpose of acquiring new knowledge without altering thereby the things known, or imprinting a new direction on the course of real events; except, of course, that part of the course of real events which consists of the neuro-cerebral processes subserving the knowledge. But these are neither the objects of the knowledge, nor events which there is any conscious desire to alter; they are the proximate real condition immediately subserving the redintegration itself as it proceeds, and throughout its course, being indeed in that character the most essential factor in the acquisition of the knowledge, effecting its change from worse to better, and not to be counted among its consciously anticipated purposes.

I turn in the next place to the second chief mode of redintegration, governed by the desire for feeling, and apply to it the same doctrine, namely that will is never frustrate. We will a desire by adopting it, and dwelling upon it as a desire. Thus it is, that, what we simply will, we will as end, not as means. To will the means to an end is nothing else than making the means our proximate end. In volition we dwell upon the end by adopting the desire for it, and this cannot be frustrate of its purpose; our will fulfils itself; but it does not extend to the procuring or securing the continuance or increase of the feeling in the future. That depends on other circumstances, which may or may not be in our power. It depends on our knowing, being able to employ, and actually employing, the right means. Now the first of these conditions is matter of knowledge. That is to say, we are thereby referred to the other chief mode of voluntary redintegration, just as we saw might be the case in the preceding paragraph. When we have discovered, by that mode of redintegration, what the right means are, and what is the first step to be taken in putting them into execution, then we select that specific idea for attention, and allow it to take effect, either in overt and transeunt action, or in imprinting some resolve or image upon the cerebral mechanism by immanent action.

We may say, then, that normally the concrete course of conscious and voluntary life consists of an alternation between the two chief modes of voluntary redintegration. It begins, let us say, in some specific interest being selected and dwelt upon, and this gives rise to thought employed to acquire knowledge of the means whereby that interest may be secured. But this very course of thought directed to acquire knowledge may itself bring new objects into view, which are attended with new interests of a specific kind, and which in virtue of these new interests give a new direction to the redintegrations governed by the desire of feeling. Normally it is redintegrations of this latter kind, that is, of feeling, which select ends, while redintegrations of knowledge discover means, and enable their selection as proximate ends. Yet it is also an ordinary experience, that a long series of redintegrations of either kind takes place, without being interrupted by the intervention of redintegrations of the other kind. This is most often, and for the longest periods, the case with the redintegrations of thought in acquiring knowledge, as when some man of science is employed for hours together in working out some difficult problem. But it is also found with redintegrations governed by the desire for feeling, as when some religious mystic is absorbed in rapturous contemplation of a specific kind of imagery. Moreover, a bias in either direction, more or less exclusive of the other, may be implanted in the Subject's character from his birth, and may also be fostered by circumstances, by training, or by indulgence, to such a degree as to make its pursuit habitual, and almost, in some cases, a virtual necessity of conduct.

Apart, however, from these extreme cases, and over and above the fact of the alternation of the two modes in concrete experience, it is found that trains of voluntary redintegration, consisting of the alternations spoken of, fall into two great classes, according as the desire which governs the whole of any one continued train of alternating re-

§ 4. Relation of these two Modes to each other.

dintegration is a desire for knowledge, or a desire for some specific end or content of knowledge.

If the desire for knowledge is the ruling motive, the whole train of alternating redintegration in the concrete is governed by Thought, and has the character of Knowledge. Thus arise the various Positive Sciences. With these we have nothing to do in philosophy, except so far as to show their connection with metaphysical analysis. This was partly done in Book II., from the side of the scientific conceptions which stand at the root of them; and has now been done, and will be done more fully in the following Chapter, for the remaining part, by showing the general relation of acquired knowledge to the operation of Thought, in the conscious agents who pursue and develop such conceptions.

The methods of science, of which so much is usually said in treatises claiming to be either philosophical or logical, and especially the methods and laws of Induction, are methods not of Thought simply, but of acquiring new knowledge on the basis of old, by means of thought, observation, and experiment together. The thought involved in them consists (1) in paying selective attention to some part or circumstance in the whole object-matter, which is either obscure in itself or unharmonised with the other parts, (2) in watching the content offered by presentation or by spontaneous redintegration, for facts which may be brought into connection with it, and (3) in thence anticipating consequences which may be tested by experiment or newly directed observation. In brief, it is a framing of hypotheses, which may support or

VOLUNTARY REDINTEGRATION.

even develop into a theory, or at least may destroy an old one which is unsatisfactory. In so far as this process involves attention to a specific content, it seems to belong almost as much to the second as to the first of the two chief modes of redintegration which alternate in the series. The difference is, that here the interest which attaches to the specific content selected does not spring from its own original pleasurable quality, but is derived to it from its supposed conduciveness to the end of knowledge, and is then enhanced by personal predilection for a subject which we have made our own. But originally it becomes an end of feeling, because it is supposed to be a means of knowing.

Turning to the various trains, made up of concrete and alternating redintegrations, which are governed on the whole by the persistent desire for a specific content or feeling, we find that from them arise the various branches of practice, in that narrower sense in which it is contradistinguished from theory, that is, from knowledge in its purest form. All branches of practice in this special sense are methods of attaining some desired change or improvement in the actual course of Nature, either our own or external to us, as distinguished from a change or improvement in our knowledge of Nature, considered as existing independently of our present action. They aim at something entirely *in futuro;* the domain of possibilities and practicabilities is theirs; those criteria of certitude which are derivable from a comparison of their objective thoughts with the real objects of a material and independently existing world, or course of Nature, are wanting to them, since *ex*

BOOK III.
CH. III.

§ 4.
Relation of these two Modes to 1 each other.

§ 4. Relation of these two Modes to each other.

hypothesi the real results they aim at do not at that time exist; their own criteria are drawn from remembered or recorded experiences of success or failure, in similar or analogous instances of practical action or endeavour.

Their variety is enormous, as will be evident if we consider that, with the single exception of acquiring knowledge, they embrace all departments of human activity, social, political, civil, military, industrial, and so on, with all their minute subdivisions and ramifications; in fact, that it is a variety limited only by that of the several desires, and groups of desires, of which human nature may be the seat. Nevertheless in the pursuit of any one branch of practice, the ultimate end or primary motive alone is fixed, which governs the pursuit. During the pursuit itself the same alternation takes place between the two modes of redintegration, which we have already observed in the pursuit of knowledge, I mean the alternation between the pursuit of ends and of means to ends. For knowledge already acquired, whether it be knowledge of laws of Nature, or of single matters of fact, or knowledge derived from recorded experience of success and failure in analogous instances, is constantly called in and employed to guide the course of action, from step to step, in the pursuit of the ultimate end in view. In short, practice in all its branches is a method, though a method of realising something which does not at the outset exist; for method itself is nothing else than the alternating pursuit of ends and means, combined by the purpose of attaining an ultimate or primary end.

§ 4. Relation of these two Modes to each other.

In conclusion it may be said, that every branch of human action, conduct, or practice, taken in the large sense in which it includes, instead of being contrasted with, the exercise of thought and reasoning in acquiring knowledge, contains in itself, in virtue of the alternation now insisted on, the rudiments both of a science and of an art. It is directed now to know, now to do or produce something, both parts of the action being combined, by virtue of the ultimate or dominant end of the whole action, in support and furtherance of each other.

I say the rudiments of a science and of an art, because the alternation here spoken of refers only to immanent actions, abstracting from the overt or bodily acts, to which during their course they give rise, as for instance, the actual performance of experiments involved in the pursuit of knowledge, or the actual intervention in the course of human affairs or of Nature, involved in the other branches of practice. It is with redintegrations alone, the immanent actions of objective thought, that we are here concerned, and in these it is, and in the alternations of mode which they contain, that the distinction, which in the concrete we know as that between science and art, has its ultimate source. Every train of conscious and voluntary redintegration, since it is guided by purpose, is a method; and every act or moment, which enters into its composition, has in it the rudiments of that alternation which constitutes method, in the two elements, of knowledge and feeling, which as its components are inseparable from it, as well as being inseparable from each other.

§ 5. We have now before us in outline the whole range of human practice, so far as it comes forward in redintegration spontaneous or voluntary. We have seen that it falls into two main branches; the first depending solely on the desire for knowledge, or aiming at cognition alone, but at the same time at cognition of every possible kind of object-matter, and therefore being co-extensive with the whole range of experience; the second consisting of a multifarious group of pursuits or activities, each of them governed by the desire for some special feeling or group of feelings; but always including cognition as a necessary condition or means of its realisation, or entering as a ministerial factor into the pursuit of it. All practice, however, as we saw in § 1 of the first Chapter of the present Book, is the object-matter of some science of practice, which analyses its processes, and systematises their laws, with the view of guiding and developing it; in virtue of which function that science of practice becomes a practical science, that is to say, an activity of thought which is both cognitive of reality and directed to realise in the future a specific purpose. It is therefore evident, that the discrimination and classification of the practical sciences must follow those of the branches of practice which are their object-matter, those being the actions which they are directed, first to analyse, secondly to promote and guide.

It is also evident, that the practical sciences, in their character as science, must be based upon that mode of reflective perception which includes self-consciousness or perception of the Ego, since, unless

VOLUNTARY REDINTEGRATION.

§ 5. The main branches of Practice.

they were placed at this point of view, so as to make part of this the most comprehensive mode of human knowledge, the results obtained by them would be destitute of all final or decisive authority, unstable and precarious. The practical sciences, therefore, in contrast with the practices which are their object-matter, take their rise, not in the simply re-active energies of selective attention, but in those complex re-actions of attention which include a perception of selective re-actions as belonging to the Ego, as well as a perception of them as selections between a better and a worse. In other words, the practical sciences are founded in that mode of reflective perception which we name Conscience; and Conscience is not reflective perception merely, but consciously attentive and selective perception; selective of the conscious action of the Subject, as its special object.

Furthermore, since conscience is no separate faculty with a constitution fixed once for all, and with an outfit of forms, laws, or principles of its own, but is a particular mode of reflective perception, and exists only in its successive moments, it is also plain, that conscience itself, with all its perceptions, judgments, and dictates, is a part of the object-matter of conscience, that is, of itself in subsequent moments, just as reflective perception is, of which it is a mode. The activity of conscience is, in other words, itself a part of practice, as the *analysandum* of practical science. And this is a most important addition to what we have hitherto, that is, up to the present Section, included in the range of human activities governed by the two main classes of desires—desire for knowledge and desire for specific feeling. Conscience, in fact, has two important functions—one to guide the individual agent in his immediate future action, by criticising his action in the past, the other to aid in the establishment of a general science of practice, by analysing and determining the laws which govern conscious action, including those of conscience itself.

In endeavouring, then, to bring human practice, in its entire range, under the survey and dominion of practical science, there are two main points to be considered;—first, the nature of thought or the reasoning process itself, which is necessarily involved in all voluntary redintegration, in whatever way it may be employed, and, secondly, the grouping of the branches of practice, which fall under the consideration of thought or reasoning as its object-matter. I will devote the present Section to the consideration of the second point, a proceeding which has the advantage of taking up the line of thought where it was dropped at the end of the foregoing Section.

Reverting, then, to the two great branches of practice governed respectively by the desire for knowledge and the desire for specific feeling, let us consider where, if at all, a further differentiation may be observed, which will break them up into smaller and more manageable groups. In the desire for knowledge this seems impossible. There is something quite unique about the whole of it, parallel, and co-extensive with the mere luxury of consciously existing, or of having a state of consciousness simply and solely as such. Thought, too, the volitional activity to which it gives rise,

VOLUNTARY REDINTEGRATION.

Book III. Ch. III.

§ 5. The main branches of Practice.

is the same everywhere, and to whatever object or content it is directed.

But the case stands differently with the other great class of desires, included under the desire for feeling; for this is always a desire for some specific feeling or content. Its unity is that of a collection of units, a similarity, not simply an identity, of nature possessed by all specific contents or feelings desired. Here it is, that it lies open to differentiation. There is no such thing as Thought which is not identical, in nature, with itself as Thought, whatever it may be employed upon. There is no such thing as Feeling which is not, as Feeling, specifically different from a whole host of other feelings. It is the nature of every feeling to have a specific quality, whether it be nameable or not, which is another question. But there is no specific quality answering to the general name of *feeling;* and therefore this name does not imply one specific thing, the same under all modifications, and definable in the abstract, as thought is. Pure thought is the object of an abstraction, but pure feeling, if taken as an object, is a fiction. In no single feeling, simple or complex, is it possible to perceive feeling pure, distinguishable though inseparable from the specific content which is itself. Some specific feeling is itself an element in every concrete perception.

The unity, then, of the desire for knowledge, and of the redintegrations which spring from it, is proximately due to the unity of nature in the object desired, namely, knowledge as obtainable by thought, and therefore ultimately to the unity of thought itself, and not to the fact of its being a desire. The

§ 5.
The main branches of Practice.

desire for specific feelings, on the other hand, has no such unity, inasmuch as its unity cannot be given by the mere fact of its being a desire, but must arise, if at all, from the unity of the object desired. But this includes all specific feelings. Hence it is for some deeply seated difference between specific feelings, or groups of such feelings, that we must look, if we would discover a further differentiation of the two great modes of redintegration already established. That is to say, we can hope to find it only within the second of those two modes, namely, redintegrations governed by the desire for feeling; always remembering, that the difference we are in quest of must be discoverable in the redintegrations of objects, and not merely in the objects themselves, that is, must exist as much in the desire, which arises only in redintegration, as in the content or object desired, if this latter is conceived as something having an independent existence in the real order of Nature.

Looking in this way at the great heterogeneous group of desires for specific feelings or contents, we find that it breaks up into two lesser groups which divide it without remainder, according as the desired feelings are or are not irresistibly forced upon us as objects of desire, that is to say, are either feelings which we must obey, or feelings which we may indulge. In other words, the distinction between desires which are imperious and desires which are optional is the distinction of which we are in search. In place of one vast heterogeneous group of desires, we then have two lesser and less heterogeneous groups, co-ordinate and apparently co-eval with each other; the second of which groups, namely the optional, has a remarkable similarity in one respect to the desire for knowledge, namely, in the fact that each of its members is a desire for the simple satisfaction of a feeling, untinged by the circumstance, which attaches only to desires of the imperious group, feeling that the non-satisfaction of the desired would be a pain, and often an unendurable one.

I will begin by speaking in the first place of those desires only which are prior to, or more strictly independent of, the arising of self-consciousness. The first group of these is formed by the feelings which flow from our bodily constitution, our bodily wants, appetites, and impulses, which force us to seek and take pleasure in the objects which satisfy those needs, and remove the pain which they involve so long as they are unsatisfied. The desires for food and drink, air, light, warmth, bodily activity, and sexual intercourse, and many other modes of escaping bodily pain and discomfort, are thus necessities of our nature. These are the imperious desires. By this I do not mean, that we have no power of modifying, restraining, and governing them, but that their non-satisfaction is always painful, the pain being of various kinds, and also varying, within each kind, in degree of intensity, from slight discomfort up to almost intolerable torture. They are imperious in the sense that, whether their non-satisfaction is intensely painful or not, and whether we can succeed or not in governing them as motives of action, we must in any case attend to them, and cannot, if we would, avoid being sensible of them as desires.

The second group of desires contains those which flow from those feelings which we take a natural and spontaneous pleasure in satisfying, whenever and wherever we are not suffering from the unsatisfied necessities of the first group, and are left, as it were, free to enjoy the world of Nature, in the midst of which we find ourselves. We then immediately take delight in pleasures of sense, sights, sounds, flavours, and, in short, beauties and attractions of every sort and kind, attractions appealing at first to a savage and uncultured taste, in all the objects and persons about us, and especially in those objects and persons which are concerned in the satisfaction of needs belonging to the former group. These desires constitute what I venture to call the optional group of desires.[1]

In the redintegrations which are governed respectively by these two co-ordinate groups of desires, we have the foundations (1) of what is strictly prudential, popularly and loosely called practical, activity or reasoning, the term *practical*

---

[1] I should perhaps warn my readers not to confuse my optional group of desires with Dr. Bain's "Optional Morality," as described in a well known passage of his *Mental and Moral Science,—Ethics.* Part I. Ch. II., pp. 434—435. 2nd edition, 1868. "The Rules of Ethics, termed also Law, Laws, the Moral Law are of two kinds:—The first are rules imposed under a Penalty for neglect, or violation. The penalty is termed *Punishment;* the imposing party is named Government, or Authority; and the rules so imposed and enforced are called Laws proper, Morality proper, Obligatory Morality, Duty.—The second are rules whose only external support is *Rewards;* constituting Optional Morality, Merit, Virtue, or Nobleness." The meaning of this is clear and definite, and quite different from my distinction between optional and imperious desires. When I class desires as either imperious or optional, it is solely in respect of the different degrees of force which they themselves possess of compelling our attention; not in respect of their being either commanded, forbidden, or permitted, either by authority, or by conscience, or by the ultimate moral law, in whatever it may be held to consist.

VOLUNTARY REDINTEGRATION.

§ 5. The main branches of Practice.

being then used in a narrow and misleading sense, and (2) of æsthetic and poetically imaginative activity or reasoning; two great and well marked lines of human motive and interest. They are co-ordinate, not only with each other, but also with redintegrations of the first mode, governed by the desire for knowledge, since they take the place of what in the present exposition stands for their common parent, the general desire for specific feeling or content. Three chief modes of redintegration thus replace the two with which we began; namely, redintegrations governed by

1. Desire for knowledge.
2. Desire for satisfying imperious feelings.
3. Desire for optional, that is, æsthetic and imaginative gratifications.

Moreover it will be found, that the same or a similar law of alternation of redintegrations obtains between each of the two new modes and the third, as was found to obtain between the former two. Nothing is altered in this respect by the fact, that two modes of redintegration are substituted for one, since each of the two stands in precisely the same contrast to redintegrations governed by the desire for knowledge, in which the one mode stood, which they have replaced. If a particular content, belonging either to the imperious or to the optional group, is selected and made the governing end or motive of a train of alternating redintegrations, then the redintegrations in that train, which are directed to acquire knowledge concerning it, are on that account an enquiry into the means for attaining the end proposed. That is to say, they are subordinated to the ends selected by feeling, but they do not cease to belong themselves to the mode governed by desire for knowledge. Taken by themselves, they still aim at knowing, not at altering, the real course of Nature.

In fact it is in this way, and for this reason, that the two modes of redintegration of feeling become the foundations, as was said above, of prudential and æsthetic reasoning respectively. They do so by combining with, and subordinating to themselves, redintegrations which, for their own part, belong to the mode of knowing. Whenever knowledge of a specific content, selected for its specific interest, is the proximate object of pursuit, the knowledge so pursued is pursued as means to a further end; and this ultimate end belongs either to the imperious and prudential, or to the optional and æsthetic, group of desires and modes of redintegration.

But here again I pause to repeat the remark, applicable alike to what precedes and to what is next to follow, that the governing desires or ends aimed at are in no case the real determinants of the redintegrations; they are but modes of the concomitant and dependent consciousness, by which alone we can discriminate and name the really operative neuro-cerebral processes, which underlie and support both the feelings desired and the modes of redintegration which spring from them. These are the really operative element or factor in the whole conscious action which "we" are said to perform in any of the three cases. Our neuro-cerebral mechanism, thought of as unconscious when thought of separately, is the real agent, our concomitant consciousness is the awareness or knowledge, not of it, but of the meaning and value of its action; and the personal pronouns refer to and express the concrete conscious agent, consisting of mechanism and consciousness together.

Hitherto I have been speaking only of the chief modes of voluntary redintegration as they exist prior to, and independent of, self-consciousness or perception of the Ego.[2] I now come to the immense change and development which these same modes of redintegration undergo, when self-consciousness supervenes upon them, in the way described in the second Section of this Chapter. A new period then begins, on the basis and as the development of the old. This development consists of two particulars. In the first place, the arising of self-consciousness adds the personal emotions, and the desires springing from them, to our previous stock of feelings and desires, (see Chap. I, §§ 4 and 5 of the present Book), and, by thus placing us in a world of persons as well as things, gives us new objects for the exercise of volition, imagination, and thought. And secondly it enables us to reflect upon our own conscious activities, perceive them as our own, compare their relative advantages and disadvantages, and thus initiate

---

[2] There is one apparent exception to this statement, inasmuch as the need for sexual intercourse, which has been spoken of above, is not manifested till long after the attainment of self-consciousness. Nevertheless, though delayed in its manifestation, it has its foundation in bodily functions which are quite independent of the perception of personality.—It is probably in substance an old remark, that nothing can have contributed more decisively than this delay, in the case of man, to the development and final supremacy of his higher or spiritual nature; a delay which gives, as it were, a start of several years to the personal emotions over the pre-personal and instinctive sexual appetite; whereby the latter, on coming into full play at puberty, finds a number of associations and corresponding habits already formed, and the channels, so to speak, in which it has to flow, already to a great extent dug for it.

new lines of practical reasoning, in the large and proper sense of the term *practical,* lines which are the development and continuation, under the guidance of reflective criticism, of those very activities which they criticise. This feature of the development, the feature of self-conscious choice and judgment combined, from which new lines of practical reasoning take their origin, is what we know as the guidance of Conscience, a guidance which thus pre-supposes and includes self-consciousness simply, of which, as we have seen, Conscience is a special mode.

In this way and at this epoch it is, that we begin to become aware, that the three main groups of desires, the three modes of redintegration springing from them, and the three kinds of trains or series of alternating redintegrations determined by the ultimate end sought to be attained by each train, are special cases or modes of Practical Reasoning in the wide, which is also the proper, sense of the term *practical,* and that all alike are liable to the criticism of reflective self-consciousness, or Conscience, which, when taken up into trains of redintegration, becomes itself a part of practical reasoning reflecting on its own activities, and judging them in point of preferability, with a view to determining future action. For reflective knowledge of our own activities, taken simply as *de facto* existents, the term self-consciousness may be retained. In other respects the three modes of redintegration, and the three kinds of trains consisting of alternating redintegrations, remain as before. That is to say, they are unaltered save, first, by the addition of a new content of specific feelings, namely, the personal emotions arising in two of them, and the desires springing from those emotions, together with the objects which are capable of satisfying them, and which are thereby proposed as objects of knowledge; and secondly by the supervening of Conscience, which, as already said, is conscious perception of a specific object, namely, the Subject's own acts of choice, governed by the specific interest of choosing better in the present or future, by means of the knowledge so acquired.

I will take in turn the two features just noted, in which the new development consists; and in the first place speak, very briefly, of the new content of feelings and objects added by self-consciousness. These may be summed up in the words,—persons, and personal emotions and passions, with the imaginations entertained concerning them. These as felt, conceived, or entertained as our own, or as affecting ourselves and our own relations to others, belong to the imperious group of feelings. Love, sympathy, eros, anger, hatred, malevolence, envy, jealousy, pride, conceit, vanity, shame, humiliation, remorse, sense of justice and injustice, indignation, scorn, and so on through the whole list of personal emotions and emotions springing from our conception of personal relations, have an immediate interest from which we cannot shake ourselves free. They combine with the pre-personal feelings belonging to the same group in the most intimate manner. We can to a great extent modify, coerce, increase, and otherwise govern them. But we cannot avoid attending to them, and making them our primary interests, after the satisfaction of our bodily needs, with which they often stand in the closest combination. They constitute in fact the very material and substance of our own moral nature.

These same emotions, interests, objects, and relations, again, when contemplated by us *ab extra* as it were, as exhibited between persons with whom we have no immediate concern, or between the persons of fictitious narratives, pictures, and dramas; or when conveyed to us indirectly and by hardly traceable channels of association and suggestion, as in the case of natural scenery and landscape painting; or by means of music operating through similar channels, though in this case without any necessary accompaniment, either of narrative, or any visual imagery, or pictured scenery; when in short we are intellectually and morally free to hold the feelings or objects at arm's length, as it were, and feel or contemplate them without anxiety on any score of our own;—then these same feelings belong to the æsthetic or optional group. It is to this group that the Plot-interest, so well described and so justly dwelt on by Dr. Bain in his great work, *The Emotions and the Will*, properly belongs. The personal emotions of this, the optional, or æsthetic and imaginative group, combine with the pre-personal feelings of the same group, precisely as in the case of the two sections of the imperious group. The pre-personal section of the optional group is more properly called *æsthetic*, the personal section *poetic*. Poetry includes imagination of every kind of personal emotion, and is itself imagination employed in rendering, enforcing, and creating new modes and combinations of it. Not words alone are its media, but everything in which imagination can be embodied by suggestion, or by which it can be conveyed to the minds of others. In this sense Poetry pre-supposes Æsthetic, which is its own pre-personal section, and which applies primarily and properly to the media of sense, and modes of handling them, in and by which the strictly poetical imagination finds its vehicle and embodiment. Yet so close is their union, that often we are unable to say where the one ends and the other begins. It is the work of poetic genius to combine the two elements in a mutually supporting unity, and often we are made distinctly aware of the real presence of both, only by the dissonance which a fault, traceable plainly to one, produces in the effect of the whole.

I turn in the next place to the second of the two features of the new development, noted above as due to the appearance of self-consciousness, namely, the conscious criticism of our own volitions which is known as Conscience. Concerning this it is only necessary here to observe that, springing as it does from self-consciousness, it is universal in its applicability, has volitions or choice of desires of every kind for its object-matter, and is not restricted to any one or two of the three lines of practical reasoning, or groups of practical science, but is the common critic of all alike, and of every branch of them. Its distinctive *differentia* is, that it judges them solely in their volitional character, that is, as acts of choice between a better and a worse, and not in their character of simply perceptive or intellective acts. The indulgence or non-indulgence (1) of the desire for knowledge, (2) of any imperious, or (3) of any optional desire, in any particular case or class of cases, is that which it falls within its province to approve or condemn. It is not within its province as conscience simply, but only (as will be seen later on) within that of certain specific forms of it, to criticise the truth or falsity of an intellectual judgment, or to test the comparative amount of gratification to be derived from any of the competing representations of pleasure or of pursuit. These can never be more than elements in the evidence, upon which its own judgments of the moral value of volitions, in their volitional character as immanent acts of choice, are formed.

Briefly, then, to state the results at which we have arrived, we find in the first place, that the whole mass of our mixed trains of voluntary redintegration, trains in which the two modes of voluntary redintegration alternate with each other, breaks up into three distinct groups, according as the mixed trains of redintegration are governed,—
  A. by the desire for knowledge of any and every kind,
  B. by imperious desires personal and pre-personal,
  C. by optional desires personal and pre-personal.
And secondly we find, that the desires which either govern, or come forward in the course of, any of these trains of redintegration are amenable to the judgments of conscience, so far as they are alternatives adopted or rejected by volition. Every such desire in a train of voluntary redintegration, and cousequently the volition into which it enters, has two distinguishable but inseparable aspects, first as

a percept or cognition, second as an action or motive of action; but it is only in the latter aspect that it is judged by conscience. In its perceptive or purely cognitive aspect it is governed by the laws of Thought and of Real Conditioning, with which conscience has nothing to do, seeing that they are wholly beyond the control of an individual's volition.

A line of demarcation runs, so to speak, right through every alternative desire and every act of choice, distinguishing therein what is amenable to the judgments of conscience from what is not so amenable, or in other words, distinguishing their strictly moral from their strictly intellectual character. Every alternative desire and every act of choice, to whichever of the three groups it may belong, and even if it is merely a desire for knowledge, or a choice of its pursuit, is subject to the judgment of conscience. Every act of cognition, since it involves consenting to the desire of knowing, is to that extent, but to that extent only, an act of volition or choice. It must, therefore, not be too hastily assumed, that the three branches of human practice, and of the arts of life or practical sciences which grow out of them, are co-incident in their limits with the three sciences of practice, Logic, Ethic, and Poetic, as these will be finally determined in the following Section, on further grounds there to be adduced.

We must proceed in the next place to scrutinise these trains of voluntary redintegration somewhat more closely on their cognitive side. It is when looked at in this character that they appear as trains of practical reasoning, and fall into three groups of Arts of Life, or Practical Sciences, depending on the three kinds of desires above mentioned. The varied contents of these groups divide the whole conscious activity of human life between them; they are the

"*Quidquid agunt homines, votum, timor, ira, voluptas, Gaudia, discursus,*"

of Juvenal (Sat. I. 85). In other words, all the fullness of conscious human activity may be exhaustively classed under three heads, as governed by desires of three comprehensive kinds, in virtue of our analytical reduction of all conscious activity to trains of voluntary redintegration.

But a further simplification in the relations of trains of redintegration to each other will be found to result, if we proceed to take each of the three modes of redintegration severally, and look at them in the light of the well known distinction between end and means, or what is ultimate and what subordinate, in the desires which are severally constitutive of each mode. And this simplification will also be found, if I mistake not, to afford the possibility of so classifying the various actually existing branches of knowledge and of practice, as to bring them under our threefold distinction of mode, and so exhibit them as cases of voluntary redintegration.

A.

Taking, then, in the first place that mode of redintegration which is constituted solely by the desire for knowledge, we find that it breaks up into two great divisions, according as the knowledge desired is an ultimate or a subordinate end.

I.

Under the first head we have the pursuit of

knowledge purely and simply for its own sake, that is to say, pure Science in all its kinds, and all its parts and details, and Philosophy in both its branches, analytic and constructive; the former of which branches again subdivides into (1) analysis of positive objective thought, and (2) analysis of practical objective thought, in which, as we shall see, Ethic is included, so far as it is a knowledge of what practical objective thought actually and *de facto* is.

§ 5. The main branches of Practice.

II.

Secondly we have the pursuit of knowledge as a means to particular ends, and subservient to particular desires, belonging either to the imperious or to the optional group; for where the knowledge sought is sought solely as a means to further knowledge, it falls under the first head, inasmuch as it is itself, not only a means, but also a part of that whole knowledge, which is the only object of desire. This subordination of knowledge to specific ends, of imperious or of optional desire, makes the reasoning in pursuit of it ministerial, and that irrespective of the group to which the ends subserved by it belong. Reasoning which is consciously subservient to ends belonging to the imperious class of desires gives us the whole group of the practical sciences, popularly so called, and this group again breaks up into two minor ones, according as the objects dealt with are personal or non-personal. To the personal group of reasonings belong the sciences of Politic, Sociology, Education, Jurisprudence, Administration, Diplomacy, and so on. To the non-personal belong the mechanical arts and sciences. And there is also a numerous group of sciences which have a mixed object, dealing with persons and things together, as for instance, War, Medicine, and Political Economy. —If on the other hand the ultimate ends of the reasoning belong to the optional class of desires, the reasoning is still ministerial, but falls into subdivisions, among which the *Technique* of the Fine Arts and Poetry may be noted as conspicuous, being directed to discover the best means subservient to the ends they aim at as ultimate, and the best modes of applying them.

B.

If in the next place we turn to the mode of redintegration which is constituted by desire of feeling, and take in the first place that which is constituted by feelings of the imperious class, we find that it also breaks up into two similar groups.

I.

We have first the selection of feelings to be gratified or secured for their own sake, or as ultimate ends.

II.

Secondly we have the selection of the means to those ends, means which, when selected, become the ends of modes of knowledge. This second branch of the mode constituted by imperious feelings thus co-incides with, or rather is contained under, the second or ministerial branch of the mode constituted by the desire for knowledge (A), leaving only the first branch peculiar to the mode constituted by imperious feelings.

C.

Thirdly we find a similar division holding good

of the mode constituted by optional feelings and desires.

I.

We have first the selection of the ultimate ends to be attained, or feelings to be gratified.

II.

And secondly we have the selection of the means to their attainment, which is a matter of art, or skill in the exhibition, interpretation, or enforcement of the desired effect, that is, a matter of *technique* in the large sense of the term. This subdivision again is contained under the second branch of the mode governed by the desire for knowledge (A), leaving only the first subdivision peculiar to the mode constituted by optional feelings.

Thus in result we find, that the second branch or subdivision of each mode of redintegration severally, though occurring in trains which may belong to any of the three groups of redintegrations, has the one common feature of being a mode of ministerial reasoning. Redintegrations belonging to the first branch, in all the three groups, on the other hand, while co-inciding in the characters of being practical, and of being governed by ends which are ultimate, that is, pursued for their own sake alone, are essentially different from one another in point of the nature of the ends which constitute them, and therefore also in their own nature as modes of redintegration determined by those ends. It is only the first branch of the first mode of redintegration which contains what is strictly and purely science or knowledge; but this it necessarily does, inasmuch as the bare act of

§ 5. The main branches of Practice.

selective attention to a content of consciousness is *eo ipso* a conscious knowledge of the content attended to, and there is no knowledge, from the simplest up to the most complex, abstruse, or ennobling, which (supposing it attained) does not fall under this description. We have in fact, in any content to which we consciously attend, what may be called the germ, or essential molecule, in the composition of all knowledge as an end in itself, that is, in other words, of pure science or of philosophy.

The first branch of the other two modes of redintegration contains (to continue the metaphor) the germ or essential molecule, not of knowledge, but of choice directed to present or future action, so as to modify, not discover, the real course of Nature. In neither of these two modes does this branch contain what can strictly be called science, but only judgments of preferability, or acts of choice, which are an object-matter of science. These are in fact the object-matter of Ethic, which, as will be seen later on, is strictly a science in the sense of being systematised knowledge, though it is also part and parcel of philosophy, being founded immediately on subjective analysis of consciousness, being also ultimate in its own department, and having no superior dictating either its end or its methods.

§ 6. The Sciences of Practice; Ethic, Logic, and Poetic.

§ 6. Two points, it will be remembered, were distinguished at the beginning of the foregoing Section, the first of which was the nature of thought or the reasoning process involved in all cases of voluntary redintegration, and the second the grouping of the several branches of practice, which fall under the consideration of thought or reasoning as its object-matter. Of these we then postponed the first, and followed up the second, wherein, by reducing all branches of human practice, so far as they involve thought or reasoning, to modes or combinations of modes of voluntary redintegration, we were enabled to group them all under three main heads, founded on the three main kinds of desire, which are their ultimate or governing ends. It remains to take up the first point, then postponed, in order to show how these groups or branches of practice are severally brought under the jurisdiction of the practical department of self-consciousness, that is, of Conscience, as the self-conscious criticism of volitions; or, in other words, to discriminate those ultimate practical sciences, which are, as it were, the grasp which metaphysic or philosophy has over the whole of human practice or conduct.

It would be a great mistake to suppose, that the nature and laws of the several branches of practice are determined exclusively by the nature of the object-matter to which they are devoted, or by that of the three kinds of desire upon which their grouping depends, and not also, and indeed primarily, by the nature and laws of rational volition or practical reasoning itself, taken in the abstract, and considered as independent of, though common to, the particular branches of practice in which it is involved, and in which, as concrete processes or pursuits, it is manifested. That grouping is in great measure arbitrary, and a matter of convenience. It will be remembered, that we broke up the whole multifarious group of practices, governed by desire for specific feeling, into the two groups governed respectively by imperious and by optional desires, in order to render it more manageable. A proceeding of this kind cannot have the effect of isolating the groups of practices which it distinguishes, and rendering the sciences devoted to them autonomous, as if each was ultimately based on laws of practice peculiar to itself, and underived from a higher or more general source. No new principles of practice have been disclosed thereby. In other words, the grouping of branches of practice, by reference to differences in their specific content, does not carry with it the establishment of separate principles of practice for each group, independent of the general principles of practice which are common to all alike, and so constituting for each group a separate and independent science. The grouping of branches of practice is one thing, the discrimination of the sciences under which they fall, and to the laws of which they are ultimately amenable, is another. We cannot straightway and at once refer the group of rational practices, or practical sciences, governed by the desire for knowledge to a separate science of Logic, the group governed by imperious desires to a separate science of Ethic, and the group governed by optional desires to a separate science of Æsthetic or Poetic, however natural and consonant to first appearances such a reference may seem.

Moreover, to treat the three sciences of Ethic, Logic, and Poetic, or any three sciences, however named, devoted respectively to the three groups of practices now distinguished, as separate and autonomous, in the sense assigned, would lead at once to a hopeless contradiction. For it is evident that, simply as sciences, they all fall under the single head of cognition or acquisition of knowledge; that is, knowledge alone is what, as sciences, they aim at; and yet we have just seen that two of them, Ethic and Poetic, if considered as the ultimate sciences to which the branches of practice based respectively upon imperious and optional desires are amenable, must be defined by aims quite different from knowledge,—some form of good or right action, as distinguished from knowledge, being the end of Ethic, and the attainment of the highest optional enjoyments that of Poetic. So that to treat these two sciences, so defined, as independent and autonomous would involve basing them severally on two different ultimate aims at once, which is an impossibility of thought. The contradiction arises from attempting to treat as the derivative of a separate principle what is in fact derived from an inseparable element of experience;—the common fallacy of Empiricism.

We see, then, that something more is requisite, for the definition and ascertainment of an ultimate practical science, than the mere demarcation, on our part, of a group of practices to which it applies, and of which it is in some sort the continuation and development. What this something more is will become evident, if we consider, that all thought or reasoning, being purposively selective attention, is volition,[1] independently

---

[1] Consequently all reasoning in its ultimate analysis is practical reasoning; a fact which shows that the separate faculties or functions, set up by an *a priori* philosophy as the Pure Reason and the Practical Reason, are fictions.

of the volition to think or reason, which initiates it; and also that, as volition, it necessarily falls under the cognisance of that mode of self-consciousness which perceives and judges volitions, which we call Conscience. In fact, thought or reasoning is practical choice, as well as cognitive action, irrespectively of its attaining or not attaining the knowledge at which it aims; and it is as practical action or choice that, in every branch and every mode, it is amenable to the judgment of conscience. The cognisance which conscience takes of all practice, including thought or reasoning, so far as it is practical in this broad sense of choosing, is the material or basis of a science which is supreme over the whole of human practice, that is, over all the three groups above distinguished, and the desires by which they are defined; a science the authority of which admits of no restriction or limitation, save such as are allowed and imposed by itself. This science which, as resting on the analysis of self-consciousness alone, is not one of the so-called positive sciences, but is part and parcel of Philosophy, is strictly and properly known as *Ethic*. It is a practical science in the sense of reviewing and guiding practice, for the purpose of better practice in the future. But in order to this, it is also cognitive, both of the practices which conscience judges, and of the action of conscience in judging them.

This difference of function will be seen more clearly if we advert to the distinction, drawn in § 1 of the first Chapter of the present Book, between a science of practice and a practical science, and to the relation between them. A science of practice, it was said, becomes a practical science, when it employs its analysis of the branch of practice, which is its object-matter, to guide its action and promote its ends. Every practical science, therefore, falls into two divisions, one of which is the basis and preparation for the other. The first division is analytical, and directed simply to ascertain the actual nature and actual laws of whatever branch of practice is in question ; and here it is simply cognitive of what is *de facto*, or really exists or happens independently of its ascertainment. In this division it is a science of practice. It is in its second division only that it becomes a practical science ; and this it does when it uses the knowledge, obtained in its first division, to promote the purposes of that branch of practice which it previously analysed. In their first division, therefore, or as sciences of practice, all practical sciences are simply cognitive, or aim at knowledge alone, notwithstanding that, in their second division or as practical sciences, they aim at other purposes than knowledge, that is, at promoting the aims proper to their own branches of practice.

When we approach them, as in the two foregoing Sections, from the side of the branches of practice to which they belong, we necessarily come upon them first in their character of practical sciences ; for every practice, consisting as in part it must, of voluntary redintegrations, is not a practice simply, but a practical science also, that is, a reasoning about some object-matter with a purpose in view ; the difference commonly recognised between them lying solely in the degree of organisation at which a practice, or combination of

§ 6.
The Sciences of Practice;

Ethic, Logic, and Poetic.

practices, may have arrived, owing to the intervention of reflection upon them, which, so far as it is analytical, is in strictness a science, or the beginning of a science, of the practice or practices in question. We saw, too, at the conclusion of the 4th Section, that every branch of human activity, so far as known to us in voluntary redintegration, contained in itself the germs both of a science and an art. In the 5th Section again, taking up the same thread of thought, we classified the practical sciences solely by reference to the classification of the branches of practice which they systematise. But this in no way contravenes the fact which we have now signalised, and which indeed the systematisation itself pre-supposes, that an analytical and simply cognitive basis must first be laid, in order that any practical science should be able to perform its function of guiding and furthering the corresponding practice in the pursuit of its ends. A practical science, to be worth anything, must at least be a science, or knowledge of independently existing facts. It follows, therefore, that the essential and fundamental part of all practical sciences, in their final shape as sciences of review, is that in which they are sciences of practice, that is, in which they are analytical of the practice to which they are devoted. Ethic as described above is no exception to this law, of which rather, as a science of reflection and review, covering all other practical sciences, it is the most conspicuous instance.

But now to turn to the branches of practice, or practical sciences, which fall under the review of Conscience, and therefore of Ethic, in the way

§ 6. The Sciences of Practice; Ethic, Logic, and Poetic.

above described, and see what this analysis, as instituted by reflection on the sciences themselves, shows and must show, in all branches of practice, with regard to the common strain or factor in all alike which constitutes them distinct and concrete practices. We shall thus be enabled to see what are the restrictions and limitations which must be accepted and imposed by Ethic itself on its own authority and dominion. For the question now proposed brings us back directly to the point recalled at the outset af this Section, as still remaining to be considered, namely, the nature of thought, or of the reasoning process itself, whether involved in voluntary redintegration simply, or in processes by which voluntary redintegrations are themselves analysed and judged. And the analysis of reasoning or thought, being thus common to practice and to the science of it, is therefore the common basis upon which all practical sciences must build. That is to say, it is the strain of reasoning, disclosed by this analysis, by which both practical sciences and sciences of practice are constituted.

Now these considerations bring us back again, by another route, to ground which is already familiar, namely, the part played by choice, and therefore also to that played by its co-element or co-elements, in reasoning processes in their simplest shape, that is, processes which aim at being simply cognitions of independently existing facts. We have now merely to come to somewhat closer quarters with this function of choosing already known to us, by following it up into acts which are acts of selective attention governed solely by the desire of attaining new knowledge of independent fact, the general line which selective attention is to follow being previously marked out for it by the concrete train of redintegration in which it occurs.

When we take the matter in this way, we see in the first place, that the other necessary co-element with choice, in the cognitive act, is perception of fact; and consequently perception of fact in reasoning processes is that part of them which is necessarily withdrawn from the jurisdiction of conscience, and therefore of Ethic, so far as it is based on conscience, as the science of review which covers all other sciences of practical reasoning. Let us see, then, more closely how this comes about, and in what the relation between the two elements, choice and perception, consists. Supposing, then, attention fixed upon something about which we wish to know more than at present, we then watch the content offered by spontaneous redintegration. If what then rises into consciousness is a well-known and constant adjunct of the fact from which we start, we are said to perceive it in that connection, and we then count it as something already known, and implicitly contained in our knowledge of the fact which is our starting point; it is no new knowledge but a recognition of old. If on the contrary no part of the content offered by spontaneous redintegration stands in familiar or constant connection with the fact which is our starting point, then what we do is to fix attention provisionally upon some part of the newly offered content, which has some similarity or relationship more or less striking with our original fact, and make it by attention a new starting point, in hope that the content next offered by spontaneous redintegration, in connection with it, may be such as to enter also into relation with our original fact, and be a fresh addition to our knowledge of it. Here it is that choice comes in, I mean in selecting from the content offered by spontaneous redintegration some fact or facts which will procure for us, mediately and indirectly, some new knowledge about the fact with which we originally begin. In acquiring new knowledge by way of thought or reasoning, everything depends upon the choice we make of these provisionally adopted starting points, or *media* of acquisition, (apart of course from the fertility of our spontaneous redintegrations), since an ill-made choice may lead us off upon a fruitless track, or even become the parent of error and illusion. It is, moreover, in this part of the process of reasoning that we have the source of all framing of hypotheses, and adoption of provisional assumptions, as a part of method.

We see, then, that even in the reasonings which are purely cognitive in aim, and the ultimate test of which lies in their conformity to independently existing fact, a large part is played by choice as distinguished from positive perception. The same is of course true, when such reasonings intervene in a course of practice, which is ultimately determined by imperious or by optional desires, as reasonings about the means requisite to attain desired ends, in which their function is subordinate and ministerial, as set forth at the end of the foregoing Section. But wherever there is choice or selection between possible alternatives, there also is necessary liability to the judgments of conscience, which is reflective perception directed upon volitional acts. Save that here a modification comes in, which is due to the particular kind of desire which governs the whole process, namely, the desire for simple truth of fact. That is to say, in the case now before us of reasonings purely cognitive in aim—the conscience by which we judge them is conscience judging by a particular standard, that of conformity or conduciveness to truth of fact, and not conscience in the full and unrestricted sense. It is a mode of self-consciousness which has been well termed the *logical conscience*. Conscience in the full sense is the necessary judge of the original choice, which determines whether the reasoning shall be entered on at all; but when it has once been entered on with the approval of conscience, then the conscience which judges its selective actions is the logical conscience only. Cognitive reasonings fall under the dominion of conscience, and therefore, when treated in the general, of Ethic, with respect to the question, whether they shall be entered on or dismissed; but are exempted from that jurisdiction as cognitive reasonings simply; except that, here also, they remain subject, in that part of them which consists of choice, to the logical conscience, which judges by a special standard. From this point of view, Logic, as the science of Thought, must be regarded, in virtue of the volitional element which all thought contains, as covering a special domain carved out, as it were, from the whole dominion of Ethic, considered as the science of practice generally.

A similar distinction holds good of that other domain, similarly carved out of the whole dominion of Ethic, the domain of reasoning directed to the gratification of optional desires, the science of which is Poetic. Conscience in the full sense is *de jure* supreme in determining whether or not any such course of practice or practical reasoning shall in any particular case be entered on. That is to say, it has to approve or disapprove the choice to be made between gratifying and not gratifying any of the optional desires which belong to the domain of Æsthetic or Poetic, and the entering or not entering upon the course of practice directed to gratify it. But supposing such a course of practice has been so approved and entered on, then it is at once withdrawn from the jurisdiction of conscience in the full sense, and is amenable, in that part of it which consists of acts of choice, to a mode of self-consciousness which we may call the poetic or æsthetic conscience, which is restricted to judge by a special standard, namely, that of beauty or harmony. The subordinate or ministerial acts of cognitive reasoning, which intervene in the course of it, are of course subject primarily to the laws of cognitive reasoning, as already set forth.

The same conclusions are confirmed, when we approach the whole domain of human practice from the ethical side. In Ethic, it is only acts of choice, that is, acts which are in our own power to do or to omit, acts therefore in which choosing and doing are one and the same thing, which are subject to the judgments of conscience. In judging of any act or choice whatever, and that whether the judgment is combined with the choice itself, making it a complex act, or is merely retrospective upon a past act, we always, as a matter of fact, draw and apply this distinction; I mean, that we always perceive, in the concrete act, a part which is purely choosing and in our own power, and a part which is imposed upon us by perception or perceived fact at the moment of choosing. Whatever belongs to the latter part, and also whatever is referred to it in consequence of a previously adopted decision, (as in the case of originally adopting lines of cognitive reasoning, or lines of optional gratification), that we exempt from the jurisdiction which conscience has over the act of choice immediately before us. It has, in fact, been exempted by conscience itself, supposing that conscience has approved the previous decision. In short, it is a fact of experience, that only the purely volitional element, or element of choice, in matters of practice and reasoning, but at the same time that element necessarily and universally, is subject to the judgments of conscience in the full and proper sense of the term, as the selective attention to volitions.

And here I recur once more to the now familiar distinction between sciences of practice and practical sciences, the former being the analytical foundation of the latter. Sciences of practice are purely cognitive in aim, and analytical of the nature and laws of those branches of practice to which they are devoted. It is only in their superstructure or development that they become practical sciences. The constant and, so far as we can see, unchangeable nature and laws of the practice which is their object-matter it is their duty as sciences of practice to ascertain. In proving this position we have had recourse to one or two of

VOLUNTARY REDINTEGRATION.

the most fundamental facts, common to all branches of practice, as the ground of our demonstration. First we have found that, in all acts of practice or of reasoning, there is a part which is fixed and imposed by facts of perception, and another part which is choice; and that of these the latter only is subject to conscience in any shape. Secondly we have found, that judgments of conscience in one shape or another are normally passed, in all cases of choice; and therefore, that the existence of conscience is a fact belonging to the constant nature of practice, irrespective of what its judgments are in any particular case. Thirdly, we have distinguished conscience in the full and unrestricted sense, in which it belongs to Ethic, from the special and narrower forms of it in which, being restricted to judge by a particular standard, or rather by comparison with a particular aim, it appears in Logic and in Poetic.

These are not facts which depend upon Ethic, Logic, or Poetic, as practical sciences arbitrarily or empirically determined by their supposed correspondence to, or identity with, three groups of practices distinguished by the kinds of desire which are their ultimate aim. They are constant facts in the nature of all branches of rational practice, however these may be distinguished and classified; facts which show that, in every act of volitional redintegration, there is an element of choice and an element of cognition, inseparable from each other, and that the former element is subject to the judgments of conscience, in whatever concrete branch of practice it may be found. Ethic is the science which analyses and systematises these judgments. It is a science defined by having, not a special group of practices, but a certain element in all practices, as its object-matter, namely, the element of choice, the element which gives their practical character to all acts of volitional redintegration or reasoning. Ethic is therefore the primary or fontal science of practice and practical science, from which all others are derived, so far as they are founded on and deal with this element of volition in concrete practices or practical sciences, by whatever marks, taken from the special aims or desires which govern them, these practices or practical sciences may be distinguished and classified.

Assuming them to be classified as set forth in the foregoing Section, what has now been shown is the relation in which two groups of them stand to Ethic, in virtue of the special modifications which conscience assumes, when the special modes of choice, subordinate to the special motives and aims of those two groups, the desire for knowledge and the desire for optional gratifications, are taken as the objects of its judgments. It follows, that Ethic is not a partial or particular science, dealing only with a particular group of practices or practical sciences, demarcated by a special kind of desires, which in our classification is called the imperious kind, but is the fontal science, supreme over the whole range of practice, by relation to which the nature and range of all other practical sciences are determined. In every case it is the element of choice in practical reasoning or volitional redintegration, which constitutes its practical character, and renders it amenable to a single ultimate science of practice, which is itself founded on an exercise of the same function of practical reasoning, as those practices are which it analyses and judges.

From this view of the kind of facts which it is the business of the sciences of practice, as analytical sciences, to watch for and insist on, namely, facts which are inherent in the nature and laws of practice itself, among which the nature and laws of conscience in all its forms are included, it follows, that it can never be the function of the practical sciences founded on them, to prescribe laws for the conduct of individuals, in any of the three main branches of practice, or in their subdivisions. This must be left to the conscience of individuals, the *de jure* supremacy of which, so far as the individual is concerned, but no farther, is expressly assured to it by the analytical science of practice, which deals with the kind of practice in question. It is not for Ethic as a practical science to dictate to the conscience of individuals in any matter of choice whatever. It is not for Logic as a practical science to limit the individual reasoner in his choice of alternative lines of thought, methods, hypotheses, or provisional assumptions, or to insist on accuracy in the judgments of which his chains of reasoning consist; this is the function of his own logical conscience. It is not for Poetic as a practical science to command or to forbid combinations of sensory or emotional gratifications, as if demanded or prohibited by immutable canons of Taste; it is the poetic conscience of the artist in living, which criticises and controls what, in the fine arts, are called the inspirations of his genius, upon which this office is imposed.

VOL. III. P

The function of the practical sciences as ultimately constituted is entirely general, and so far as individuals are concerned, purely ministerial and consultative. They record and compare, criticise and classify, the results of experience, and the observations of moralists, reasoners, and artists, draw conclusions from them, and enforce those conclusions by exhibition of instances and examples, as well as by precept and exhortation. But all this is for the instruction, guidance, and enlightenment of the individual conscience, and is not intended or suited to fetter or supersede it. The attempt to use the results of any practical science in that way can lead to nothing but legalism, dogmatism, and conventionality.

Over all the volitions of the individual his own conscience is supreme. All feelings and all conscious acts whatsoever fall within its domain of surveillance, and the very highest acts of virtue cannot exceed the scope of its commands. The ever-present difficulty with most men is to make their actual will, choice, and action, conform to its distinctly recognised behests. Its appearance works the transformation of simply practical into moral action, and as a function it is the highest tribunal to which an individual can appeal in justification of his own acts. The exercise of all other functions, harmonised by the supervision of this, constitutes the whole Art of Life, the whole Practice of right living. We have, however, already seen, and it must not be forgotten, that the office of conscience includes the revision of its own previous judgments. In this way it is, that by the judgments of his own conscience, as well as by his own acts which are subject to them, the individual stands or falls. He falls most grievously, if he surrenders his conscience to a conscience keeper.

From this we see the nature and limitations of all those ethical theories which fall under Ethic as a practical science. Differ as they may in other respects from one another, it is essential to them all alike to be founded on conceptions dictated or approved by the conscience of their deviser. On the other hand, their application to the individual case must always be made by the conscience of the individual. The judgments of others on an individual's actions, though passed in accordance with a sound ethical theory, can be probable judgments only. As general judgments they may be irrefragable. But as judgments of an individual's action they require his own echo and *imprimatur*; they must be valid *in foro conscientiæ*, that is, must be felt by the individual to be true of himself here and now. Judgments of right and wrong, concerning what is nominally the same action, are not identical, when taken as generalisations of Ethic, with what they are when taken as particular insights or imperatives of the individual's conscience. Many puzzles and apparent contradictions in morals are caused by confusing these two ways of apprehending the meaning of moral judgments.

In what remains of the present Book, I shall confine myself to Ethic, Logic, and Poetic, as sciences of practice, with but few and occasional excursions, if any, into the domain of the practical sciences called by the same names. Not that I in any way wish to depreciate them in the latter character; but, as already said, the ground they cover is too vast to be effectively entered on in a general treatise on philosophy. Enough will have been done for the purposes of the present work, if I succeed in making it evident, that these sciences, if they are to have any value as practical sciences, must be treated on a metaphysical basis, that is, founded on a metaphysical analysis of experience, as part and parcel of philosophy, and not dealt with as if they were positive sciences concerned solely with the Order of Real Conditioning, and therefore had their ultimate basis in some one or more of the positive sciences, such as psychology or anthropology.

CHAPTER IV.

THE FOUNDATIONS OF LOGIC.

§ 1. I take Logic first of the three sciences distinguished in the foregoing Chapter, because in its first or analytical department, or as a science of practice, it deals with the laws of those processes which are Thought, or the Action of Thinking, in its simplest shape, that is, involve the co-element of volition or choice in one form only, namely, as volition or choice governed solely by the desire for further knowledge. But in every complete act of thought, this co-element is twice operative, first as an act of selective attention to a particular content or object-matter, secondly as an assertion of one out of two or more mutually exclusive alternatives concerning it, in consequence of that prior act of attention. Choice for the sole purpose of knowing, but exercised first as attention, then as assertion, is the single volitional co-element involved in the thinking processes which are the object-matter of Logic as a science of practice. This co-element, therefore, which we may call pure or abstract thought, together with the fact that it has inseparable co-elements, or in other words, the fact that it is always exercised in or upon some content, though irrespective of what that content may be,—

that is to say, the thinking process itself, and the laws to which it is subject,—are the special object-matter with which we have now to deal.

For, considering that thought, in this which is its simplest concrete shape, enters into all processes of voluntary redintegration, and is one fixed and unchanging element in them, an element moreover which conditions and limits them, and from which there is no possibility of escape, whatever may be the particular purpose which they are directed to realise,—whether it be a purpose to attain some particular kind of knowledge, or to promote the well being or the well doing of human agents, or to secure the greatest and best kinds of optional gratification,—considering this, it will be evident, that, in order to understand any of these aright, it is necessary first to gain some insight into that which they all alike pre-suppose, namely, the laws of Thought in its simplest shape, in which it is the object-matter of Logic in its analytical department, or as a science of practice.

I therefore begin with Logic in this department, or as occupied with the laws of thought simply; and I also begin the consideration of it, in this department, by first distinguishing these laws, as laws of thought simply, from the laws, if any, which govern method; taking what is called method in thought to depend upon the peculiarities of some particular content selected for investigation, or the peculiarities of some particular kind of knowledge aimed at, and therefore holding it to fall more properly under the second department of Logic, in which it appears as applied logic, or as a practical science. The laws of method are laws which govern it by advising and directing choice, within the general domain marked out by attention for the purpose of knowing simply, pre-supposing this initial choice already made, and having the acquisition of some particular kind of knowledge as its ultimate aim and purpose.

Turning, then, to Logic as the analytical science of the thinking process simply, we find that it deals with the laws and processes of thought in another respect than that already mentioned. It deals with them as distinguished both from the concrete but less perfect knowledge with which thought starts, and which we therefore call perceptual or pre-logical, and also from the concrete and more perfect knowledge at which it arrives, by means of its own process and that prior knowledge combined, and which we may call logical or conceptual knowledge. It deals, not with concrete reasoning as the process of obtaining knowledge, but with thinking as a contributory element in that concrete process. Logic, both as a science of practice, and as a practical science using the results of analysis as guides to truth, and for the detection of sophistry and error, was first cast into systematic shape by Aristotle, the hypothetical syllogism being the chief later addition to his work. Here we have to do with it only in its purely analytical part, or as a science of practice.

Beginning, as most convenient, with the general relations which thought bears to perception, we find that there are certain definite operations or steps in the process of thinking, which are inseparable from it as a process, and by which its nature can most readily be perceived ; just as the nature of simple sense-perception is perceived by noting differences in its content, that is, different perceptions simultaneous and successive, contributing to compose the stream of simply perceptive consciousness. These operations or steps in the process of thinking are distinguishable both from the perceptual knowledge with which it starts, and from the conceptual knowledge at which it arrives, and receive names from Logic (which is the science of the process) as abstract conceptions or forms of thought, necessary to it as a volitional process dealing with phenomena of consciousness, and impressed by it upon the concrete result of conceptualised knowledge, in which the process issues. These abstract conceptions or forms of thought fall under three heads.

First, in dealing with the percepts from which it starts, thought converts them into *universals* and *singulars* (also called *particulars*) by the observation of differences; and this conversion yields the abstract concepts of *genus, differentia,* and *species.* The conversion of percepts into concepts, which are either universals or singulars falling under universals, is effected by the lowest and simplest act of thought, namely, the act of attention for the purpose of further knowledge. The abstract concepts of *genus, differentia,* and *species,* are a schema established by Logic, the science of thought, on the basis of the distinction between universals and singulars; a schema whereby any percept, on being converted into a concept, may be brought to logical definition, have a place assigned to it in a *scala generum,* and be treated thenceforward as a known and labelled subject of the kingdom of thought.

Secondly, in dealing with the combination or separation of concepts, thought expresses *judgments*, affirmative or negative, and yields, when systematised by Logic, the abstract concepts of *subject, predicate,* and *copula,* in one mode of predication, and those of *antecedent* and *consequent* in another mode, namely, in that which expresses judgments hypothetically, by treating what might be the subject of a categorical proposition as a supposition, and not simply as a fact. The original act of purposive attention here becomes more complex, becomes an act of comparison, or attention to the relation between two or more percepts, or perceptual features in concepts, supposing the percepts already conceptualised.

Thirdly, in dealing, not now with the original percepts, nor with their combination or severance by judgments, but with reasoning in the narrower sense of *discourse* of reason, that is, with the relation between judgments, whereby something different from what we had in the judgments separately comes out as the result of comparing them, the same essential act of thought, that is, the same act of purposive attention, assumes the form of *syllogism;* and syllogisms again have two forms, according as they follow the line of categorical or of hypothetical judgments. In the former case they consist of two categorical *premisses* and a categorical *conclusion;* in the latter, one of the premisses is hypothetical. These abstract conceptions and forms of thought, though first distinguished and named by Logic, are thus founded on really experienced differences and really different processes inherent in the thinking process, when considered in connection with its perceptual content of whatever kind, and irrespective of its particular differences. Together with those which express the nature of the act of purposive attention, in which Thought itself as a pure process originates, and by which it is at every step supported, I mean what are called the Postulates, they constitute the analytical basis of the whole science.

The foregoing brief description is sufficient to indicate what science it is which I consider to be properly designated by the name *Logic*, when taken, as it most commonly is, for the science of thought as a whole, apart from its application to acquire any particular kind of knowledge. Owing to its purely analytical character,—analytic, not of an imaginary, separate, and self-contained thinking activity, but of the thinking process as we find it in experience, distinguishable only by abstraction from the content with which, from time to time, it deals,—it is identical with the science known as *Formal Logic*, the science which selects and establishes forms and modes of thinking, both as guides to thinking with unerring correctness in the present, and as tests by which fallacies in trains of past thinking may be detected and exposed.

Thus even the purely analytical and formal Logic has a department or a function which is practical; and this function is capable of considerable development, namely, by applying the forms discriminated and named by its purely analytical branch to the practical though perfectly general purposes of Dialectic, or the art of logical discussion, whether it be discussion carried on between different persons, or between different trains of thought in and by one and the same person. It then becomes what we may call an *ad hominem* science, proceeding from definitions as adopted by persons, and working out by purely formal processes the conclusions to which they lead, in consequence of the suppositions which either tacitly or openly are involved in them. This was avowedly its nature and origin in the mind of its first systematiser, or creator of it as a science, Aristotle; though it is true, that he also proceeded to show, on the ground of its necessity and universality, that the knowledge gained by positive science could be brought within its formulæ, and have its conclusions tested by them; which he did in the treatise known as the *Posterior Analytics*.

It is evident that there is a wide difference between a science or theory of this sort, which formulates the laws and modes of pure thinking so far as they are at once necessary to thinking and the source of formulæ conducive to dialectical discussion, and any science or theory which formulates those laws and modes of concrete reasoning by which facts may be observed, experimented on, and marshalled, so as to discover the general facts or laws of Nature, of which they are cases, and by which they may figuratively be said to be governed. Any science of this latter sort undertakes virtually (assuming the nature of thought itself already known) to guide thought aright in the pursuit of knowledge; by giving general rules for directing choice, at any juncture in the pursuit of the knowledge aimed at, where alternative suppositions are open to us, or for weighing the evidence for and against given hypotheses, or opposite probabilities; the value of this guidance, and of the method pursued in consequence, being determined in the last resort by the conformity of their results when obtained, not to known laws of thought, but to known facts of concrete experience.

These two theories or sciences, namely Formal and Applied Logic, are therefore essentially different, although they have one fundamental element, namely thought, in common, because the object-matter is different with which they deal, and the purposes different in view of which they deal with it. The object-matter of the former, that is, of Formal Logic including Dialectic, is pure thinking, taken as a constituent element discernible in all concrete thinking; that of the latter, or Applied Logic, is the method or methods followed by concrete thinking in any department of positive or practical science, methods which consist in observing and ascertaining positive facts of particular kinds, instituting experiments, forming and verifying hypotheses; always resting ultimately on the assumption of one or more facts of a certain kind, taken in their common-sense form and taken as ultimate, such as the real existence of Matter and the external world, of conscious agents in it, or of percepts given separately as data to conscious percipients, beyond which those who use the methods in question do not for the moment press their enquiries; and always guided by the specific purpose of making ever further and further acquisitions of positive and ascertained knowledge, on whatever basis has been assumed as ultimate. If the assumption were made, that Thought was an agency constitutive or productive of its own content, instead of pre-supposing it, then what is now called Applied Logic or Scientific Method would necessarily appear as identical with Formal Logic and Dialectic, and what are now regarded as Laws of Nature would appear as identical with the Laws of Thought, which on that assumption would be the only Reality. It is hardly necessary to say, that this assumption is the principal foundation of the Hegelian philosophy. But to return.

The scientific methods now described are usually summed up in the one word *Induction* or the Inductive Method, and the theories which deal with them should properly be called theories not of Logic but of Methodology. Well-known instances of such theories are those of J. S. Mill and of Mr. Herbert Spencer, the latter laying down as the ultimate canon of all reasoning what he calls *The Universal Postulate*, by which is meant, that the inconceivability of the negative of any fact, conception, or proposition, is our sole and sufficient test of its being necessarily and universally true.

It was a most important and indeed invaluable step out of the dense Empiricism which then wrapped the whole English world of thought, when Mr. Herbert Spencer first brought forward this light-giving conception, because it decisively shifted the centre of philosophy, as then understood in this country, from the objective to the subjective aspect of existence, and established the true idea of philosophy as a *knowing;* not as a knowing of this or that object, or even of Being or Existence as a whole, when taken, as by Empiricists, whether Idealist or Materialist, it usually is, as something which is already known before knowing begins. Nevertheless the *Universal Postulate* of Mr. Spencer is nothing more nor less than the Postulates of Logic,—the laws of Identity, Contradiction, and Excluded Middle, which (if I may be allowed the expression) are a trinity in unity, belonging to the pure process of thinking,—expressed in a form suitable for application in concrete reasoning from assumed data.

I am, then, very far from intending any polemic against these or similar theories. What I am anxious to show is, that, since they deal with the methods of acquiring positive knowledge, and not with the laws of pure thinking involved in, but always distinguishable from, those methods, they are not theories of Logic but of Methodology, or more strictly, are theories of Logic, not as a science of practice, but as a practical and applied science, dependent as much on the particular object-matter, and end in view from time to time, as on the laws of thought made use of therein. Induction is a method of acquiring additional knowledge from already given data, not a law by or under which thought, as distinguished from other modes of consciousness bound up with it, necessarily moves; although, since it involves thought as one at least of its necessary constituents, it must obey its laws, and exhibit their validity in every instance of its exercise, and that whether the results to which it leads be true or false. In short the two sciences are essentially different, as well as being identical in point of their common foundation. Methodology tells us what steps to take in observing and dealing with what are assumed to be facts, if we want to acquire a systematised knowledge of all facts of that kind; Logic tells us what steps we cannot help taking in reasoning, if we reason at all, whether the truths aimed at by Methodology are the result of our reasoning or not.

Induction includes all methods of concrete reasoning which start from a basis of already assumed or ascertained facts. It is of the concrete reasoning in Induction or Methodology that Mr. Herbert Spencer must be thinking, when he tells us that the lowest act of reasoning, which nevertheless he calls a *syllogism*, has always *four* terms. According to this, all reasoning would be reasoning by analogy, and capable of expression as a sort of qualitative sum in arithmetical proportion, which is in fact the expression which Mr. Spencer gives it. But all concrete reasoning in pursuit of truth varies with the various matters dealt with, and is liable to error; pure thinking, which is in all cases its constituent element *qua* reasoning, is exempt from error, and has the same unchanging validity which universal laws of Nature have. The errors which occur in concrete reasoning are due, not to its element of pure thinking, except so far as the fact of its involving choice enables errors to be made, but to defect of attention to some of the other elements bound up with it, the perceptual matter of representation and imagination, in and with which it moves, and which makes it concrete. It is part of the business of Methodology or Logic applied to any particular object-matter, to tell us upon which of the elements we should direct our attention, if we would attain truth as our result. Logic tells us what we do and cannot avoid doing in the act of attending to any element in relation to the rest. If the result of inductive reasoning is false—that is, not in harmony with the results of similar reasoning which are known to be true—we lay the blame on the induction, as being founded on insufficient or wrongly estimated facts. But we never dream of blaming the laws of thought as misleading or erroneous.[1]

Similarly, to some extent, with the results of Dialectic, inasmuch as therein we start from, and may introduce in the course of the reasoning, assumed definitions and conceptions, concerning some particular object-matter, and taken provisionally as expressing truths. This brings elements into our reasoning which are not taken from the laws of pure thinking, and renders Dialectic also concrete. But the difference is, that it is the very purpose of Dialectic to detect and eliminate all errors of this kind, errors which are due to the assumptions, definitions, and other conceptions, imported into the reasoning process; assuming that the error, if any, must be due, not to the laws of thought, or the formulæ expressing them, which are established by Logic as an analytical science of practice, on which Dialectic itself is founded, but always to the extraneous matter which is brought in by one or the other disputant, or by both, in the definitions and conceptions with which they begin, or which they introduce in the course of the dis-

---

[1] On this point of the source of error in reasoning, as well as on the whole of the present Chapter, see my Aristotelian Address, *What is Logic?*—delivered Nov. 1889, and published in the Proceedings of the Aristotelian Society, Vol. I., No. 3, 1890, pp. 1 to 31.

putation. And the same applies to the arguments which a man holds with himself, where the two disputants are represented by two principles, and the two trains of thought flowing from them, in his single consciousness.

There was a period, before the revival of letters and the new birth of the positive sciences in Europe, when Logic was held to involve certain indisputably true ideas in its own framework, ideas, that is, bound up with the very laws of thought itself, as for instance, those of Being, Essence, Substance, Cause, Property, and Accident; and when, in consequence of this, Dialectic was held to be an infallible method of acquiring true knowledge of fact, by a process which was really concrete reasoning, but which was falsely supposed to be reasoning in its utmost abstraction and purity. But when the true methods of concrete reasoning in pursuit of knowledge, from a basis of assumed or ascertained fact, all of which are included, as already said, in the Inductive Method, were discovered, and more or less rapidly took complete possession of the whole field of experience, then the disputations of Dialectic, which seemed to aim at the very same results by deduction from, or evolution out of, the original conceptions essential to all thought, fell more or less rapidly into total discredit and disuse, at least wherever enquiry was free, and there was no foregone conclusion of a theological or philosophical nature, which their maintenance was supposed to favour, and might serve to uphold.

The Inductive method then gradually but in the end completely ousted and supplanted the Dialec-

§ 1. Logic and Method.

tical. A new Logic thus seemed, but only seemed, to take the place of the old. For the fact was overlooked, that it was only so far as both methods were methods of acquiring knowledge on the basis of assumed fact, not so far as both involved the same laws of pure thinking, that the old Dialectic was replaced by the new Induction. The change did not touch the laws of pure thinking, which were involved in both alike. It was, therefore, not Logic, as a science of practice, which was displaced and supplanted; neither was it Dialectic, as a method of purely logical reasoning; it was the false dialectical method of acquiring knowledge on the basis of assumptions bound up with purely logical processes, as in the noted instances of "survival," Spinoza, who evolved his Ethic from the conception of Substance and its Attributes, and Hegel, who evolved his Encyclopædia from the concept of Being, combined with the purely logical law of Contradiction. Logic as the theory of the laws of thinking is common both to the method of Induction and to that of Dialectic, and continues as immutable as are the laws of thinking themselves, which constitute the one unvarying strain or element in every method of acquiring knowledge, an element which, as will I hope appear still more clearly as we proceed, is always distinguishable, though never separable, from the concrete process in which it is involved.

§ 2. Logic and Reality.

§ 2. Having thus distinguished the Laws of Thinking, which are the object-matter of Logic in its first part, as a science of practice, from the Precepts of inductive reasoning which are Method, and belong to Logic in its second part, or as a practical and applied science, the question next in order concerns the relation which these laws bear to real existence in the fullest sense of the term, namely, to those objects thought of, which are real conditions as well as real conditionates. This question, however, concerns the laws of pure thinking in no other way than it concerns the concrete reasoning in which pure thinking is an element. It concerns thought generally, whether pure or concrete. The question stated broadly is, What is the relation of Thought to Things? When, for instance, I judge that crows are black, or that Her Majesty is at Windsor, I plainly do not mean to assert anything whatever about *my thought* of crows, or *my thought* of Her Majesty ; I do not mean, that my thought of crows involves the thought of blackness, or that my thought of Her Majesty at the present moment involves the thought of her being now at Windsor. I mean to assert something about crows as realities, and about the Queen as a real person. And yet, since my own thought is all that I can by any possibility have immediately present to my thought, in thinking about anything whatever, it seems impossible to suppose that my judgment can relate to realities as distinguished from my thoughts about them; impossible, therefore, that realities should ever be present to my thought at all, and consequently, that to suppose that my judgment relates to realities is an illusion and a mistake.

Now that it is an illusion and a mistake, or in other words, that reality is undistinguishable from illusion, seems to me an unavoidable consequence of making the initial assumption of ordinary

Empiricism, that the meaning of *Reality* in the full sense of real condition is given by perception alone, independently of thought; and still more obviously, if that assumption takes a more specific form, as for instance the assumption, that Mind and Matter are similarly known independently of thought, as two realities of opposite natures. Assumptions of this kind lead directly and inevitably to scepticism, the fallacy of which is only detected, when the initial assumption is found to be merely a common-sense mode of thinking, made to do duty as a fact of experience which can be a basis of philosophy. Unless indeed an issue is sought for a time, by making the assumption made by Hegelian Empiricism, namely, that Thought is the only real and permanent existent, creative of minor and transient realities by intus-susception; in which case the very same difficulty of distinguishing between what is real and what is unreal, or between reality and appearance, revolves upon us in a more complex shape,—the only change being that what before was called an Existent, as a part of Existence, is now called a Concept, as a part of Thought,—a shape in which the difficulty consists in distinguishing between Thought itself and its content, whether taken as parts or products. In other words, the Idealist's device of re-naming Existence, and calling it Thought, does nothing to relieve us of the sceptical idea, that reality and illusion are the same.

I do not propose to enter into any polemic with either of these opposite forms of Empiricism. Not with the Hegelian form of it, because the analysis of the two foregoing Books has, I trust, sufficiently shown, that no mode of consciousness, whether thinking or anything else, is a real condition or agent. Not with the English form of it, because the same analysis has shown (1) that we have no positive conception of, and consequently can have no positive evidence for, Mind as a real agent, and (2) that the meaning of *reality* is revealed solely in and by purposive attention to consciousness, or experience as it is actually experienced; so that the question of the relation of thought to reality may here be taken as already decided by the analysis of Book I., and decided in a sense which is non-sceptical with regard to reality. I refer especially to Chapter VIII., Sections 4 and 5, in that Book, where the filiation of the conception of objects real in the full sense of being operative as real conditions was traced to that of objects thought of, and the existence of such fully real objects, independently of our objective thought of them, was shown to be an imperatively necessary inference from the facts of experience. Thought deals with such realities, when once they have been conceived and inferred, by the very same laws which guided it in originally conceiving and inferring them. The meaning of our conception of them, and consequently the reality and efficiency of their existence, independent of our conception, are unchanged;—discovered not created by thought. It remains only to ascertain those laws, to which both the original discovery and the subsequent dealing with the realities discovered are subject, laws which are the object-matter of Logic.

Nevertheless, before proceeding with the analysis of spontaneous and voluntary redintegration, from the point reached in the foregoing Chapter, and showing by that analysis what the true genesis of Thought is, as a specific mode of consciousness conditioned and determined by further action of the same cerebral processes which also condition and determine spontaneous redintegrations and the laws of association, something more must be said on that relation of Thought to Things which is such an embarrassing puzzle to English Empiricism. The puzzle exists only for the empiricist, not for the metaphysician; for it arises solely in consequence of beginning the enquiry into experience by assuming reality as the object of knowledge, instead of beginning it with analysis of experience as a process-content of knowing. This analysis soon reveals to us what the terms *reality* and *object* mean, as parts of the process-content of a knowing. Whereas, if we begin by assuming reality and objectivity as known before we begin our enquiry into experience simply, we render the very experience into which we enquire a special experience, namely, one defined and limited by that upon which it is supposed to be directed, and we are moreover forced to assume our Self as a real Subject of that special experience which we receive (as we suppose) from the assumed object and the assumed reality. For the assumption of an object experienced unavoidably involves that of an experiencing Subject.

These two methods, then, are widely different. The analytical method, in which we analyse experience simply as a knowing, is experientialism; the opposite method, which proceeds by way of assumption of something independent of experience, is empiricism. Now assumptions are good in science, when they are warranted by previous metaphysical analysis; they are never good in philosophy, the fundamental principle of which they contravene; and to introduce them into the study of philosophical questions is the certain way to turn those questions into insoluble puzzles. By dealing thus, instead of analytically, with the present question, we treat a question of philosophy as if it was a question of psychology, and of psychology based on warranted, not (as in this case they are) unwarranted assumptions. Such are the two methods of philosophising, one true the other false. And, as already said, the puzzle now in question arises only when the wrong method, the method of empiricism, is adopted in philosophy.

The empiricist's puzzle arises thus. He assumes a supposed objective reality to begin with. But he finds, that reality in its fullest sense, that is, the existence of objects which are real conditions as well as real conditionates, is always *inferred*, and never immediately perceived. How can he be assured, that the reality which he infers is identical with the reality which he has assumed? To put it briefly, no such assurance is possible. He himself has destroyed the possibility of it by assuming *himself* as the Subject, or knower, of an assumed reality which he calls Object. For, inference being a process entirely within consciousness, no inference can assure him that what he infers as a reality or realities independent of himself is not a creation of his own mental activities, and therefore dependent wholly on himself, whose reality he has also assumed without any knowledge of its, that is, his own real nature.

The truth of the matter is, as was fully shown in Book I., in which the experiential method was adopted, that objective reality in its fullest sense, namely, the existence of objects which are real as conditions, and not merely as conditionates, is always matter of inference, and never given immediately to consciousness. Therefore it cannot legitimately be made an original assumption. The only things given immediately to consciousness are perceptions which are part and parcel of the process-content of consciousness itself; and out of these we both construct the objective thoughts of concrete and real objects, and also infer the existence of material objects thought of, as the real objects of those objective thoughts.—I say material objects thought of, because these are the only real objects, in the full sense of the term, for which we have any evidence. There is no *a priori* reason against inferring immaterial real objects, in the same full sense of the term *real*, if only there were facts enabling us to construct the objective thought of them, and evidence showing their real existence as objects thought of. No testimony in their favour, even though professing to be drawn from direct personal experience, can have any evidential weight, unless it be shown, that those who give it have had the precise point to be proved clearly and distinctly in view, as it is exhibited by the method of subjective analysis of the phenomena of experience without assumptions. The question, however, as to immaterial real objects in the full sense is a digression from the train of argument now before us.

Resuming that train of argument, I remark in the next place, that on the subjective and analy-

THE FOUNDATIONS OF LOGIC.

tical method of philosophising the puzzle in question does not arise at all. There is no chasm to be bridged between a reality assumed and a reality inferred, for the simple reason that there is no reality assumed; and therefore the reality inferred is the only reality with which we have to deal. We infer from the data of experience as it is actually experienced, that there are real material objects thought of, the meaning of *real* and *material* and *objects* being ascertained by analysis of the data, and that these real objects follow lines of operation of their own, quite different from, and independent of, the lines followed by the objective thoughts, of which they are the real objects. It is true, that objective thoughts follow lines of sequence, combination, and separation, which are closely dependent upon the lines of operation followed by one class of real objects thought of, namely, the operative processes in physical nerve and brain substance. But these are not all the objects thought of by objective thoughts, though all the latter arise in dependence upon some one or more of the former. I mean that, while every objective thought is proximately conditioned upon some brain process, that brain process upon which it is conditioned need not be, and only rarely is, the object of that objective thought. The objective thought, say, of a black crow is dependent upon some neural process in the thinker's brain; but the real crow, and not the neural process, is the real object of that objective thought. The neural process is the real object of another objective thought, that which images the process; and this objective thought depends in turn upon another

BOOK III.
CH. IV.

§ 2.
Logic
and
Reality.

neural process, which is its proximate real condition, but not its object thought of.

We infer, then, from the data of experience, that there are real material objects thought of, which exist and operate independently of the objective thoughts which represent them; and we find, by going over this whole process analytically, as we did in Book I., that our whole knowledge of real objects in the full sense is inferential, or in other words, that our consciousness is never immediately aware of those objects, but only of certain features or elements in them, which are also parts of the process-content of consciousness, from which the inference of their reality in the full sense is drawn, though drawn in most cases instantaneously, at least by adults. It is this instantaneousness, all but simultaneity, of the inference which hides its inferential character from our view, and gives rise to the common-sense notion, that our perception of real objects in the full sense of the term is immediate.

Hence it is, that the empiricist's assumption of reality as the object of knowledge is possible. He takes the common-sense notion of real objects immediately present to consciousness as something *per se notum*, and belonging to the very essence of experience itself. And this assumption it is which, as we have just seen, commits him to the impossible task of identifying his assumed with his inferred reality, a self-made difficulty from which the metaphysical enquirer is wholly free. The only reality, in the full sense, of which we know anything at all, is an inferred reality, mediately and not immediately present to consciousness.

THE FOUNDATIONS OF LOGIC.

The connection of this explanation with the question of Logic will now be evident. Logic deals with the laws of thought and inference as processes of consciousness, and not with the brain processes upon which they immediately depend, to which they owe their character of being activities, and the reality of which is itself an inferred fact or object. Now inference is employed in two main directions, under which all other directions may be brought, namely, (1) in constructing our objective thoughts and distinguishing them from objects thought of, and (2) in establishing the real existence and operation of certain objects thought of, and thought of as independent of the existence of the objective thoughts by which we bring them into consciousness. The only way in which we can bring real objects into consciousness is by having objective thoughts of them. They are brought within our ken, in the first instance, by inference from objective thoughts, and all further knowledge of them is gained by modifying and correcting objective thoughts, or amplifying them by the incorporation of new experience. The idea that any part, either of consciousness, or of thought which is a mode of it, taken as part of a knowing, and not as an existent, can penetrate, assimilate, be identified or in contact with, or in immediate presence of, its real object (in the full sense of the term) is absurd. These are metaphorical ways of speaking drawn from our experience of the operation of matter upon matter. The only way in which a real object of any kind can be present to consciousness is by consciousness knowing it, and knowing it (when said of consciousness, not of the Subject) means containing an objective thought of it which will be verified by, or be in harmony with, other objective thoughts representing it or other real objects.

The same analysis applies also to the Subject, as an objective reality in the full sense of the term. We know it by inference only, and not by immediate intuition; and therefore cannot legitimately assume it as a datum independent of experience. Neither can consciousness itself be a real object thought of in the full sense of reality; it is a knowing, and a knowing only, of such objects among others. When we speak of consciousness as a real existent, it is a a real existent only as a conditionate, not as a condition. It cannot, and does not, act and re-act with real objects which are real conditions. With this view of the nature of objective reality we must perforce acquiesce, however repugnant it may be to our common-sense prejudices. But it will be found, to say the very least, as fully adequate as that of a reality assumed *a priori*, to meet all the legitimate requirements of philosophical explanation and theory.

Thought, then, apart from its real conditions, belongs entirely to consciousness, of which it is a mode, and consists in first forming and then manipulating objective thoughts, whether these have real material objects represented by them or not. They are formed originally, by means of consciously and purposively selective attention, out of the imagery and other content offered by spontaneous redintegration, in the way which has been already described, and to which it will be necessary presently to revert. This action is the origination of thought. But thought taken as an already formed product, that is, as the result of the action of that selective attention (when completed in the way presently to be explained) upon spontaneous redintegrations, consists wholly of objective thoughts, including their relations to one another. It will be remembered for what reason and in what sense thoughts are called objective. It is because they are objects of reflective perception, objective to consciousness itself, of the process-content of which they are parts, and in which they are perceived from the moment of their formation, which is also the moment of their beginning to recede into the past of memory.

Every objective thought, when formed for the first time, is thus an object of reflective perception; that is, we are conscious of it as a freshly formed state of consciousness, just in the same way as we are conscious of a simple sense-presentation. But when, after having once faded from the view of consciousness on its first formation and perception, it is recalled, that is, represented, in memory, it becomes itself an object thought of, being the object of a freshly arising representation, which is the objective thought of it. Objective thoughts, therefore, may be themselves real, though not material, objects thought of, that is, not real objects in the full sense of the term *real*. An objective thought may thus both *have* a real object thought of, which it represents, and also *be* a real object thought of, namely, in or to another objective thought, by which it is represented.

Thus, to take the old instance, when I say *crows*, or that *crows are black*, I mean real crows. I am then expressing in language an objective thought, which has real crows for its object thought of. I may also speak of my thought of crows, and say that my thought of crows contains the thought of blackness. In that case I am expressing an objective thought which has another objective thought for its object thought of. In both cases alike my thinking moves entirely within, and is a modification of, my panorama of objective thought; and the laws by which it moves, so far as it is pure thought, are the laws of Logic, or more strictly, the laws of pure thought made known by Logic, in its first department, or as a science of practice.

It is this perpetual representation and re-representation of objective thought by objective thought, quite as much as the varying combinations into which objective thoughts enter with one another, which constitute the well-known intricacy of thought-life, as if it were a massive pile of tangled net-work, and make the clue to its mazes difficult to find. It is in discovering and holding fast this clue, that the rules and forms instituted by Logic as distinguished from its fundamental Laws, find their special task and justification.

We have thus distinguished two kinds of objective thoughts, one which has real existents in the full sense of reality, and the other which has other objective thoughts, for its objects thought of. But there is a modification to be mentioned, springing from the relation of these two kinds of objective thoughts to one another, which practically results in the formation of objective thoughts of a third kind. Real existents in the full sense, as distinguished from the objective thoughts of them, can only be brought before consciousness by objective thoughts of them *as such*, that is, as real existents in the full sense. This follows from the facts, that objective thoughts may themselves be objects thought of, that in this sense they are also themselves real existents, and that their existence follows lines quite different from those followed by the real objects in the full sense, of which they are the objective thoughts. When I think of a real object or a train of real events as really taking place, my doing so means my having at the moment an objective thought of the real object or train of events. So far the objective thought is nothing but the subjective aspect of the object or events thought of. But if I go farther and think of the real object or train of events as being independent of my objective thought, that is, of what was its own subjective aspect,—which it is when both are taken in their character of real existents,—then I modify my objective thought of the real object or train of events, so as to make it include the representation of this independence in the objects thought of; and this new form of it is what I call an objective thought of the real object or train of events *as such*, that is, as real in the full sense of the term *reality*. I thereby think of the real object or train of events in connection with their own real conditions, co-existents, and re-acting conditionates, and disconnect them from the objective thoughts associated in my consciousness with those objective thoughts of which they are the objects.

The objective thoughts representing the real objects are the starting point of this proceeding ·

they are the subjective aspects of the objects which they represent, and represent the nature or *whatness* of those objects. But from the moment that both aspects are taken as real existents, and the genesis and history of the two aspects are seen to be divergent,—which is in fact to distinguish one of them as belonging to the object-matter of psychology, not simply of metaphysic, and the other to the object-matter of some other positive science,—then it becomes necessary to introduce, or rather notice and record, a modification of the objective thought, which is originally the subjective aspect of the real objects, so that the new form of it may represent the fact of independence on the part of the real objects thought of. We cannot have the real objects brought into consciousness at all except by having an objective thought of them, and we cannot have them brought into consciousness *in their independence* of objective thought, except by having an objective thought of them *as independent*, which is what I have called above an objective thought of real objects in the full sense *as such*.

We have, then, in result, three kinds of objective thoughts,—1st those which represent real objects in the full sense of reality, but represent them in their nature or *whatness* only ; 2nd those which represent other objective thoughts as their objects thought of; and 3rd those which represent real objects in the full sense *as such*, that is, represent them in their real connection with other real objects, which are real in the same full sense of the term, that is, are real conditions as well as real conditionates. It is by means of objective thoughts

THE FOUNDATIONS OF LOGIC.   257

of this third kind that thought deals with the real objective world in the full sense of the term *reality*, which is the world of real conditions; and they it is which supply the answer to the question with which we began—-What is the relation of Thought to Things?—apart of course from that relation of real conditioning, by which our thought itself depends upon one class of real existents, namely, nerve and brain processes, for its own genesis and existence.

§ 3. I now revert to the actual origination of Thought out of the imagery and content offered by spontaneous redintegration. The brain may be figured as an aggregate of living organic machinery for continuing to produce physical nerve processes similar to those which have once been received or otherwise set up within it, processes which are accompanied for the most part by states and processes of consciousness, of which they are the proximate real conditions. During the periods of youth and maturity at any rate, the growth and internal development of this living machinery, and the corresponding wealth of the consciousness which it can turn out, increase with every new impression received and process set up in the brain substance. And as each physical and neural impression and process is, at its origination, received and set up in connection with others, so also it is liable to be revived by and to revive others, when it or they are revived by stimuli received either from without or from within the brain substance; revivals which are also for the most part accompanied by their own dependent states or processes of consciousness.

VOL. III.   R

By revival of a physical brain impression or process is meant, not of course that the two or more occurrences of it are one and the same, *unum numero*, but that each separate occurrence after the first is the occurrence of an impression or a process closely similar to the first, taking place in a closely similar manner, in the same or very nearly the same group of nerve particles. This close similarity of the separate occurrences, which we call repetition or revival of the first of them, is not a fact known by direct observation, but one which we infer, and then make use of in accounting for the observed close similarity of the states and processes of consciousness which depend upon them; the physical impressions and processes being the *hypotheta*, or real conditions which we assume by hypothesis, in order to explain the occurrence of states and processes of consciousness so closely similar to each other as to be called in ordinary language revivals or repetitions of the same state or process of consciousness.

But more than this is requisite to account for the phenomena grouped under the general head of memory. What is called a revival or repetition of a state or process of consciousness is in fact the simultaneous or nearly simultaneous occurrence of two closely similar states or processes of consciousness, (which occurrence of two we call memory of a third), depending, as we must suppose, upon the simultaneous or nearly simultaneous occurrence of two nerve processes, closely similar, both to each other and to that which was the original real condition of the original state or process of consciousness said to be revived or repeated. The *whatness* of these three states or processes of consciousness is or may be so closely similar as to seem identical, and render them apparently or at first sight undistinguishable one from another, which is what we call being identical in point of kind; although in fact, as we have seen in a former Chapter, what are perceived as repetitions or revivals of a former state or process of consciousness in memory are not re-appearances of one and the same state or process of consciousness,—as if they could be compared, say, to the successive appearances of a single candle at the different windows of a gallery, along which it should be carried,—but the original and its repetitions alike are numerically different occurrences of contents so closely similar in point of kind, as to be numerically distinguishable from one another only by the circumstance, that the context in which each of them occurs is perceived to be different. This very circumstance, however, necessarily involves some difference, however small, in the several percepts themselves, both at the moment of first repetition, when we are said to remember or revive the first perception, and at subsequent moments of re-representation, when we are said to remember former remembrances.

At the same time, though the fact of the minute differences in representation and re-representation of long familiar experiences is beyond question, it by no means follows, that in remembering we remember each remembrance in the series, distinct from others, or from the original experience, by means of its minute differences, whether intrinsic or in respect of its context. A single blurred remembrance is usually all that we retain, comparable to our perception of the trees on either side of a long straight avenue, seen from one end of it; a remembrance which nevertheless may be practically and essentially faithful, notwithstanding that it may cover and include a countless series of experiences in a single image.

This process of spontaneous redintegration is continually going on, and the general laws or uniformities which prevail in it are those known as the Laws of Association of Ideas, laws which are stated, it must be remembered, in terms of consciousness, not in terms of the cerebral processes upon which consciousness depends. The process, moreover, is continually taking up into itself new sense-presentations, which, on their first ceasing to be perceived as presentations, become liable to revival as representations, and subject to the laws of association. The sense-presentations are in perceptual form when first perceived, and no change is made in them, in this respect, by their revival as representations. All spontaneous redintegration, prior to and apart from thought, consists of imagery in perceptual form, though enriched by emotional feeling, which has an intra-cerebral as distinguished from an extra-cerebral origin. This whole process-content of spontaneous redintegration, subject to the laws of association, is the perennial source of the matter or pabulum of thought.

It is true that thought, being re-action attended by consciousness upon process attended by consciousness, must be conceived as nearly, though not quite, co-eval with the spontaneous redintegrations out of which it arises, and which supply its matter or pabulum. In so considering it we adopt the historical point of view, which is that adopted by psychology, and also that which we adopt, side by side with the metaphysical point of view, in the present Book. The beginning of reasoning, therefore, historically and psychologically speaking, is all but co-eval with spontaneous redintegration ; just as spontaneous redintegration is all but co-eval with sense-presentation, and as the objectification in retrospective perception is all but co-eval with reflective perception, or consciousness, in its lowest terms. There is thus some historical priority, which is quite independent of priority in order of our understanding the phenomena as a whole, in all these cases ; that is to say, in the simplest states of reflective perception as compared to their objectification ; in sense-presentation as compared to spontaneous redintegration ; and in spontaneous redintegration as compared to reasoning or thought. Without the previous existence of the simplest states of reflective perception, the perception of them as objects of a subsequent reflective perception would have had no historical existence ; without the previous existence of sense-presentation, the spontaneous redintegration of sense could never have arisen ; and without the previous existence of spontaneous redintegration, selective attention to its varied content would have been impossible—as impossible as to take a second step in walking without taking a first, notwithstanding that the process of walking is the same in every step we take, and in every part of each step, however minutely we may divide it.

It seems evident, moreover, that thought does not arise directly from, or directly operate upon, sense-presentations. We may, indeed, and often do attend selectively to sense-presentations, simply for the purpose of experiencing them with greater clearness or intensity. In some cases falling under this description, the act of selective attention, which initiates thought, terminates in an act of attention simply, that is, an act of attentive perception of a singular object, and the thought (so to call it) which it originates is then at an end. With this class of cases we are not now concerned. But in those cases where acts of selective attention continue to sustain the thought which they originate, the selection resides, not in the singling out particular objects for direct attention in isolation, but in the adoption of the desire to attend to them, as a means of knowing better the objects attended to, in the sense of perceiving their relations to other parts of the content of consciousness, and so rendering the whole more easily comprehensible. The sense-presentations to which in these cases we may directly attend are then, as it were, incorporated with our thought, as a means of attaining its desired end of further knowledge. Yet even here, whenever we appear to reason directly about a new or strange sense-presentation, what we immediately reason about is not the presentation itself, but its representation, even though the sense-presentation is continued throughout the whole process. For in reasoning we connect the sense-presentation with previous representations, and in so doing repeat the presentation itself as a representation, only recurring from time to time to the continued sense-presentation to correct or revivify our representation of it, for the purpose of comparison with other representations.

As for instance, suppose I am walking out on a misty day, and see an object looming indistinctly through the mist, and question whether it is, say, a bush, a post, a horse, or a man. I at once compare the sense-presentation with other remembered presentations, and my reasoning, as to what the sense-presentation really means, consists in my comparing one representation of it with another, until on coming up to the object the final sense-presentation decides which of my representations, if any, was the right one, that is, which was closest to the real object, or what new representation I must form in order to be in harmony with the fact of sense. Now all sense-presentations, taken *per se* and prior to representation of them, have the same character of uncertainty as to *what* they are or mean, that the supposed indistinct object seen in the mist has. Apart from representations of them they have no meaning at all, form no part of memory, and consequently supply no material for thought.

The Thought, then, with which we have to do, is something which springs up perpetually from, and perpetually re-acts upon, the process of spontaneous redintegration and the material offered by it, no matter what stage we pitch upon for examination in the lifetime of an individual, and no matter what place the individual may occupy in the whole history and evolution of humanity. And the task now before us is to trace the operation by which the whole and every part of the panorama of objective thought receives organic form, yet only so far as purely redintegrative processes are employed in its construction, and again, within these, only so far as the operation consists in what is common to the whole and every part, not specially determined by anything peculiar to particular kinds of content, or by particular purposes connected with them.

From this it is plain in the first place, since thought is a volitional modification of the content offered by spontaneous redintegration, and has no power to summon up a content unaided by suggestion, that its modifying action must consist in attention to some feature in the suggested content, and the dismissal of others, which that attention involves. In other words, the action which is the basis of all thinking is that of consciously and purposively selective attention. And in the next place, since such selection pre-supposes some interest or other to be taken in the feature selected, which is said to determine its selection, and the action of thought is common to every kind of content, we see that the determining interest also must be general, not confined to any particular kinds of content, but capable of arising in all alike. I mean, that the feature attended to must have at least an interest of this general kind, if the attention to it is to generate thought, irrespective of whatever special or peculiar interest it may possess besides.

Now all thinking is a consciously forward-looking process, directed to come to some conclusion, or attain some insight, which we are not previously in possession of. And it has been shown in a former place (Book I. Chap. III. § 4), that simple attention to a content of consciousness is the original basis of our perception of future time and experience, as distinguished from past and present; and thus that all attention is expectant of a future, as well as retrospective on a past experience. When the feature attended to, which is said to arouse the attention, has a distinctly perceived interest attaching to it, the expectation is coloured in a particular way corresponding to that interest; we then contradistinguish our future expectation from our past or present experience, and selectively attend to the latter, in view of a purpose to be fulfilled by the expected content. This selective and purposive attention is the action which originates thought.

In the Section just quoted we were speaking more particularly of attention arising in connection with sense-presentations. But the very same thing which holds good of sense-presentations, in relation to attention, holds good also of trains of spontaneous redintegration in relation to acts of selective attention and thought. Spontaneous redintegration *per se* is simply the continuation or repetition of sense-presentation in a weaker form and altered order; with emotional content, it is true, in addition to or rather in combination with it, but still containing nothing which either forces or enables us to distinguish a future from a past or present content, nothing which makes us recognise the distinction of its *de facto* expectation of a future, as we afterwards call it, from its *de facto* remembrance of a past content. The associated imagery of representation goes on in a continuous current, rising above the threshold of consciousness and receding into the past of memory, just as the series of sense-presentations does, of which it is the representation. The consciously drawn distinction between expectation of a future and remembrance of a past experience is due to simple, and not consciously selective attention, as much in the case of spontaneous redintegration as in that of sense-presentation, which are in fact inseparable, though distinguishable, elements in the one concrete stream of consciousness, which we are now considering in its redintegrative aspect only.

Now it will be evident, from the account given above of the play of spontaneous redintegration under the laws of association, combined with the distinction between a remembered and an expected experience, that an altered or distorted remembrance, that is, an imagination not true to the experience which gave rise to it, will frequently occur as an expectation, and will frequently also prove to be in conflict with remembrances which are comparatively unaltered, and the truth of which may be proved by their harmony with each other, and with new sense-presentations which, when taken up into the train of redintegration, serve to verify them. Whenever this occurs, that is to say, whenever we find an imagined expectation out of harmony with a true remembrance, say, the remembrance of a sense-presentation which has occurred immediately before it, commonly called a fact of experience, there will be a shock of surprise, a sense of discrepancy, a dislocation of the order of conscious experience, which will be felt, in our first experience of it, as wonder, bewilderment, uncertainty, and intellectual uneasiness. We shall then for the first time attend to the discrepancy, that is, to the facts which are anticipated by imagination and the newly presented and accurately remembered facts which falsify the anticipation, or in other words, to the two discrepant contents and the point or points in which they differ, with the desire of harmonising them, and so dispelling the uneasy surprise, wonder, and bewilderment. We shall put our first question, *Why* or *How* they come to differ. We shall exercise for the first time our power of consciously selective attention to redintegrative contents. A conscious desire of knowing, that is, of having a future state of consciousness different from the actual one, and different in respect of the disharmony of the actual one, will for the first time arise.

Fundamentally, then, and both in respect of its essence and in respect of its origin, the reasoning process consists in the adoption of the desire to restore a state of harmony to consciousness, on the basis of actually experienced but discrepant facts, the discrepancy of which has disturbed a harmony which previously existed, and has, as it were, ruined for the moment its primal paradise of unsuspecting repose. The attention which adopts the desire of restoration is fixed upon the point at which the discrepancy occurs, that is to say, it is selective of the point at which the content of consciousness consists of two discrepant perceptions, and selects that content from the other parts of the whole process-content of consciousness presentative and representative. And this account holds good in cases where we have representations alone before us, just as much as where the discrepancy is between a representation and a presentation. In fact it has already been shown, that, even when presentations are in consciousness, it is the representations of them with which we really reason. One train of redintegration may give rise to expectations, or anticipated consequences, in representation, which are discrepant with consequences anticipated in virtue of other trains of redintegration. That is to say, the whole ground of redintegration is covered and ruled by the fact of discrepancy, and by the desire thence arising to replace it by a new or renewed concord, namely, by harmonising the discrepant facts, and showing how they may be conceived as consistent with one another, in whatever way this desired result may in different cases be attained; I mean, whether by retaining both facts and referring them, as particular cases, to a more general fact occurring with modifications due to different circumstances, or by retaining one or more as facts, and dismissing others as fictions.

The whole process of concrete reasoning is thus determined by, and, as it were, developed out of, the perennial desire to harmonise the discrepant facts of experience; or in other words, is an attempt to reduce all facts which may come forward in sense-presentation, or may be offered by spontaneous redintegration, or may result from thought operating on spontaneous redintegration, or from thought again operating on those results, to a single systematised scheme of conceptions consistent with itself in all its parts. And selective attention to every discrepancy, with a view to collect facts, either from new sense-presentations or from the content offered by spontaneous redintegration,—for there are no other ultimate sources than these,—is the means whereby thought operates in effecting the desired harmony. For the most part we have recourse, not to new sense-presentations, but to what is already included in the content of spontaneous redintegration. And this we do by taxing our memory to bring facts to distinct recollection, which the mere fact of their being suggested at all makes us think likely to throw light on one or more of the facts which we begin by attending to as the seat of the discrepancy.

This taxing of memory is the well known process called *hunting*, θηρεύειν, by Aristotle. What we do in *hunting* for a forgotten fact is this. Since thought has no power of summoning up an idea from absolute nothingness, that is, without having some inkling of what it wants to summon, the hunting is only possible in cases where we have, in memory, some trace, however slight, of the fact said to be forgotten, some dim sense of its effect upon us, or some dim outline of the relation in which it stood to other facts. On each of these in turn, the effect and the related facts, we then fix our attention, and deepen the impression by dwelling on them, trusting to spontaneous redintegration under the laws of association, in consequence of the stimulation so received from attention, to re-instate in memory the fact with which they have been connected, and the specific features of which we have now forgotten.

There are two Laws to which the whole process of concrete reasoning is subject; one of them founded on its psychological nature as a process dependent on the action of a living and sentient Subject, the other on its character as a process of conscious thought. The former is known as the Law of Parcimony,—*Frustra fit per plura quod fieri potest per pauciora*,—a law which expresses the preference which a sentient being feels for doing whatever it has to do with the least possible effort, and by the shortest possible route. The latter is known as the law of *Ratio sufficiens cognoscendi*, a law which we may express by the precept, *Make no assertion in thought without a sufficient reason for knowing it to be true.* What it means is, that in reasoning the nexus between the facts which we are endeavouring to harmonise must be capable of being pointed out in the objective thoughts representing those facts; whether it be the thought of some intrinsic similarity, or some similarity of relation or analogy, or of their dependence one upon another, or of their common dependence upon the same real condition or set of real conditions.

Both laws, however, are rather practical precepts guiding choice, and applicable to concrete reasoning, than strictly speaking laws by which the pure action of Thought moves, and without which it would not be Thinking at all. Nevertheless the complete fulfilment of both precepts, in organising the entire content of objective thought, would be the complete attainment of Truth, so far as possible to humanity, Truth of which no further criterion or test would be either needful or possible; since our objective thought would then be a Knowledge, in or concerning which the arising of further doubt would have been precluded, which is the ideal goal which all reasoning is an endeavour to attain. Short of this ideal, degrees of Truth may be said to be attained (though always liable to reversal or alteration by further knowledge), in proportion as more and more facts, represented by objective thought, are ascertained and harmonised, and as larger and larger fields are consequently included in the organisation of objective thought.

It must of course be remembered, that there are many processes, included under the wide term concrete reasoning because they contain the element of thought, which are not directed to establish the systematised scheme of conceptions spoken of above, that is, are not suited for incorporation in the methods of science or of philosophy. We may for instance selectively attend to a representation or to a presentation, for the sole purpose of being more clearly and distinctly conscious of it, perceiving it or feeling it more definitely or more intensely. Or again we may "hunt" for a forgotten name, circumstance, event, person, spoken phrase, and so on *in indefinitum*, simply for our own gratification in reconstructing our personal experience, or as the means to some particular ulterior purpose. Or again we may be governed by one or more of the countless desires which lead us to busy ourselves with our ordinary occupations, or with the news of the day, or with amusements and pleasures of various sorts; and every one of these desires will lead us to fix our attention upon objects of different kinds, without any idea that we are thereby pursuing knowledge for its own sake. Still, so far as any one of these acts or operations is part of a series governed by the desire for harmonising a discrepancy in redintegration, to that extent and for that reason it makes a part in concrete reasoning, the proximate purpose of which is knowing and knowing only, and which is subject to the laws of pure thought. This desire is the sole element which constitutes any operation a ratiocinative action, not the greater or less degree of dignity or of prudence which may characterise the particular motive or ulterior determinant of our choice, nor the degree of clearness or of intensity which we may attain in attending to particular objects. It is in the pursuit of a systematised scheme of consistent truth, that the desire of knowing is seen for the longest unbroken periods, and in the greatest degree of isolation consistent with its being seen as an element in concrete reasoning. And this is why we naturally choose that pursuit as the instance which best exhibits the action of pure thought, though doing so often induces us to mistake the concrete pursuit of scientific or philosophic truth for the element of pure thought which it involves and exhibits.

In pure thought, that is, in selective attention governed merely by the desire of harmonising discrepancies, and its immediate consequences, we are not governed by any positive or specific anticipation, or foreseen object of desire, as we are in all cases of concrete reasoning, and even in that mode of it which has some particular systematised scheme of consistent truth as its foreshadowed end or τέλος. The object aimed at by the pure act of thought is always either negative or indefinite; either to escape the uneasiness of a discrepant experience, in which it is negative, or to attain a greater degree of insight, or some clearer conception than we have at present, in which it is indefinite. In neither case do we positively foreshadow or anticipate the specific goal of our desire. This circumstance constitutes a great difference between pure thinking and every one of the concrete modes in which it is involved, and more perhaps than anything else throws light on the nature of pure thought. No specific satisfaction or pleasure is its guiding motive; but on the contrary, thought itself is a pre-requisite of the idea of any specific satisfaction or pleasure as an object of future attainment. Desire,—not desired pleasure or satisfaction, but desire for something as yet unknown, desire born of the uneasiness of not knowing,—is the motive power in reasoning *qua* reasoning, impelling us to go forward, by attention to the content offered through non-volitional channels, to the attainment of greater insight into the relations of objects, though what the nature of that insight will be we know not. From this it is evident, that a comparison of specifically anticipated pleasures, followed by a selection of that which we judge the greatest, is not necessarily and universally the condition, or the pleasure so selected the motive, of volitional action, as some empiricists appear to think.

On the whole, then, we find, that the immediate material of thought consists of the imagery and emotional content of spontaneous redintegration, the parts of which are connected together, prior to thought, under the laws of association, have the form of individual or single percepts in time, or in time and space together, as the whole, taken together, also has, and are brought before us in a continuous succession of present moments of consciousness. At the same time, those parts of the whole which represent sense-presentations of sight and touch, and on that account have spatial extension as their perceptual form, are perceived in redintegration as spreading out on all sides from

BOOK III.
CH. IV.

§ 3.
The Material and Origination of Thought.

the perceived image of the Subject; which latter constitutes, as it were, the centre of a spatial panorama in the three dimensions of space, a centre which, in respect of time, is always moving forward, along with the rest of its panorama, into the future, and having the previous state of the whole spatial panorama, including itself as centre, for the proximate object of its consciousness. For this panorama, which has already been described in Book I. as the panorama of objective thought, includes the representations of concrete real objects which have been formed by the operation of thought upon the material offered by spontaneous redintegration previous to thought, and which, when formed, have themselves taken their place in spontaneous redintegration, and therein recur, or tend to recur, in accordance with the laws of association, just as if they had been representations of simple sense-presentations from the first. And the further products of the operation of thought on these complex images, when once they have become habitual and familiar as representations of complex real objects, likewise take their place in the panorama of objective thought, so that they too must thenceforward be counted as part of the material which spontaneous redintegration offers to the action of all thought which is subsequent to their incorporation in the panorama.

The whole moving panorama of objective thought, which is the material continually offered to thought by spontaneous redintegration, is therefore also continually being enriched by the action of thought upon it; an enrichment which consists partly in the formation of new images, partly in the modification of old ones, as well as in the sweeping away of some, which advancing thought shows to be fictitious, and not images of anything permanent or real. But both spontaneous and voluntary redintegration, both the material of thought and thought itself, with their products, are alike confined to the subjective aspect of real existence in the full sense, and move within the circle of objective thought, the total panorama of which is in fact constituted by their united action. They make no part of the real panorama thought of, which is real in the full sense of *reality*, that is to say, the objects and events constituting which are real as conditions as well as conditionates. Thought is part of the panorama of objective thought, not of the panorama of real material (or immaterial) objects thought of, in the sense of being itself a real agent. Thought is a knowing, not a knower, not an agent knowing or known. It supplies us with knowledge of the panorama or world of real conditions, by the modifications which the thinking Subject introduces into the panorama of objective thought. Its mode of origin out of, and connection with, that representational panorama is what I have endeavoured to make evident in the present Section. The task of the next Section will be to exhibit some further effects of its operation on its material, effects in harmony with the uniform laws of its own nature, as a process initiated, and at every step attended, by that special mode of volition which I have named selective attention for the purpose of knowing.

§ 4. The two panoramas spoken of at the end of the foregoing Section, the one real in the full sense of the term, the other consisting of images and thoughts which represent the real one, have two points in common, at which the phenomena of each meet and coalesce with one another. The first blending-point consists of the contacts and pressures taking place between our bodies and material objects external to them, which are the very things perceived or mirrored in sense-presentations of touch; which latter are taken up into our objective thought, first, of the material objects in which they are actually presented, and then of all material objects whatever. At this point, that is, in touch and its sense-presentation, the two panoramas blend and are identical; that is, their *whatness* and their existence coincide; and this blending constitutes the nexus between them in the character which they bear of opposite aspects, subjective and objective, of each other.

The second blending-point is the psychological moment of thought, or selective attention to the objective-thought panorama for the purpose of knowing; which moment belongs in respect of its content to the subjective panorama, of which it appears as a modification, and, in respect of its being an action, to the physical energy of brain substance, which is its proximate real condition as an existent mode of consciousness, and belongs to the panorama of reality in the full sense. Thought in the strict and proper sense of the term, that is, as distinguished from perception, is not the subjective aspect of the whole of reality simply, but only of the whole as modified by the action of selective attention. The reality which we perceive by thought is a conceived reality. Real conditions and the relation of real conditioning are among the realities of perception only as these are modified in conception. At the same time, thought itself in the same strict sense, being a mode of consciousness as an existent, cannot be conceived except as a conditionate immediately depending on some physical action in the material world. The genesis of thought is an instance of real conditioning, and that modification of perception which is due to it, and which we call thinking, is the origin of our conception of real conditions. In thought, the highest known kind of real conditions, brain substance, conditions that mode of consciousness which alone is adequate to the conception of a world or panorama of real conditions in any form. The sense of touch thus lays the foundation, upon which thought builds the conception of Real Existence in the full sense, as at once the Object and Condition of consciousness in its entirety.

Recurring to what was said in the foregoing Section as to the two features noticeable in concrete reasoning, its forward movement as a psychological existent, and its content as consciousness perceivable reflectively, a similar remark will be found true of the action of pure thought itself, initiated by selective attention. It is a mode of consciousness which both retains a selected object in memory by dwelling on it, and while doing so proceeds to bring consciously into connection with it whatever object rises next into consciousness from the stores of spontaneous redintegration, which rising of a new object constitutes the consciousness of its forward movement. The question, then, is, What is the nature, or law, of this double action of retention and progression, taken by itself, irrespectively of the particular objects which are retained, and the particular objects brought into connection with them? This is the question to be considered in the present Section. And closely connected with it is the further question, What change, if any, is made in the perceptual form of the objects which are dealt with in this manner, in consequence of their being so dealt with?

It is obvious in the first place, that, of the two universal forms of perception, time and space, time alone and not space is the form to which Thought is subject, as a forward movement of consciousness into the future. Space and the perceptions which occupy it are among the particular objects present to thought in its forward movement, but are no part of the forward movement itself, which is a process of consciousness consisting only in the succession of objects more or less complex, which are to be connected with a previously experienced object or objects, retained in memory during the succession.

But consciousness is not only a succession of perceived moments or contents, each experienced as a definite state of consciousness; it is also, within every such moment, a continuous change or flux. Not one of what we roughly call definite states of consciousness remains for even an infinitesimal duration of time exactly what it is at a given instant or point of time. From the moment of its rising into consciousness above the threshold to its disappearance, it is always undergoing change both intrinsic and in relation to its context, owing to the fact that it is throughout that period receding into memory. How then can any state of consciousness be retained in memory exactly as it was when selectively attended to, so as to be brought into connection with other states, which are also subject to the same continuous flux? It is plainly impossible. What we do in selectively attending to any state of consciousness is virtually (though not explicitly) to assume and define it as that state of consciousness which existed at a given instant or point of time, namely, the instant of attention; to which state our actual perceptions of it as retained in memory are, in point of exactness, approximations only, since they include or may include both more and less than is included in the state taken as existing at a single selected instant of time.

There is thus a duplication of the content of an empirical present moment, owing to the action of attention ; its modification into a thought by selective attention does not destroy it as a percept, but both its modified and its unmodified form exist, in a certain important sense, side by side with each other. For (1) it retreats into the past of memory as a perception, though recoverable again in perceptual form by memory proper, and (2) it is retained in present retrospective consciousness as a thought expectant of comparison with the contents of future moments. That is to say, the act of selective attention arrests and retains it in the form of a thought representing a percept, which, as a percept, is recoverable only, if at all, by memory proper, after its disappearance below the threshold.

Every state of consciousness, by which I mean to include thoughts as well as percepts, to which we selectively attend, is duplicated and arrested as just described, by the action of selective attention whenever directed upon it, no matter what its specific content may be. We volitionally fix upon a certain feature of the time stream, having appreciable duration as an empirical present, and distinguish it from others by reference to the instant of time at which we attend to it. And thus it is that we are enabled (1) to distinguish between the action of pure thought and the concrete reasoning in which it comes forward, and (2) to show the law or mode of its action as an action distinguished by abstraction, but still an action *sui generis*, irrespective and independent of all particular differences in the specific contents attended to or dealt with by it, though not of the fact that there is difference between them. It consists in retaining in consciousness a volitionally selected content as one and the same, or self-identical, and distinguishing it as retained and identical with itself from changes which it undergoes as part of the flux of consciousness, in changing into or being succeeded by other contents in the actual course of redintegration. And since this action is one and the same in kind, irrespective of all particular differences in the contents dealt with, we can and do formulate it as an action by using symbolic terms, which express all contents indifferently, as well as the relation which the action itself introduces between the content originally attended to and any content or contents which might otherwise have been confused with it, so far as, and no farther than, that relation is due to the action itself.

The symbol usually adopted to express the object of selective attention (whether percept or already concept at the moment of selection) is the letter A; and the invariable nature of the action of selective attention for the purpose of knowing is expressed by what are commonly known as the Postulates of Logic, but which are in reality axiomatic statements of the act of selective attention, as well as pure instances or expressions of the movement of Thought itself. They are:

1. The Postulate of Identity, A is A.
2. The Postulate of Contradiction, A isn't not-A; or, No A is not-A.
3. The Postulate of Excluded Middle, Everything whatever is either A or else not-A.

These three Postulates are statements of the nature and operation of the act of selective attention for the purpose of knowing, each severally stating one of the three aspects of it, which together exhaust its full significance. The first says of the object or content selectively attended to, that it is taken as it was as that moment, that is, unchanged by its being part of the flux of experience; or that the A spoken of is *itself*, being its own predicate. The second says of that object, that it is exclusive of everything not included in it at that moment, that it is A and A only, so that, however often it recurs in thought, it is taken to contain exactly what it contained at the moment of first attending to it, and is not subsumed under, but commensurate and convertible with, its predicate, the second A of the first Postulate; whatever is not so commensurate and convertible being called Not-A. The third Postulate expresses the fact, that the division drawn by the second between A and not-A is exhaustive, and does not admit of an intermediary, that is, of anything which is partly the one and partly the other, as any change, having duration, from A to not-A would be. The truth of each Postulate involves and implies the truth of the other two, and all three severally as well as conjointly express, in terms of thought, that is, in the form of judgments, the single action of selective attention ; which was what I meant in calling them above a trinity in unity. They are three inseparable aspects of one and the same act, each implying the others, and conveying its whole nature either expressly or implicitly. And thus each separately may be used in Logic as an ultimate Canon for testing the truth or falsity of concrete arguments.[1]

---

[1] This unity of the three Postulates, the fact that they are expressions for one and the same fundamental act of thought, is well brought out and insisted on by Sir William Hamilton in his *Logic*, Lecture VI., Vol. I., pp. 96 to 100. For Aristotle's statements of them, see first, as regards their use in applied Logic, *Anal. Post.* Book I. Cap. 2, p. 72, a, line 12, ἀντίφασις δὲ ἀντίθεσις ἧς οὐκ ἔστι μεταξὺ καθ' αὐτήν, in which *Excluded Middle* is used to define *Contradiction*, and *Identity* is implicit in the restrictive expression καθ' αὐτήν, as may be seen from the further statements at Cap. 4. p. 73, b, l. 23, ὥστ' εἰ ἀνάγκη φάναι ἢ ἀποφάναι, ἀνάγκη καὶ τὰ καθ' αὑτὰ ὑπάρχειν, and l. 28, τὸ καθ' αὐτὸ δὲ καὶ ᾗ αὐτὸ ταὐτόν, οἷον καθ' αὑτὴν τῇ γραμμῇ ὑπάρχει στιγμὴ καὶ τὸ εὐθύ· καὶ γὰρ ᾗ γραμμή, the point being, that where you are reasoning about anything in its already ascertained nature, you must keep to that nature, and not reason from what is incidental to particular cases only.—And secondly, as regards their being essentials to the reasoning process itself, see *Metaphysica*, Book III (Γ) Cap. 3. pp. 1005, a, line 20, to 1005, b, l. 34 ; Cap. 4, pp. 1005, b, l. 35, to 1007, a, l. 15 ; Cap. 7, pp. 1011, b, line 23, to 1012, a, l. 28 (more particularly for *Excluded Middle*) ; and also Book X (K), pp. 1061, b, line 34, to 1062, b, l. 11.—In all these statements the Postulate of *Contradiction* is the most prominent, and that from which Aristotle seems to start. But, besides the third postulate of *Excluded Middle*, they all plainly involve the first postulate of *Identity* ; for it is only as an expression of this postulate that we can regard Aristotle's repeated insistance, in varying phrases, on the fact that every name or word must have one and only one meaning, ἕν τι σημαίνειν,—οὐθὲν γὰρ ἐνδέχεται νοεῖν μὴ νοοῦντα ἕν (Γ. Cap. 4. p. 1006, b, l. 10), if reasoning is to be possible. We may say therefore, that the Postulates of Logic, as we now have them, are found stated by Aristotle, the first formulator of the science, as essential to reasoning, and in inseparable connection and interdependence ; though they are not signalised by him as expressions of one and the same single act, which is the differential characteristic of thought, nor laid, in that character, at the foundation of Logic, which is the science of thought.—Still earlier than Aristotle, however, a virtual scovery and demonstration of that ultimate law of pure thought, which we express by the Postulates, are found in Plato's

THE FOUNDATIONS OF LOGIC.

Book III. Ch. IV.

§ 4. The Law of Thought and the Nature of Concepts.

The act of selective attention for the purpose of knowing is thus expressed by Postulates or Axioms which have the form of judgments. But the act itself is not, by itself alone, a judgment; it is only the necessary initiation or first step to framing one, judgment being the form taken by that very knowing, when attained, in view of which the act of selective attention was performed. We have still to consider the completion of the act of Thought, which the act of selective attention initiates, and the nature of which in fact it implicitly determines. What, then, is the nature of a completed act of Thought?

The act of selective attention is an act of volition which interrupts the non-volitional current of ideas, gives it a new direction, and imprints a different

---

Parmenides, and that as the main purpose of the Dialogue. Plato there contrasts the consequences of affirming the pure thought of unity, εἰ ἕν ἐστιν (137 C. κ.τ.λ), with those of affirming concrete or existent unity, or unity sharing in being, ἕν εἰ ἔστιν (142 B. κ.τ.λ); and then farther contrasts the consequences of assuming the negatives of those propositions with each other; the result being to show that, while all real existence is concrete, pure unity exists only as a step in the process of thinking, though a step which is necessary to the thinking of anything and everything. Now affirmation of the pure unity of the Dialogue (εἰ ἕν ἐστιν) is exactly equivalent to the A is A of the Postulates, and affirming or denying the existent or concrete unity (ἕν εἰ ἔστιν) of the Dialogue is similarly equivalent to positive categorical Predication, affirmative or negative, as in A is B, A isn't B, supposing both subject and predicate to be taken in their lowest terms, or as simple units. The foundation is thus laid, in the concrete nature of real existents, for the discrimination to be drawn by later logicians between categorical propositions *de inesse*, in which *whatness*, *i.e.*, some attribute or accident of the logical subject, is affirmed or denied, and categorical existential propositions, in which the fact of existing, whether affirmed or denied, takes the place of the predicate. The differentia of Real Existence in the full sense, τὸ ὄντως ὄν, is left for future determination.—Moreover, that ἄτοπός τις φύσις, as Plato calls it, *Instantaneity*, τὸ ἐξαίφνης (156 D), which he imagines will in some way account for change of state in concrete existents, becomes less enigmatical if we consider, that what Plato must really have been thinking of was the act of arrest or selective attention in conceiving and judging. This act introduces an ideal division, occupying no duration, into the time stream, just as the act of counting mathematically does. And this division marks the origin of the act itself, I mean that act of selective attention which turns any

character upon it. We then no longer receive unhesitatingly the ideas or percepts as they occur in the non-volitional stream of consciousness, but we question them, asking as it were whether they are or are not in harmony with the idea to which we have selectively attended. The perception of either their harmony or their discord with it, in answer to our question, is a judgment; and there is no judgment which does not pre-suppose an implicit question or doubt, involved in the act of selective attention for the purpose of knowing, an act of attention to what we afterwards, that is, in Logic, call the *subject* of the judgment. The act of selective attention renders the percept or idea attended to expectant of some other percept or idea (to be supplied from the store of memory by spontaneous redintegration) which will harmonise, that is, will coalesce with it, so as to form a single but complex idea. The discrepancy, real or apparent, of the percept attended to with the course of spontaneous redintegration in which it occurred was the very circumstance which led us to attend to it, with the view of finding something with which it would not be discrepant. We thus found the subject of our judgment; and the twofold fact, that it has a

---

percept attended to into a concept; and the sustaining of which turns the forward-moving process of redintegration into a judgment, the subject of which is distinguished as expectant of a predicate by the act of attention at its origin. The *locus* of the act of judging, in relation to the completed judgment, is therefore marked by that ideal division between subject and predicate, which is represented by the copula, affirmative or negative, in categorical propositions. The obscurity which could not but attach to this act, in the infancy of psychology, was increased by the fact that generalisation is involved in all conception and judgment; so that time relations are therein *ipso facto* abstracted from, unless of course they happen to make part of the object-matter of the conception or judgment, as well as of the process itself.

definite nature or *whatness* at the moment when it is attended to and made the subject of a judgment, and that this nature or *whatness* can be retained in memory, is what is expressed by the Postulate of Identity, A is A. What we now want to find, and what the subject is expectant of, is what we afterwards, in Logic, call a *predicate* for that subject. For the second A, in the judgment expressing the Postulate of Identity, does not stand for a predicate of the first A, but for the fact that A, that is, the subject of any logical judgment, has in reasoning one and only one meaning.

From this it follows, that judgments are of two kinds, affirmative and negative, according as a suggested predicate will coalesce or will not coalesce with a given subject. The perception of either fact constitutes the nexus or *copula* between the two terms of the judgment; and in the copula resides the assertion, or volitional adoption in thought, of this perception, the assertion being affirmative in the case of coalescence, and negative in the case of repugnance or non-coalescence. A judgment, therefore, is the completion of an act of selective attention. And the effect of this completed act of thought is to transform a certain portion of the current of spontaneous redintegration into a train of voluntary redintegration, consisting of parts which are named, in Logic which is the theory or science of Thought, *subject, copula,* and *predicate,* a train which, when expressed in language, is called *Predication,* and takes the form of a *Proposition;* as for instance, again to use symbolic terms, A is B. In which it will, I think, be clear, that no contradiction to the Postulates is involved, notwithstanding that

BOOK III.
CH. IV.

§ 4.
The Law of Thought and the Nature of Concepts.

B is obviously a case of not-A; since the Postulates express the self-sameness and mutual exclusiveness of the terms used in thought, and as terms of thought, while propositions or judgments, in the full and usual sense of the words, express relations which obtain between different terms, building upon that very self-sameness and exclusiveness in the terms themselves, which are secured by the Postulates, and without which no proposition or judgment of thought could be valid, or even possible as a rational act.

Let us next observe what changes are wrought by judgments, or complete acts of thought, in the ideas or percepts which are offered as their material by spontaneous redintegration, and which in consequence become terms of judgments and contents of thought. In the first place they clearly drop the order of sequence which they had, or may again have, in trains of spontaneous redintegration, and appear in a different order determined by their congruity with one another. They have been re-born, as it were, in a new character, as members of a kingdom of thought; and now form trains of voluntary redintegration, in consequence of the volitional action of selective attention completed by judgment. A selected idea or percept is no longer connected, simply by juxtaposition or interpenetration, with those which precede, accompany, and follow it in spontaneous redintegration, but is connected, by perception volitionally acquiesced in, with those which will harmonise or coalesce with it into a single complex idea or percept, from whatever part of the spontaneously occurring order they may be taken, whether they originally occurred next to it in that

THE FOUNDATIONS OF LOGIC. 287

order or not. They do not cease to be percepts, in the sense that they are contents of consciousness occupying time, or (in the case of contents of sight and touch) time and space together; but they add to this a new character, in consequence of their volitional birth into a new order and arrangement, the character of being volitionally grouped by reference to their observed congruities *inter se;* and in this character they are named and known as Concepts, and the act of perceiving their new relation and adopting them into the new order is named Conception;—in contradistinction from their former names, Percepts and Perception, terms which now receive another and a narrower meaning than before, and are now used to mark their contents and the consciousness of them in their pre-volitional and pre-ratiocinative state. And it may be worth noting, that we have here another instance of terms having a twofold meaning, in the larger of which the term is inclusive of opposites, one of which is expressed by itself, the same term, in its narrower meaning. *Percept* in the large sense includes *Concept*, and yet in Logic is used as its exclusive opposite.

But what are the congruities or harmonies, or what are the modes of coalescence, which determine the new volitional and ratiocinative order, and the concepts which are to take the place of predicates of any selected and given subjects? It is impossible to suppose that these can be dictated by any *a priori* forms inherent in the activity of thought itself. This supposition would be possible only on the assumption, that there was an immaterial agent, or faculty, dealing with perceptual matter extraneous to itself, as a man deals with material objects which he possesses; and this empiricist assumption has been abundantly shown to be groundless, and indeed untranslatable from words into meaning.

Neither can these congruities or modes of coalescence be dictated by the law of movement of Thought or Judgment itself, as formulated by the Postulates, unless we falsely understand the Postulates to express general modes of Predication, instead of expressing the nature of Predication in relation to the terms between which it moves. As, for instance, when Hegel, at the first step in his *Logic*, predicates Nothing, or Not-being, of Being, and *vice-versa*, so bringing them under the Postulate of Identity taken as a mode of predication; notwithstanding that Nothing, or Not-being, exists only as the logical contradictory of Being, and therefore, by the Postulate of Identity in its true sense, must always mean Nothing, or Not-being, and can never be predicated of, still less predicated convertibly, that is, identified, with Being, which is its purely logical contradictory. By thus using the Not-being of the Postulates as a predicate, Hegel makes the Postulates self-contradictory, and thereby, since he cannot avoid thinking by them in their true sense, introduces a radical confusion of thought into his whole system.[2]

---

[2] It is worthy of note, that Hegel in his larger Logic, when comparing Being, *Seyn*, under the head A, with Nothing, *Nichts*, under the head B, does not venture to assert of *Das Nichts*, as he asserts of *Das Seyn*, that it is immediate, *unmittelbar*. This point of resemblance is by him omitted. And this ought logically to have prevented him from asserting the simple identity of the two, under the head C, *Werden*; for there is a very palpable difference between them. The difference is, that *Das Seyn* has a content, *Das Nichts* has not. We cannot have a presentation of *Das Nichts* alone, for such a presentation would be identical with *no presentation*. Thought cannot *begin* by conceiving *Das Nichts*; there must be a positive content to begin with; unless, indeed,

THE FOUNDATIONS OF LOGIC.

It has also been shown, that thought as such is governed by no purpose more specific than the general purpose of obtaining further knowledge concerning any point or circumstance of interest to the thinking being. And from this it follows, that even the idea of congruity, harmony, or coalescence, is not present to it as a guide in adopting predicates for its subjects, or as a standard to which a predicate must conform in order to be adopted. The fact of congruity, when a congruous idea or percept is presented by spontaneous redintegration, is self-evident, and the gratification attending its perception is the sole and sufficient motive for its adoption by thought as the predicate for a judgment, and for our acquiescence in its adoption so long as it continues. It is, in short, a fact of experience in the strictest sense. It is known to be supplied by experience because it is supplied by spontaneous redintegration. We welcome congruities when they are suggested, without recognising that congruities are that of which we are in search. The

BOOK III.
CH. IV.
———
§ 4.
The Law of Thought and the Nature of Concepts.

---

pure Thought is creative of its own content, which is the fundamental but wholly unwarranted assumption of the Hegelian system. We can conceive *Das Nichts*, in the first instance, in and by the act of conceiving *Das Seyn*, but we cannot conceive *Das Seyn*, in the first instance, in and by the act of conceiving *Das Nichts*, because *Das Seyn* is already presupposed in first arriving at the conception *Das Nichts*.—It is true, that in the act of conceiving *Das Seyn* as including all contents, we also necessarily conceive *Das Nichts*, or No content, as its purely logical contradictory; but this does not supply *Das Nichts* with a content, still less with one which is predicable of, or renders it identical with, its contradictory *Das Seyn*.—It is not till Hegel comes to the first Note, *Anmerkung* 1, on the following page, that he quietly slips into calling *Das Nichts* an *unmittelbare Negation*. Now the act of negating may be called immediate, *unmittelbar*, being nothing but the act of purposive and selective attention which initiates thought; but the thing supposed to be negated, the concept *Nothing*, is not immediate, since, having no content of its own, it arises only in the act of conceiving *Being*, the content of which is pre-supposed. It is difficult to imagine that Hegel was wholly unaware of this confusion between the act of negating and the content supposed to be negated, by which he allowed himself to be deceived.—At the same time, the idea of the Reality of "Nothing" (*Das Nichts*), involved in this confusion, is apparently

VOL. III.   T question, then, is, What constitutes a congruity; what specifically is meant by congruity, harmony, coalescence, or any other word which we may use to indicate predicability in ideas or percepts; or in what respects must these ideas be congruous with those of which they are to be predicated?

Now there are just two modes in which one percept or idea will directly and immediately harmonise, coalesce, or be congruous, with another. One mode occurs in cases when the ideas are perceptibly similar, the other when they are perceptibly dissimilar. But similarity is of itself congruity, and observable similarities are offered in legions by experience. When for instance I selectively attend to a particular case of blackness, say in a crow, and spontaneous redintegration offers me other cases of it, as in coal, jet, ash-buds, ink, and so on, I perceive their congruity with the particular quality on which I have fixed my attention in the crow, group

---

necessary to Hegel's system, since it is this idea alone which at once enables and compels Thought, to which all agency is by assumption attributed, at a certain point in its career, to negate itself as the whole of Thought, and become the content of its own otherwise abstract categories, that is, Matter, or Real Nothing (the only sense in which Idealists can allow Matter to be real), in the perceptual forms of time and space; and which again compels Matter (being essentially Thought), at a certain point in its career as the object of *Natur-philosophie*, to negate itself as Matter and become Mind *(Geist)*, in which shape Thought is finally re-united with itself, after its temporary masquerade as Matter. The whole Universe is thus conceived as Thought's negation of its own negation of Itself. Expressed in terms which are terms at once of common sense and of theology, what we have in this system is (1) in the *Logic*, the Divine Plan of creation forming itself, (2) in the *Naturphilosophie*, the issuing of the Material World out of that Plan, and (3) in the *Philosophie des Geistes*, the return of the Divine Thought, indefinitely pluralised by appearing in the form of Matter, into the unity of the one Divine, Real, and Absolute Mind.—This is genuine Scholasticism, being founded on the unwarranted assumption of a real energy inherent in Thought, which is a direct descendant of Aristotle's "faculty" psychology, though very much out of harmony with that form of Scholasticism which is accredited by the Church of Rome.—There is a criticism of Hegel in my *Time and Space* (1865), pp. 195—201; and again pp. 364—402; a criticism which I should now think somewhat too sympathetic. Nevertheless the objections which it brings forward have not, so far as I know, been seriously met.

THE FOUNDATIONS OF LOGIC.

together these instances of the quality as similar, and mark the group as a single object or idea by giving it a single name, *blackness*. The judgment, of which blackness in the crow is the subject, will then run as follows, *This quality in the crow is blackness*. Blackness in the crow coalesces with other instances of blackness to form a single general idea, or as it is technically called in Logic, an *Universal*. This kind of congruity based on similarity of cases otherwise different is the ground and origin of all classification, the gamut of shades in a single colour for instance, or the perceptions of each of the different senses as forming a single group.

The other mode of direct and immediate congruity is based on the perception of dissimilarity as its prerequisite, and this mode also is suggested and warranted by experience alone. It takes effect when, having fixed my attention, say as before, on blackness in a crow (but of course before any knowledge of the crow as a real object), I find that it coalesces with other and dissimilar qualities in the crow, as for instance, its shape and tangibility. Noticing one by one all the qualities which thus coalesce with one another in the crow is in fact building up the idea of the crow as a single complex percept representing a single real object, though the reality (as real condition) of the object represented is not now in question, but only that of the complex percept or objective thought representing it. There is no necessity that the object so built up should represent a material real object, a "remote" object of perception, as it has been called above, or a real event or process in material things, as for instance, the fall of a stone, the trotting of a horse, the discharge of a cannon. I may build up a group of dissimilar percepts which have no single material object thought of as such behind them, and yet are suggested by spontaneous redintegration when one of them has been selectively fixed on by attention for completion in thought. The colours of the prismatic spectrum, or the notes of an often heard tune, are instances. I will however keep for the present to the former illustration.

The difference of this from the other mode of congruity is, that what it builds up is not a general or universal thought, but a single or individual complex object, as for instance the one objective thought of a single crow, without taking into account any other instances of blackness or of crows, or any other instances of the other qualities belonging the crow, except the repetitions of it and them in spontaneous redintegration. Though I go through concepts, as defined above, to the formation of this single complex idea, that of the single crow, yet I retain or re-introduce the perceptual character of every quality, representing it as it is originally perceived in sense-presentation and subsequently repeated in spontaneous redintegration; and therefore also retain or re-introduce the perceptual character of the whole complex idea, that of the crow, as the union of these qualities. If I now make the blackness of the crow the subject of my judgment, then that judgment will run as follows, *This quality (blackness) is one of the qualities constituting this complex object (the crow).* It is in this second mode of observing congruities that thought directly contributes to build up the objective-thought panorama of the material world; it is its operation in this mode which was intended, when it was pre-supposed and expressly reserved for future analysis, in the account given of that process in Book I, and again in Chapter II, § 5, of the present Book, when treating of the laws of association;— promises which have now been partly fulfilled, reserving what more remains to be said for a later Section.

Returning to and comparing the two modes of coalescence just described, we see at once that the second is based upon and pre-supposes the first, in every instance of it. The order of spontaneous redintegration having been broken by paying selective attention, for the purpose of knowing, to some particular member of it, and the order of thought having thus been initiated, then we find at once, that the perception of similarity and that of dissimilarity are involved in each other, that we cannot perceive one without perceiving the other also. Now the first mode of coalescence consists, not indeed in this perception simply, but in the immediate acceptance of similars as congruent, and the rejection of dissimilars as incongruent. But the second mode of coalescence does not consist in the immediate acceptance of dissimilars as congruent, as the first in that of similars, which would be a self-contradiction. It pre-supposes the perception of similarity and dissimilarity, and then proceeds to observe the way in which perceived dissimilars coalesce with one another, though they are dissimilar, namely, first by their common and simultaneous occupation of one and the same portion of time, or of time and space together, as in ordinary material objects, whether at rest or in motion, and secondly by the constant and immediate sequence of one upon another, in which case they would properly be called events or processes. In the case of dissimilars, the perception of their dissimilarity is a separate act, which precedes the perception of their coalescence into single complex ideas or percepts, whether as things or events.

Now this subsequent coalescence of dissimilars in thought is given by perceptive attention to the fact of constant connection between them in point of time and space relations, whether this connection is one of sequence or simultaneity, as it is given originally in sense-presentation, and repeated in spontaneous redintegration. It is thus a simple case of what is called (unanalytically) observation or registration of certain facts of experience; but nevertheless one which is only possible on condition of our having previously broken up the stream of experience as it actually occurs, which we deal with as represented by spontaneous redintegration, into parts determined by selective attention to special contents or percepts in it, the recurrences or repetitions of which parts are separated from one another by heterogeneous matters in the actual course of experience, and therefore of spontaneous redintegration also, in its simplest and earliest instances, which in fact are neither more nor less than memories. The constant accompaniments of these selected contents are what we then register as coalescences of dissimilar contents into complex ideas or percepts, representing the real objects or real events of the material world. This is in fact the very process which was described in Chapter II., § 5, of the present Book,

—a passage which I would beg my readers to refer to again in comparison with the present,—only that it is now connected with the act of selective attention which originates Thought, and shown to pre-suppose the distinct perception of similarities and dissimilarities as such, before it proceeds to register the coalescences of dissimilars into concrete objects and events. The fact that we perceive those coalescences as concrete objects and events is due to thought, but the nature or *whatness* of the concrete objects or events perceived is due to their constant combination in sense-presentation primarily, and then to their consequent habitual combination in spontaneous redintegration, under the laws of association.

Whenever any such complex percepts have been formed in thought, by the operation of selective attention and thought upon spontaneous redintegration, they take their place, as complex percepts, in the content of spontaneous redintegration again; and that, whether they are percepts representing real objects or events in the full sense of *reality*, or whether they represent modes of consciousness which are real only as conditionates, as for instance, the prismatic colour spectrum, or the overtones which follow the hearing of a particular note. In every case alike they take their place in the content of spontaneous redintegration as percepts, not as concepts. The conceptual action of thought is subsidiary and mediatorial only, and subserves their formation, but does not contribute anything to their nature or *whatness* as perceived objects. But after this, and for this very reason, they are again open to the conceptualising action of selective attention and thought, precisely in the same way as if they were simple representations of single sense-presentations. The perception of a single crow, for instance, becomes in the subsequent action of thought a concept, and therefore also a general or universal thought, embracing all the similars of the first, that is, all crows wherever and whenever found, as its particular instances.

The case is quite different with the objects formed by thought in the first mode of coalescence, a process which, I need hardly say, goes on, in actual occurrence, simultaneously with the second, although they are here taken separately for purposes of analysis. These objects take their place at once in the stream, not of spontaneous, but of voluntary redintegration; they are concepts as distinguished from percepts; and although they may be conceptions of real objects in the full sense of *reality*, as in the case of crows just mentioned, they are themselves real only as objective thoughts, and objective thoughts which have a volitional form impressed upon them, though, like all concepts, they derive their whole meaning from the percepts out of which volitional and conceptual action has framed them. Blackness, for instance, though an immediate conditionate of nerve or brain activity, does not exist in Nature in the same way as the different perceptions of black quality do, which are perceptions of the sense of sight. The object expressed by the word *blackness*, a general term, is an artefact or manufactured article, which has reality only so far as it has truth, that is, can be retranslated into perceptions of black quality, out of some of which it was originally formed by thought

An appeal to experience, in the acquisition or correction of knowledge, is never an appeal to such conceptions, but always an appeal to the perceptions which they professedly embody in conceptual form. The same holds good of the general conception *crow*, which has real existence only as a volitionally formed thought, and depends for its meaning, and for its truth, entirely upon the particular percepts, that is, the particular crows, which are or may be objects of sense-presentations and of the spontaneous redintegration which reproduces them.

All concepts, then, whether simple or complex, taken as pure concepts, or in their conceptual nature only, that is, prior to their retranslation into perceptual form, and considered simply as a knowledge of real objects, have an abstract, artificial, incomplete, and provisional character. They are steps in the process of arriving at complete insight, or truth. The reason of this is, that they are founded upon the *whatness* or nature of perceptions, including their features and relations of every kind, formal as well as material, all of which fall under the two heads of similarity and dissimilarity, with tacit abstraction from their existential, which is also their individual character. My perception of whiteness in a mass of snow to-day is not individually one with my perception of whiteness in the same mass of snow yesterday. The individuality and the existence of a perception mutually involve each other. In forming concepts from perceptions we generalise the perceptions, that is, we treat them as belonging solely to the order of knowing, and not to that of being, or as existents. Their characteristic purpose is to attain a knowledge of the *whatness* of objects, that is, to afford Definitions; provisional or tentative definitions at the outset, final and complete definitions and systems of definitions in the end; though no definitions can be definitions of individuals *as such*, since they go no farther than to characteristics which are conceivably common to more members than one of even the lowest distinguishable species or variety. In order to complete our knowledge of an individual, supposed to be already known as a member of such a variety, recourse must be had to mathematical processes. It is mathematic which deals with the analysis of individuals as such, beyond the limits of actual sensibility, just as it is mathematic which measures and numbers the parts of individuals, within those limits. Two individuals otherwise indiscernible must at least differ *numero*, or, as we may also express it, in point of place in time, or in space.

But so far as logical or conceptual thought goes, the whole of pure science or theory may conceivably take the form of a complete system of definitions, embracing the whole of Nature, or applicable to it in its character of real existence, and rendering it intelligible in that character. Still, before concepts can be applicable to anything so as to render it intelligible, they must first have been distinguished from what they are to be applied to, and thought of in separation from it. And this separation in thought originates in the tacit abstraction, just noted, from the existential and individual character of percepts, prior to their being modified so as to form concepts.

To which the remark must now be added, that, in so forming concepts, the individuality lost by the percepts re-appears, as it were, in the concepts generalised from them, each of which is thereby taken as an individual idea, expressed or expressible by a single name or symbolic term, and having its existence in the world of objective thought, in which it occupies a definite place, determined by its relations of similarity, contrast, or contrariety, to other concepts similarly individualised. The whole of objective thought may thus come to be occupied by concepts only, in seeming independence of the perceptual world, from which, by abstraction, it has been derived.

From this it follows, that every pure concept, or logical universal, is subject to a threefold distinction, in respect of its relation to the perceptual world from which it is derived, and to understand which it is properly applied. Let us first take the case of a simple concept, say *blackness*. The first act of selective and expectant attention paid to any perception of the quality of blackness makes that perception a concept, whether it is followed by and coalesces with similar perceptions or not; for it is held fast by attention and becomes expectant of further knowledge. As expectant it is a concept, and potentially an universal. If similar perceptions follow it, with which it coalesces, it receives a content as an universal, and becomes an *ens unum in multis* (or *one thing in many instances*), its content then consisting of a number of similar concepts, each of which is taken up from perception, and compared with those preceding it, by selective attention being paid to them. The completed concept, or universal, thus consists of concepts, and is their unification, or their character as forming an unity of kind or *genus*; while at the same time its real experiential basis lies in the percepts from which it is originally derived. This purely perceptual content, which is its basis, I have proposed in a former work to call the *Intension* of the concept or universal.

On the other hand, the concepts of which it immediately consists are properly called its *Comprehension*. These in the simple case now before us would be different shades or varieties of blackness, taken in their abstract quality or *whatness* only. The intension and comprehension of a concept are distinguished from one another solely by the one being in perceptual, the other in conceptual, form ; by which is meant, that one, the intension, belongs to the perceptual world, existing as an individual percept, or series of percepts, and the other, the comprehension, to the world of thought, consisting of percepts already compared to one another, and having individuality only as an unity of kind, that is, a *genus*, formed by thought, and being in fact the conscious grasp our thought has over a multitude of similars.

But this distinction also enables a separation to be made between them in thought, whereby the comprehension becomes capable of separate treatment, apart from the intension which is its basis. When so separated, it can be applied either as a means to render the purely perceptual world intelligible, which is its legitimate use, or to serve as the basis for futile and mischievous speculation, by first illegitimately hypostasising it as a prior condition of perception in order of real existence, instead of *vice versa,* and then taking whatever concepts are so hypostasised as belonging to a system of types or patterns upon which the really existing world was framed; whether these types are supposed to exist in their own right from all eternity, or to have their being as thoughts in an eternal and Divine mind. The illegitimate hypostasising of the comprehension of concepts, including, be it remarked, that of pure thought itself as an agency, is nothing more nor less than the fallacy commonly but inadequately described as that of making entities of abstractions.[3]

This parent of fallacies is the parent-fallacy of Scholasticism in all its forms and modifications. Strange to say, it was professedly derived, in medieval times, from Aristotle, notwithstanding that he was the detector and exposer of it in his great master Plato; derived from him by treating certain of his conceptions, notably those of substance, attribute, and cause, and more especially, perhaps, those of final and of formal cause, not as stepping stones to better knowledge, but as truths which might be made serviceable in building or supporting the fabric of a dogmatic theology, that is, as means of maintaining a foregone conclusion.

---

[3] The fact that all nouns substantive and adjective in language are general terms has already been noticed, as explanatory of the readiness with which we commit the fallacy of making entities of abstractions. Side by side with this must be placed the fact, that in grammar most if not all nouns substantive are construed with verbs active or passive describing action, whether they are names of abstractions or not; as, *e. g.*, Perception informs us; Thought compares and judges; History relates; Law governs; Truth is distorted; Silence is imposed; and so on. We thereby, so far as language goes, personify and make an agent in the one case, and make a real concrete object in the other, of whatever abstraction a noun substantive expresses. For language in its entirety, syntax as well as vocabulary, is formed on the lines of common-sense thinking, prior to analysis

Book III. Ch. IV.

§ 4. The Law of Thought and the Nature of Concepts.

302   THE FOUNDATIONS OF LOGIC.

BOOK III.
CH. IV.
———
§ 4.
The Law of Thought and the Nature of Concepts.

It lies at the basis of Spinoza's *Ethica*; it governs Hegel's so-called *Logic*, whose whole philosophy, systematised as it is with wonderful ability, may thus be regarded as the very completion and consummation of a consistent Scholasticism. It continues, of course, to appear in what may be called by way of distinction orthodox Scholasticism, that is, Scholasticism subservient to the dogmatic theology of the Church of Rome ; as for instance in Father R. F. Clarke's *Logic* (Stonyhurst Series, 1889) pp. 5, 104-106, 141-142, and 163-164,[4] or again, in Father Thomas Harper's great work, *The Metaphysics of the School* (Vol. I., Book III., Chap. II., Art. III., Prop. 53, page 301), where he says, that, if Plato intended his εἴδη to be thoughts in the Divine Mind, on which as types He made the world by the *fiat* of His will, his doctrine would so far be unexceptionable ; not so, if on the contrary he intended to exhibit them as self-existent types, imposed upon the Divine Mind as necessary modes in which He must create, if He created a world at all.

But whatever may be the value of the results to which the making entities of abstractions may lead, or to which it may be made to lead by judicious handling,—and doubtless both to the Church of Rome, and to the crowd of visionary speculations of every kind, socialistic as well as theological, which may gain entrance into otherwise well regulated minds by covering themselves with the respectable names of Fichte, Schelling, Hegel, Schopenhauer, Von Hartmann, and others, this

---
[4] Also cited by me in a paper, *Universals in Logic*, to be found in the proceedings of the Aristotelian Society, Vol. I., No 3. 1890

THE FOUNDATIONS OF LOGIC.

value is great,—nothing can alter its inherent nature as fallacious itself, and a parent of fallacies wherever it is adopted, whether consciously or unconsciously. But to return.

What has just been said of simple concepts is also true of those complex concepts which are formed by the combination of dissimilar perceptual qualities into single complex objective thoughts. Every simple percept which goes to the formation of a complex one, say for instance the perception of a crow, passes so to speak through the logical mill of conception, and becomes part of the concept as well as of the percept of a crow, before that percept-concept can be reconverted, by the familiarity due to spontaneous redintegration, into the purely perceptual image or idea of a crow. And again, when this process has once taken place, then the percept-crow, so formed, is treated in conception precisely as if it were a simple percept; that is to say, becomes a starting-point for a new conceptual process, in which it is fixed on by attention and made expectant of further knowledge, whether that further knowledge will be by way of similarity or dissimilarity with the content to be combined with the image attended to.

Supposing it in the first place to combine by way of similarity, then we have the concept-crow as a complete concept or universal, embracing all the varieties of crows, and having or capable of having its definite place in the *scala generum* of Nature, just as the concept blackness embraced all the varieties of blackness, and had its definable place in the same *scala*. There is no typical blackness, no typical real crow, either in thought or in reality,

BOOK III.
CH. IV.

§ 4.
The Law of Thought and the Nature of Concepts.

which is the unity of blackness, or of crows, of all perceivable varieties. But both universals alike are throughout abstractions; each of them is a concept which unifies in point of kind the group of concepts which is its comprehension, and which is clearly distinguishable from the percepts prior to conception, on which it is founded, and which in that character constitute its intension.

Supposing it, on the other hand, to combine by way of dissimilarity, then the further knowledge of which it is expectant will consist of facts and circumstances in its genesis and history, its habits, haunts, and conditions of existence generally, as these are learnt primarily from sense-presentations, and then repeated in spontaneous redintegration, in order to become immediate subjects of thought and reasoning. The whole content of any percept-crow is covered by these two ways of conceiving it, either separately or in combination. This last remark is intended to show that, although Thought alone is not Knowledge, but one of the indispensable means by which systematic knowledge is acquired, yet its laws, of which Logic is the science, are of a nature sufficiently wide to embrace an exhaustive knowledge of all positively knowable realities, since we can neither think of nor imagine any positive knowledge of them, which does not fall under one or both of the two heads, (1) what they are in their nature, and (2) what they are in their real genesis, history, and development, as members of an order of real conditioning.

We have now before us two out of the three distinct characters mentioned above as applying to concepts or universals, namely, their Intension and their Comprehension. Of these the comprehension constitutes the pure concept itself; its intension being distinguished from it as containing the percepts from which it is derived by attention, generalisation, and abstraction. And before going farther it may be well to take more explicit note of a consequence of this process, which is involved in the formation of every pure concept, simple or complex. It is this, that, in arresting the course of purely perceptual consciousness by selective attention to any part of its content, we interrupt the course of purely perceptual experience, abstract for the moment the contents so attended to from the time and space relations in which they stand to their original perceptual context, and so prepare them, as it were, to take their place in a purely conceptual order, which place will be determined solely by their relations of *whatness* or kind to other concepts, whether of objects or of processes, which have been similarly framed.

In this circumstance of arrest and abstraction, which is essentially bound up with the process of conception, and is plain evidence of its limited and derivative character, we have the foundation for Spinoza's famous doctrine, " *De natura rationis est, res sub quadam æternitatis specie percipere*," (*Ethica*, Pars II. Prop. XLIV. Coroll. 2), a doctrine which, owing to the meaning which Spinoza attaches to *æternitas*, implies the notion, that certain universal features in all experience must be conceived as existing without any relation to time at all, or, as modern Hegelians sometimes express it, are 'out of time altogether.' It is one thing to abstract consciously and for a purpose from the time relations of objects to their context, by considering them in their *whatness* only, as we do in logical thought, and quite another to imagine that they can be thought to exist without existing for any duration of time whatever. For crude imaginations of this kind, Hegel's assumption of concrete thought as creative of a world of concrete concepts,—meaning by *concrete*, that with him too all concepts have a content, though with him it is a content of their own, inherent in their own nature, and not traceable ultimately, as subjective analysis shows it is, to perception,—is a better, because more recondite, foundation, than Spinoza's assumption of a Substance of infinite and infinitely numerous attributes. On the other hand, it is less suitable to account for the existence of a physical order of Nature, than Spinoza's further assumption, that extension is one of the attributes of his eternal Substance.

The third and last of the distinct characters or relations mentioned above comes into view, when we consider the application of concepts to render intelligible the world of ordinary experience, a world which, as we have seen, exists in perceptual form. Our knowledge of the world of common-sense or ordinary experience has indeed itself been formed by selective attention, thought, or conception, operating upon perceptions as they actually occur, so that the experience which concepts are now applied to render intelligible is in fact to a great extent the creation of conception, in the way we have seen. But this process, not having been recognised for what it was while being employed, has long been forgotten when we first begin to watch it with a view to unravel the mystery of knowledge, and first distinguish percepts from concepts therein. True it is, that, whenever an object or group of objects appears as part and parcel of ordinary experience, then it is also distinguishable from the process by which it was formed in knowledge, out of the perceptions of experience as it actually comes to us. But this is not a distinction which the facts of ordinary experience compel us to draw in the first instance. And if, without drawing it, we take any such object or group of objects of ordinary experience as ultimate facts in Nature, then the first distinction which meets us is one forced upon us by the discrepancy between the conceptions we form, during the process of attaining a full knowledge of it, and what appears to be the object or group of objects as they really exist, since we perforce in imagination antedate our knowledge of a world of real existents. Thus the separation in thought between the comprehension of concepts and the world of common-sense objects, which they are employed to render intelligible, lies in some sort on the surface, and may be said to be worked for us by Nature itself; whereas the corresponding separation between concepts and the percepts from which they are really derived, in experience as it actually comes to us, a separation which is marked by the distinction between the comprehension and intension of concepts, is one which has had to be discovered by analytical efforts consciously made.

Now a concept properly and strictly consists of what we have called its Comprehension. It is the unity of kind of a number of percepts, expressed by the use of a single term for them, and abstracting from their existential and individual character. But in the world of ordinary experience, which concepts are employed to render intelligible, this existential and individual character is all important, and can no longer be abstracted from. A concept, therefore, when applied to explain the real world, stands in a new relation to the group of percepts which it unifies, a relation different from that which subsisted while it was in process of formation. These percepts, taken in their connection with the really existent world, now appear as the real instances or real objects which give the concepts a real meaning, and serve to verify their truth. In this relation they constitute the *Extension* of the concepts. Thus in the case of a simple concept, all the real instances of blackness, or all black objects *qua* black, are the Extension of the concept blackness, the real particulars or singulars to which it applies, and of which it must be predicated. In the case of complex concepts it is the same. All particular real crows whenever and wherever existing are the Extension of the concept crow, or the domain of reality which that concept includes as in a boundary, but of course with limits liable to alteration by additional knowledge.

When a concept is spoken of as such, it is its Comprehension, as distinguished from its Intension on the one hand and from its Extension on the other, which is or should be intended. It is in this that its conceptual character consists. The distinction between the Comprehension and the Extension of concepts has long been established, and is a familiar doctrine. But their Intension, that is, the perceptual content which is their original foundation in experience, is not usually noticed by logicians, as in any way distinguishable either from their Extension or from their Comprehension;[5] whereby attention is confined to concepts in their strictly conceptual nature, without regard to their origination out of perception as it actually comes forward in experience. The distinction is also ignored as a matter of course by those Empiricists who begin with the assumption of ready made complex objects as the primary data of experience, reducing thereby all general terms to the rank of mere collectives. I proposed it originally in my *Philosophy of Reflection* (Vol. I. p. 322); but besides the too great brevity of the treatment there accorded it, I also fell into the mistake of transposing the application of the names *comprehension* and *extension*, calling extension what I now call comprehension, and *vice versa;* which was running needlessly counter to well established logical usage;—a mistake which I have since taken occasion to retract.[6]

The importance of the Comprehension of concepts will be evident, when it is considered, that all Definitions are framed out of and by means of it, definition being a strictly logical act, or act of thought. Definition is a process which moves by selective attention, marking out, within the limits of any single concept, which in its character of unity is taken as the *genus*, a special domain, that is, one or more of the concepts which are its

---

[5] See for instance Sir William Hamilton's *Lectures on Logic*, Vol. I., Lect. VIII., Paragraphs 24 and 25. I mean, that he uses *Comprehension* and *Intension* as synonyms.

[6] See my Address "*What is Logic?*" in Proceedings of the Aristotelian Society, Vol. I. No 3, 1890, pp. 19 to 22.

comprehension, distinguished from the rest by possessing some mark or marks peculiar to them, which are called the *differentia* of that special domain, or *species*.

It is evident that this is a process which may be repeated over and over again, to any extent, and to any degree of minuteness, so long as any perceptual differences are observable in the phenomena of Nature, or in the manner of their occurrence, combination, or grouping; since every perceptibly different feature in experience may become the foundation of a new concept, which then becomes a *species* with regard to the concept next above it in ascending order, and a *genus* with regard to all that are next below it in descending order, if any should be found to possess a characteristic difference, in comparison with it. There is nothing in the logical nature of thought to prevent this process gathering up the whole of Nature into a vast and complicated system of definitions, provided only that Aristotle's rule is observed, of taking the proximate genus only (*genus proximum*) as the subject of the differentiation; that is, of passing over no observable difference, in the generic concept, which might become the foundation of a species intermediate between that generic concept and the specific *differentia* of the species which it is proposed to define.

Some few remarks are still necessary in conclusion of the present Section. Thought, it has been shown, is a mode of consciousness depending upon a certain kind of cerebral activity. But inasmuch as the sense of effort for a purpose in this mode of consciousness is the only immediate evidence we have of the actual exercise of that cerebral activity upon which it depends, we may conveniently include that exercise under the term *thought*, that is, may speak of thought itself as an activity, provided always we bear in mind, that the activity and its exercise really belong to the cerebral organ or organs, and not to their dependent concomitant, the mode of consciousness. The onward movement of Thought,—which is not to be identified with its synthetic as distinguished from its analytic character, being equally necessary to both,—is due to the fact, that Thought, being a psychological function of consciousness as an existent, forms part of the time-stream of consciousness. It is not due to its possessing the property of Negativity, inherent in itself and all its parts, or Concepts, whereby it evolves one by negating another, and then negating its previous negation. No concept can negate itself. The true Negativity of Thought is no source of movement, but is that purposive arrest or limitation of the content of the time-stream, the nature of which is expressed by the Postulates.

Now hitherto we have watched the procedure of this activity of Thought as exemplified only by instances of the simplest kind, namely, in constructing and classifying conceptions of familiar real objects and processes of the simplest kinds, from classes of data which are perpetually occurring in everybody's experience. Hitherto, therefore, it might possibly seem as if Thought had no other office but that of observing and registering the phenomena offered by Nature, and therefore that Thought and Knowledge of Nature were one and the same thing, whereas in fact, that activity which is Thought, and the laws of which are studied by Logic, is but a contributory, though an essential one, to the attainment of a Knowledge of Nature, and of the laws which it obeys.

But in so imagining we should be losing sight of an element in Thought which is an essential characteristic of it, and which is involved in the simplest and most familiar, as well as in the most complex and unfamiliar instances of its exercise, though veiled from observation in the former by the overwhelming mass of facts of sense-presentation, which leaves Thought no alternative in considering them, but to recognise them as occurring always in the same or very similar combinations, that is, forming the same real objects and processes. The element which I speak of is the volitional element, the element of choice, in that act of thought which completes the first volitional and expectant act of selective attention, and issues in the formation of a provisionally complete concept. The percept attended to by the act of selective attention, which act initiates thought, is expectant of some new percept with which it will combine; and this new percept must be offered, as we have seen, by spontaneous redintegration from the stores of presentative and representative experience. To complete the act of selective attention is either to join or to disjoin, in thought, the content selectively attended to and the content offered by spontaneous redintegration; it is to affirm or to deny, in thought, the latter of the former; it is, in one word, to Judge; the discrimination involved in which act differs from that belonging to feeling or sense in simple perception by this very element of volition in selection and assertion.

The completing act in a thought, then, is a judgment. And we see from this analysis of it, that there are always alternatives offered to thought, however strong the evidence for or against any of them may be, alternatives between which it has, as thought, to choose, and to one of which it has to assent as true. This choice must be made, and this assent given,—both of them (if considered as two) volitional acts, —or there is no judgment, no provisionally completed thought. True, it is always of something in its character of a fact, real or supposed, that the affirmation or denial in judgment is made; that truth and falsity in judgments mean accordance or disaccordance with real things and real events as verified or verifiable by perception; or again, that truth to fact, that is, Knowledge, is the end and aim of all thought and judgment; and therefore that the essential nature of thought is to judge according to the weight of evidence, that is, in conformity to the principle of Sufficient Reason, so that, wherever this principle is lost sight of, the act *pro tanto* ceases to be thought or judgment simply, and becomes an activity of a mixed or compound nature, according to the kind of extraneous motive which is allowed to stand in the place of evidence.

But this does not destroy the volitional character of the act by which one alternative is adopted and another rejected. The act of choice indeed, the assent, the adoption or rejection of an alternative, may as an act, together with the deliberation or succession of acts leading up to it, be of all degrees of strength, vigour, or intensity, from the lowest degree of hesitation or wavering, to the highest degree of certitude or assurance; which is a necessary consequence of the fact, that the evidence in favour of any particular decision, as compared with the evidence against it, or in favour of an opposite one, may be of all degrees of weight, clearness, or cogency; and both facts together constitute the main difficulty of thinking rightly and well. They also let in the possibility of self-deception, and illusion as to what we really think in accordance with the principle of Sufficient Reason, in contrast with what we only wish to think; and thereby open the door to much arguing in favour of foregone conclusions, and much refusal to admit the validity of well-supported demonstrations. Nevertheless no judgment, no thought, is possible without consciously adopting an alternative. Volition, which is choice, is an essential element in thought, from its initiation by attention to its completion in judgment, and also, we may add, to its further development, or differentiation, in the combination of single judgments into trains of reasoning, by means of inference and syllogism.

§ 5. Having shown how Thought educes concepts, definable by their comprehension, and as its own special creatures, out of percepts which it receives by non-volitional channels, I proceed to consider the nature of its action in dealing with the concepts which it has so created; not that the one proceeding is different in nature from the other, but that it is convenient to treat one separately from and later than the other, for the sake of the greater distinctness gained by having concepts as already known to deal with. Thought consists in the completion of an act of selective attention (which is always expectant) by an act of assertion which involves comparison; that is to say, the lowest complete thought may be distinguished into those two acts,—every act of thought, complete in this sense, being a Judgment. Comparison is necessarily involved in the completing act, because there is necessarily difference in the perceptual content attended to in that completing act. This complete act of thought, as we have already seen, is that which forms concepts (I mean provisionally complete concepts definable by their comprehension) in the first instance; and all concepts as such, and in their character of a Knowing (that is, as distinguished from what they are in their psychological character), are general or universal, not singular as percepts are, and embrace not only the particular objects which originally give rise to them, but also whatever particular objects (whether past, present, or future, in point of existence) may be found to fall under them in virtue of similarity.

The dealing of thought with its concepts so formed, and with every part of their content as concepts, is effected in no other way than by repeated acts of thought, that is, by repeated judgments, all of which move by, and are analysable into, the three constituents which, when expressed in categorical propositions, are known as their *subject, copula,* and *predicate;* each of the three corresponding to an essential part or element in the judgment, and logical propositions being simply logical judgments of thought expressed in language. This is at least true of the categorical form of judgment, which is the simplest and most fundamental form of it; and with the analysis of this it will be best to begin.

An affirmative categorical judgment asserts the coalescence of its subject with its predicate. But what is here meant by assertion, and what by coalescence? And first of assertion. *Assertion* means, as it has meant hitherto, the intracerebral conscious act of assenting to something as true, which is involved in the second or completing act of thought, affirmative or negative, the characteristic act which completes the distinction of thought from perception. It is, as it were, the backbone, flexible but strong, of all thought and reasoning, hostile to all willy-nilly, shilly-shally, and flabbiness. In that character it is, that it is expressed in logical propositions by the copula, *is* or *is-not*. *Is* expresses the act of affirmation, *is-not* of negation or denial. To regard the copula as unessential is to refuse to thought the expression of that in which it most essentially consists, the expression of its nature as an act, without which it could not be an act of judgment. This act of assertion, and no content other than assertion, such as belongs to the terms which are the subjects and predicates of judgments and propositions, is what is expressed by the copula; and therefore the copula can no more be wiped out of the meaning of propositions, than the act of assent out of the act of thought or judgment.

In the next place, what is here meant by coalescence? We have seen what it means in the first forming of concepts out of percepts. But what does it mean, when one already formed concept is said to coalesce with another, that is, in dealing with concepts already formed by previous acts of judgment? Its meaning is this, that subject and predicate coalesce into a single concept, in virtue or in respect of some feature of their comprehension, which has been already noted as similar in that comprehension, and therefore common to both of them conceptually taken. When I now say *Crows are black*, I mean that crows possess some mode or variety of blackness, as a feature which is common to them and other objects, which possess some mode or variety of it also. Whether I think of the comprehension of crows and the comprehension of blackness, or of the extension of crows and the extension of blackness, in both cases I subsume crows as the subject under the predicates, black in the one case, black things in the other. Either of these may be taken as the true meaning of *Crows are black*. It is a judgment in order either of comprehension or of extension, and not in any order of intension (real or supposed), which would give no connection between concepts, its only place in Logic being in the formation of them out of percepts. It does not mean, that certain modes of blackness are constituents either of the objective thought of crows or of crows as objects thought of. Statements of that kind have been shown above to express distinct perceptual observations in their building up of concepts, whether simple or complex; and this process we now leave behind us. It is with the application of concepts to render realities intelligible, that we are now concerned; and from this point of view the judgments in question are themselves among the realities which require elucidation in Logic.

Putting this together with what has been said concerning the meaning of the copula, as expressing the act of assertion, it is evident that the relation, which constitutes the coalescence of the concepts called subject and predicate into a single (perhaps only provisional) concept, is a relation, not of identity or equality between them, but of subsumtion of the subject as the smaller term under the predicate as the larger. The blackness of the crow is a particular case of blackness generally;—this is predication in order of comprehension. Or, the crow is a particular case of black things generally;—which is predication in order of extension.

Nor is it possible to predicate one concept of another in the reverse order, that is, by taking the subject as the larger concept, and subsuming under it the predicate as the smaller. I cannot say, for instance, *Blackness coalesces with crows,* or *Black things coalesce with crows,* into a single concept, meaning that certain varieties of blackness, or certain black things, do so, without either falling back into statements expressing the formation of concepts out of percepts, or else again making use of the opposite order of predication, which is the true one, as in *Some varieties of blackness are among the features found in crows;*—unless indeed I content myself with registering an already perceived identity, as in *Some black things* (meaning crows) *are crows,* which expresses no advance in thought, but drops all reference to the comprehension of the terms, which is their specially conceptual character, and treats them simply as complex percepts.

The reason which makes the order of subsumtion necessary is founded in the nature of thought itself. It is that, in an act of thought, we always begin with an act of selective attention, which determines what is to be the subject of the judgment we are about to pass, thus treating it as a singular, while leaving the predicate open and undetermined in its native generality. For that act of selective attention involves our treating the concept selected by it as a singular for the moment, whatever its nature may be, whether one or many, simple or complex, and regarding it, if many or complex, as a single concept determined or determinable by its definition, and including those instances, and those only, to which the same definition will apply,—a definition being always logically convertible with the thing or concept defined, just as in the case of the Postulate of Identity.

For this reason the predicate in every categorical judgment is always taken as a whole, real or possible, of which the subject is taken as a possible part. An affirmative categorical judgment is one which subsumes the part under the whole, including the subject in the predicate; and a negative categorical judgment is one which refuses that subsumtion, and denies that inclusion. And for the same reason, propositions which express the same judgment assume a different form according as we adopt the order of comprehension or that of extension in thinking. In the first case, keeping to the same instance, the blackness in crows, treated as a single thing, is what makes us subsume them under the general predicate *black*; in the second, crows, treated as a single class, are in virtue of their blackness subsumed under the larger class of black things generally. But in both cases alike the coalescence takes place in respect of one single

BOOK III. CH. IV.
§ 5.
Judgment and Syllogism.

feature, which is common both to the subsumed subject and to the including predicate. The meaning, therefore, of the assertion made in simple affirmative categorical judgments is subsumtion, or coalescence by subsumtion, of the subject under the predicate.

From this it follows, that no single judgment can of itself import the equality, complete identity, commensurability or convertibility, of its subject and its predicate. For, since in every single affirmative judgment the predicate is provisionally taken as larger than the subject, it is plain, that to assert their co-incidence another judgment is requisite. Whenever a single judgment (in which co-incidence is not itself the predicate) seems to make this double assertion, it is not a single judgment, but two judgments in one proposition. In these cases, to which definitions belong, the predicate of the proposition, if taken in turn as the subject, will be found included in the new predicate taken provisionally as the larger term, and thus the limits of both will be determined as co-incident. Thus in Man is a laughing animal, if we make laughing animal the subject and man the predicate, we state that laughing animals are limited to men, as before that men were limited to laughing animals. The two judgments are therefore commensurate, applying to one and the same set of perceptual facts, or facts perceptually taken. And this is possible, because the larger scope of predicates as compared to subjects is a volitional fact, due to selective attention for the purpose of knowing, and true only of concepts, which are creatures of thought and are adopted as means of dealing with the perceptual facts which they are intended to represent.

For the same reasons it cannot be the meaning of the assertion, or of the copula, in simple categorical judgments, to affirm or deny the real existence either of the subject or of the predicate as objects thought of. Judgments in which the real existence of the subject as an object thought of is asserted are called Existential judgments. In these, real existence as an object thought of is made the predicate of the judgment, and the copula carrying the assertion expresses, as before, the coalescence or non-coalescence of the subject with it, as for instance, "There is a world"; or "There are milestones on the Dover road"; or "There are Chimæras," namely, as the content of objective thoughts treated as themselves objects thought of; or "There are no such things as Chimæras," namely, as real existents in the full sense of reality. In cases like these, the copula and predicate together are expressed by the single word or words *is* or *are*, *is-not* or *are-not*, in the sense of existing or not existing as realities of some sort or another. All that, in them, is added to the determination or knowledge of the subject is the fact of its existence or non-existence, to whatever kind or mode of existence or reality it may belong, from existence as a primary percept to existence in the full sense of real condition. But this is both an unique and important fact; and as a fact it is predicable affirmatively or negatively of any given content of consciousness, as for instance when I say, as above, *Chimæras do not exist, save as objective thoughts.* Existential judgments, therefore, in which existence is a predicate, must be carefully distinguished from simple categorical judgments, in which the words signifying existence are used as the copula only, the copula as such having no content, save as the expression of the act of judging. If it is required to affirm or deny the existence or reality of anything spoken of, that is, of the subject, it must be done by means of a separate existential judgment.

The place and function of existential judgments, in Thought and Logic, will be seen more fully when we come to speak of modal concepts. Meantime it is enough to establish their radical difference from simple categorical judgments. To suppose that these latter affirm or deny the existence either of their subject or their predicate, or that this is the meaning of their copula, is to falsify their nature as acts of thought dealing with concepts, and to treat them as simply statements of the fact, that the subjects spoken of are now present to the speaker's consciousness;—as if they meant (to keep to the above instances), *What I am now aware of is what I am accustomed to call a world,*—or *milestones on the Dover road.*—or *Chimæras,*— or *a world from which Chimæras as real in the full sense are absent.*

This view of the meaning of the assertion in simple categorical judgments, which makes them all involve existential judgments by obliterating the distinction between the two kinds, renders them wholly useless and futile as acts of thought leading to knowledge, inasmuch as it resolves the linked chains of reasoning, which concepts form when taken in their comprehension as general terms, into a phantasmagoria of successive contents of consciousness, each consisting of perceptual and conceptual material in fusion; the very circumstance of fusion, or as it is euphemistically called, the "concrete" nature of the successive contents, apparently forbidding the possibility of reducing them under any general law of sequence.

For the discovery of the law of such sequences of fused contents, if any law of them there be, must at least include and be founded in the true distinction between concept and percept, and between volitional and spontaneous redintegration; since it is in combinations of these in a state of fusion that the sequences themselves consist. We can show the existence of a law of sequence for percepts, as in spontaneous redintegration; likewise of one for concepts, as in volitional redintegration; but for fusions of both, in which the aid derivable from their distinction is *ipso facto* renounced, what uniform law of sequence can be imagined possible? And are the sequences and their law to be regarded as the work of Man, or of Nature, or of Consciousness *per se*, as a 'self-existing agency,—or of all three in a state of fusion?

The first consideration mentioned in the foregoing paragraph seems to have been wholly neglected by Hegel, when propounding his famous law of Negativity, or Negation of thought by thought, which he supposed to lead up, in every case, to the emergence of a richer and more articulate perceptconcept, than that with which the sequence began. What Hegel really did was not, as he probably imagined, to lay bare the secret psychology of the Absolute Mind *(der Absolute Geist)*, but to show that most if not all the conceptions, which were, or had been, accepted by science or by philosophy, could be reproduced, with more or less straining, by an ingenious arrangement of percept-concepts, evolved one out of another, by a continual application of his supposed law of Negativity. The truth in my opinion is, that to take fused or so called "concrete" percept-concepts as ultimate and unanalysable is a pure assumption on his part, and an assumption at variance with analysis. It is again an assumption, consequent on the former, and equally at variance with analysis, to maintain, that conception, which can admittedly modify what it has received, can also originally produce what it has not received; or again, that thought, when taken in its lowest terms, has the percept-concepts of Being and Nothing *(Das Nichts)* either already known to it as its essential and necessary content, or else revealed in and by its ever necessary act of logical contradiction,—a pair of opposites which negate each other, and which result, on that negation being denied, in the richer and more articulate concept of Something *(Etwas)*. To admirers of invertebrate systems of thought, built on unanalysed foundations like these, it must doubtless be a great relief to hear, that existential judgments, by which real existence can be positively affirmed or positively denied, have no separate *locus standi* in Logic.

According, then, to the analytical view of judgment which I am here maintaining, a proposition expressing a single categorical judgment is the simplest, most precise, and most accurate way of expressing a definite opinion or thought upon any matter of fact whatever. This property it derives from the nature of the thinking activity, which is ascertained by Logic as the science of Thought.

But its chief value consists in this, that it can express the *minimum* of opinion, consistent with its being opinion at all. Every thought from the least to the greatest can be expressed by one or more logical propositions, and every step in a train of reasoning can thus be brought in turn clearly into consciousness, for comparison with others, with its own contradictory, and with the grounds or reasons for and against its truth. For these must likewise be expressed for this purpose in logical propositions of the same structure. On the basis of conflicting judgments, expressible in logical propositions, thought meets thought, both within the same consciousness, and also between opponents who meet to maintain each his own opinions. This sifting of thought by thought conflicting with it, whether in one man's consciousness or between disputants, which is Dialectic, is the immediate purpose of reasoning in its strictly logical character, and is of course widely different from what has been called above a *method* of acquiring and correcting knowledge by observation, hypothesis, experiment, and verification, on the basis of assuming the existence of a real world of Things, Persons, and Events, as preliminary to the whole process, the reality of which basis is not considered to be in question at all.

Thought or the Thinking Activity, on the contrary, of which Logic is the theory, makes no assumptions whatever. I speak of it as an activity, it will be remembered, in virtue of the brain activity, on which it immediately depends. In this sense it is a mode of conscious activity which goes its own way, and does its own work as a knowing, without

326   THE FOUNDATIONS OF LOGIC.

BOOK III
CH. IV.

§ 5.
Judgment
and
Syllogism.

necessarily recognising the nature of what it is doing, or laying down the forms or laws under which it exists and operates. It is Logicians who discover these, by analysing the processes of concrete reasoning in which it is involved, and disengaging it, not only from such concrete methods as those mentioned at the end of the last paragraph, but also provisionally from the modes of speech in which it is expressed; until some of those modes, such as, for instance, those of subject, copula, and predicate, are found to owe the very form in which they exist to the modifying action which the thinking activity itself exercises upon purely perceptual material. The thinking process, when thus disengaged by abstraction and considered by itself, is then found to be everywhere the same; although in the concrete it makes part, now of an inductive method aiming at the discovery of laws of Nature, now of a conversation carried on in the terms and phrases of ordinary language, now of written compositions or oral discourses, and now of a train of dialectical argument between disputants, or again of a train of meditation within the consciousness of a single individual.

Everything in pure thought, therefore, every concept and judgment which it produces, and in which it is, as it were, embodied, is provisional and liable to question, being nothing but a volitionally instituted means for sifting our ideas of fact, and expelling inconsistencies and contradictions from the systematised scheme of knowledge which it is our main object to attain. No concept or idea of any kind is exempt from this sifting and questioning process. A reason must be given for adopting every concept, framing every hypothesis, and asserting or assenting to every judgment. The so called assumptions of thought are made for the purpose of being questioned, not for the purpose of being accepted without question. That is to say, they are not assumptions of fact, but challenges of disproof. And this character they owe to their volitional origin.

We can now see the true nature and origin of Syllogisms. I again confine myself to the simplest form of them, the categorical affirmative syllogism, which, with the light which it throws on its opposite, the categorical negative syllogism, will be sufficient for the present purpose. I make, let us suppose, a statement in the form of a judgment; say, to take a well-worn instance, *Caius is mortal.* But the question is, How do I know it? Why do I assert it? What is my *ratio sufficiens cognoscendi?* Answer: Because he is a living organism, and all living organisms (for reasons assignable by physiology) sooner or later cease to live. In syllogistic form:

 A living organism sooner or later dies,
 Caius is a living organism,
∴ Caius will sooner or later die.

My original judgment thus becomes the *quæstio*, or conclusion, of a syllogism, and the two premisses taken together are, not statements of the physical or other real conditions which will determine the death of Caius, or of living organisms generally, (though these are the ultimate basis of the belief), but statements of my proximate reasons, which if true are sufficient reasons, for thinking my original statement to be true. They may be valid, or they may not. But valid or not, they are the immediate *causæ cognoscendi* of my opinion, not *causæ fiendi* of Caius' mortality. They are, so far as they go, analytical of my judgment that Caius is mortal, being statements of my reasons for adopting that opinion, reasons which, if genuine and not invented *ex post facto*, were implicitly involved in its formation. It is true that, if genuine and valid, they must be the results of inductive processes, but the steps in these processes are not that which they express.

Each of the premisses again is open to question in the same way. And in support of each I may be called upon for two new premisses, which in like manner will be analytical of it as a judgment of mine, and assign the immediate *causæ cognoscendi* or reasons for my thinking it true. And so on in indefinite regress, a regress which finds its ultimate basis and termination only in judgments connecting or disconnecting concepts which are immediately translatable into perceptual facts, and are therefore undeniable, whether they be affirmative or negative. Judgments of this kind are the basis upon which the whole train of reasoning depends for its validity. But the whole process of proof, from beginning to end, is analytical of knowledge, not of the facts known in their character of real existents, unless and until their reality as facts, in some of the modes of reality, has been recognised by thought exercised by way of existential judgments; and so also is the process of disproving the truth of the original statement, supposing it to be attempted.

The syllogism, then, is the simplest, most precise, and most accurate, form of assigning a reason, or

THE FOUNDATIONS OF LOGIC.

causa cognoscendi, for knowing the truth of any judgment whatever. This reason is contained in the "middle term," which the two premisses introduce between the subject and predicate of the *quæstio* or conclusion, which is the original statement made, and for which a *ratio sufficiens cognoscendi* is required, the establishment of which may extend over a long regressive series of syllogisms. The "middle term" is to syllogisms what the copula is to judgments which connect concepts originally. As the copula contains the affirmation or denial of an immediately perceivable relation between the subject and the predicate of judgments which connect concepts in the first instance, so the middle term contains the reason for affirming or denying a relation between the subject and predicate of judgments, where the presence or absence of the relation is not immediately perceivable, but requires proof, as in the case of the judgment *Caius is mortal.* And the subject of the *quæstio* is then subsumed under its predicate (1) by its being subsumed under the middle term, which makes the minor premiss of the syllogism, and (2) by the middle term being subsumed under the predicate of the *quæstio*, which makes its major premiss.

The middle term, then, is essential to the syllogism, is indeed its distinctive characteristic, and determines the fact of its having three, and only three, terms. It contains the *causa cognoscendi*, or reason, of our knowing that one term is a case falling, or (where the conclusion is negative) not falling, under one other term, thus enabling syllogisms to take acts of thought in their utmost simplicity and minuteness, and do one thing, and one only, at a time; for a negative conclusion simply denies the subsumtion of its subject under its predicate, without making any further statement about it. But why is such a thing requisite at all? And first, what is meant by a *causa cognoscendi?* It may be defined as any known fact or conception which, in answer to a previous question or doubt about another fact or conception, connects or disconnects the latter, that is, exhibits it as coalescing or refusing to coalesce, with some formerly accepted piece of knowledge; thereby, in cases where the conclusion is affirmative, bringing the two into connection, or establishing a relation between them, in thought; and, so far as that relation goes, making them parts of a single concept or idea. The ultimate *causæ cognoscendi* are facts of immediate presentative or representative perception; but it is essential that they should be perceived as answers to previous doubt, in order to their character as *causæ cognoscendi*, or reasons, being perceived.

Now, since all judgments and reasonings require some *causa cognoscendi* in the sense just assigned, in order to being volitional acts of judgment or reasoning at all, as distinguished from simple perceptions simply attended to, it is evident that the whole fabric of our reasoned knowledge tends more and more to become a chain or network of causes and consequents in the order of knowing, as opposed to the order of being; and any breach in this concatenation, from the absence or failure of a *causa cognoscendi*, is a flaw in that systematised scheme of knowledge which is the ultimate end and purpose of thought. The essential function then, of a *causa cognoscendi* is to knit together two pieces of knowledge, by bringing them into a relation which makes them parts of a single whole. The middle term in syllogisms is nothing more than a *causa cognoscendi* which effects this union or combination in the simplest way, namely, by bringing two extreme terms together into one concept, under the simplest possible relation appertaining to conceptual union, that of part to whole. It is, in short, nothing more than the last step in that process of unification, which we have previously traced in thought, from its origin. Without volitional unification of single sense-presentations into concepts, and of less general into more general concepts, by judgments mediate and immediate, no such thing as a systematised scheme of knowledge is possible. Without it, single process-contents of consciousness, even if hanging together in groups or series formed by habitual association, would still be fragmentary, and would no more form an intelligible or comprehensible system than they actually form in trains of purely spontaneous redintegration, such as we have, for instance, in dreams.

It seems clear, then, that no more accurate or complete account of the process actually followed in connecting judgments in thought for assigned reasons, that is, of reasoning as distinguished from thought simply, can be given, than that which is exhibited and formulated by the syllogism. It expresses the *minimum* or atom of reasoning, in this sense of the term, just as judgment expresses the *minimum* or atom of thought simply. But its completeness and accuracy can only be seen when we remember, that what it formulates is a process of reasoning simply, not a method of acquiring knowledge which includes the combination of various modes of thought, various modes of observation, and physical intervention on the part of the observer and reasoner, as in performing experiments for the purpose of bringing his hypotheses to the test of perception.

Such a concrete process is the Inductive Method in its purity, that is, when it is set free from the empiricism with which it is usually associated; and as such is plainly different from the process of pure reasoning which it involves, notwithstanding that it moves by means of it at every step. Knowledge is the immediate or proximate purpose of this method; in fact, consists of this method and its results together. But knowledge in this sense is not the proximate but only the ulterior purpose of reasoning; reasoning being but one of the elements, although, owing to its being common and essential to the whole and to every step, it is the most important element of the method in its entirety. This distinction has a decisive bearing on the true meaning of *Logic*, which, if what I have maintained is true, is the theory, not of Knowledge, but of Thought. A Logic of Induction would not be Logic, but Epistemology.

Now we have already seen how the various operations of Thought, selective attention, comparison, assertion or judgment, generalisation, formation of concepts, construction of single complex objects of conception and perception together, and combination of judgments in the syllogism, enter into concrete inferential processes, for of such concrete processes we had instances in Book I, when busied with the analysis of our common-sense knowledge of the real world around us, and of ourselves as part of it. But inferential processes do not stop short at that point, in the construction of our knowledge of the real world, which we reached in Book I, I mean the point at which the conception of Real Conditions, and of an Order of Real Conditioning, was first acquired. There is a great difference between forming ideas of objects and processes which are wholly given, though piecemeal and at different times, in sense-presentation, and forming ideas of the processes and laws of processes, which combine or dissever objects and processes of the simpler kind, and of the results which follow from such more recondite separations and combinations, which as processes are not open to direct observation. Here it is that we enter upon processes which are inductive as well as inferential. The difficulty here lies, first in framing, by imagination, conceptions and hypotheses which will be verified by observations, either of their expected results, or those of experiments instituted to bring those results under observation, and secondly in devising experiments suitable for that purpose.

Here lies the great field, not only of the positive sciences, a brief review of which was attempted in Book II., but also of all sciences which aim at the discovery of matters of fact of every kind, whether belonging to past, present, or future time, such for instance as the facts, persons, events, and actions, which have constituted the history of mankind in past ages, down to their minutest particulars, or those which will continue to constitute its future course. In all such concrete processes alternatives are everywhere

334 THE FOUNDATIONS OF LOGIC.

present in forming judgments, and even the methods to be followed by speculation and research are matter for choice, assent, inference, and verification of inference, in point of their comparative value and fruitfulness.

Logic in its Second Part is a practical science, which has the unalterable nature and laws of thought for its foundation, these being the object-matter, the analysis of which constitutes the theory, on which both its formulas and its rules, as well as its precepts for their practical application, are based. The first or theoretical part of Logic is simply analytical, ascertaining facts concerning the nature and laws of thinking; which are thus found to be fixed and immutable in the same sense that the most comprehensive Laws of Nature are, the Law of Uniformity for instance, which I have elsewhere shown [1] to be involved in the Postulates of Logic, and discovered in Nature by virtue of them. These and the other laws of thinking in accordance with them are the foundations of Logic. The analytical foundations of Logic are therefore a part of Metaphysic, not of psychology, nor of any positive science. In Logic as a science of practice, Thought is occupied in analysing its own nature, and formulating its own laws.

The remaining part of Logic is institutional, containing a system of rules and forms, based upon its analytical foundation, and intended to serve as modes or standards by which we can be guided, both in thinking and in discussion with others, so

---

[1] In *The Philosophy of Reflection*, 1878, Vol. II., Ch. IX.

THE FOUNDATIONS OF LOGIC.   335

as to avoid the errors which in all concrete reasoning spring from that cardinal and perpetually recurring fact, namely, that alternatives are offered to choice in every judgment passed on the non-volitional content with which thought is inevitably bound up, and also to detect fallacies or errors in reasoning into which we have already fallen ourselves, or which lurk in the arguments of our fellow disputants. It is the volitional element in thought which makes error and fallacy possible, though imperfection or feebleness in the perceptive powers and processes often renders them practically unavoidable. The roots of error and fallacy are in choice alone. Whatever assertion, out of two or more, a man chooses to make, the Laws of Thinking will be satisfied. The Postulates do not tell us what assertions we ought to make, or what to predicate of any given subject. And this institutional part of Logic may again be divided into the system of forms and rules relating to concepts, judgments, and reasonings, and the system of precepts for practically applying those forms and rules in actual thinking and disputation.

Thus, even as a practical science, Logic is not a method for discovering laws of nature, but a system of rules and standards for sifting and testing arguments for or against conclusions to be drawn from provisionally adopted premisses, and for or against premisses which must be adopted if given conclusions are to be received as true. In all matters of opinion, such as, for instance, the interpretation to be put on oral or written testimony, or on historical documents, or on the commonly received maxims of any practical science, such as jurisprudence or

BOOK III.
CH. IV.
§ 5.
Judgment
and
Syllogism.

political economy, in short in any domain where the facts are not ascertainable by immediate observation or experiment,—there it is that the aid of Logic is of the highest value, and practically indispensable. In whatever part of any subject discussion is admissible, there Logic is valuable. How interminable would discussions be, if, for instance, *petitio principii*, or *quaternio terminorum*, and the like, were not admitted to be fatal flaws in an argument, the moment it was convicted of them. Without Logic, half the affairs of life would be handed over to the overbearing insolence of unsupported assertion. I by no means welcome the discredit into which Formal Logic has fallen, and seemingly continues to fall; a discredit, be it said, partly deserved, partly undeserved. Undeserved so far as it is owing to the mistake of identifying Formal Logic as a whole with its practical and institutional part; but deserved on account of the excessive development of its institutional part, the bulk of which can serve no purpose but that of formal discussions of subjects, the truth concerning which is ascertainable only, if at all, by positive and scientific methods, discussions which are based for the most part on purely arbitrary definitions, and in which victory not truth is the end proposed.

§ 6. To complete our sketch of the essential features of Thought which lie at the foundation of Logic as a science of practice, it remains to speak of that other kind of judgments, with their dependent forms of syllogism, which was mentioned at the outset in § 1. I mean hypothetical judgments. These are not, like categorical judgments, assertions of the simple fact of the coalescence or non-coalescence of concepts; they are assertions of a relation between two judgments, called the antecedent and the consequent, a relation which is one of expectance in the former and dependence in the latter, and which is expressed in language by a proposition of two clauses connected by the conjunctions *if* and *then*. The antecedent judgment is passed only in expectation of a consequent judgment, and the consequent judgment is passed only in dependence on the antecedent, fulfilling its expectation; and these two judgments thus take the place of the subject and the predicate in simple (not existential) categorical judgments and propositions.

Similarly, the place of the affirmative copula, *is*, in simple categorical judgment, is here taken by the conjunctions *if* and *then*, expressing and affirming the relation between the judgments which they connect. The function of the affirmative copula is here distributed, instead of being concentrated as in categoricals. On the other hand, the negative categorical copula, *is not*, has no representative in hypothetical judgments; negative hypothetical judgments there are none. The reason is, that the hypothetical form of judgment involves affirming a relation between its antecedent and its consequent as such, though either or both of these may be negative. Hypothetical judgments may be defined as assertions in conceptual form of a perceived relation between two facts, when each is taken as perceivable separately from the other. Thus, *if there are crows, then they are black*, is the hypothetical form of the categorical judgment, *All crows are black*.

The impossibility of negative hypothetical judgments is a characteristic and important fact. We cannot in a hypothetical judgment simply deny a relation between antecedent and consequent, as we can simply deny a coalescence between subject and predicate in a categorical judgment; in other words, we cannot make a hypothetical judgment negative, while keeping it hypothetical in form; because a positive relation between the antecedent and the consequent, which are its terms, is just that by which its form is constituted, being an assumption which is bound up with it merely as a forward-moving or (as some would say) synthetic process. It must be remembered that all judgments are synthetic in the sense of forward-moving, even categorical judgments of identity, as in *Crows are Crows*, inasmuch as we move forwards from the *Crows* of the subject to the *Crows* of the predicate, and add the latter to the former, in the act of making them; and the same is true of negative categorical judgments also, as in *Crows are not Jackdaws;* we move forward and come to *Jackdaws* subsequently to *Crows*, in making them. The reason for this is, that every judgment is psychologically a forward movement in time, in the genesis of consciousness as an existent, apart or distinct from what it is as a knowing of the terms which are its content. It is in vain to look for pure synthesis in judgments taken merely as acts of knowing, unless we supply by unfounded assumption (as Kant did) a transcendental source, out of which, *proprio marte*, purely synthetic *a priori* judgments are producible. And even then that source must be in fact psychological, as Kant's supposed transcendental Subject necessarily was, without his leave being asked in the matter.

§ 6. Hypothetical Judgments and Modal Concepts.

Analytically, on the other hand, that is, in point of meaning and content, or what is the same thing, considered merely as acts of knowing, these simple categorical judgments express, the one identity or coalescence, the other non-coalescence, between their terms, without any restriction being imposed on their meaning by the fact, that they are also forward-moving as psychological processes. But this is different in hypothetical judgments. In them we begin with the facts expressed by the antecedent and the consequent, taken as perceivable separately from one another, and consequently the mere fact of bringing them together in a judgment implies the perception of a relation between them. If there were no perceived relation, there could be no assertion. Hypothetical assertion is only possible on condition of affirming some relation between antecedent and consequent. Hence a negative judgment in hypothetical form is impossible. Try for instance to state *No crows are white* in hypothetical form. You will find that you cannot make the judgment negative as a whole, but that you come to some hypothetical form like this, *If there are crows, then they are not white*, in which the negative belongs, not to the copula of the whole, *if—then*, but to the proposition which forms the consequent of the whole judgment.

The syllogisms which arise from hypothetical judgments, taken as their major premiss, have their form determined by that of those judgments. A hypothetical judgment admits of an inference being drawn from it in two cases, (1) if its antecedent is affirmed, (2) if its consequent is denied. Either the one or the other will furnish a minor premiss or subsumtion to the original proposition, major premiss, or sumtion, from which a conclusion follows; this conclusion being, in the first case, the affirmation of the consequent, in the second case the denial of the antecedent, of the original hypothetical judgment or major premiss. As for instance:

1. If a bird is a crow, then it is black,
   This bird is a crow,
   Therefore it is black. } *modus ponens.*

2. If a bird is a crow, then it is black,
   This bird isn't black,
   Therefore it isn't a crow. } *modus tollens.*

This brief description, without going into further detail, is enough to show the essential nature of hypothetical judgments and syllogisms, which is all that concerns us here.

I proceed to draw some conclusions which the foregoing description warrants. The characteristic which differentiates hypothetical and categorical judgments from each other consists in the different use which they make of the form of time in asserting. Both alike pre-suppose and employ general terms, which are forms of thought as distinguished from perception; both alike are dependent on the Postulates; both are forward-going, as psychological movements; both have a meaning or content which is analytic of the perceptual material with or upon which they operate. The difference is, that, while categorical judgments refer all the material with which they deal to a single point of time represented by the copula, and so view the subject and predicate of discourse as simultaneously present at the moment of assertion, hypothetical judgments, taking their material in detail, and each part of it as separately perceivable, represent the relation between its parts as one of sequence, and throw everything out, including even what may in point of fact be a necessary connection between simultaneously existing attributes, into a time-relation of former and latter in order of knowledge. This difference in their mode of dealing with their material is the only essential difference between the two forms of judgment, and from this difference all others are derived.

In both kinds of judgment alike, it is the panorama of objective thought that is being modified or remoulded, the order of knowledge that is being corrected or completed, in and by the act of judging. It matters not what the objects thought of may be, nor to what time or place they may belong, nor in what order relatively to one another they may occur. The relation between the objects thought of as antecedent and consequent, which is itself part of the object thought of in a hypothetical judgment, is thought of as belonging to the order of existence and real conditioning, notwithstanding that the objects thought of may be either real conditions, or existent and conditioned states of consciousness indifferently. Both classes of existents are spoken of in *If a crow, then black*, and *If not black, then not a crow*. In both cases it is real crows and really existent perceptions of colour which are spoken of, not our thought of crows or our thought of perceived colours. And in every case it is the order of knowledge, or panorama of objective thought, and that only, which is really modified by judgments, and by syllogisms and trains of reasoning which are systems of judgments. In every case alike, judging and reasoning are conscious acts by which we aim at either correcting or enlarging our knowledge of facts, acts by which we consciously move forwards into the future with that end in view. They are present moments of reflective perception or experience, of a special, that is, an intellectual, conceptual, and volitional kind.

Nor does the fact, that in hypothetical judgments and syllogisms we adopt the mode just described of throwing out our material into a time sequence, and expressing it in the form of a relation between antecedent and consequent, make the existence of the objects thought of in that way one whit more problematical or conditional than it is in categorical judgments and syllogisms. Every general term includes an *If*. We have seen that general terms are prospective, and such as to cover all cases, whether existing in the past, the present, or the future, which may be found to correspond to the characteristics which the term expresses. The mode of assertion adopted by hypothetical judgments does no more than bring out into distinct statement this peculiarity which is latent in all general terms; as for instance, in saying of the general term *crow*, that if anywhere or at any time there are crows, they must possess the

THE FOUNDATIONS OF LOGIC.

attribute of blackness, or else not come up to the definition of a crow, instead of simply stating, as if it were a matter of direct intuition, that all crows are black. Whether there are or are not any real crows in the world is left wholly undetermined, and equally undetermined, by both forms of judgment. It is a fact which they both alike leave for existential judgments to assert, that is, either to affirm or deny.

This brings me to the circumstance which invests hypothetical judgments with their main and peculiar interest. It is this. The mode of assertion which they adopt, or more strictly embody, in the act of looking forward to knowledge yet to be acquired by modification of the old material, brings into the clear light of consciousness the fact of alternatives in thought both or all of which are possible to thought, or conceivably true to fact, at the moment of judging but only one of which can be really true, in the sense of corresponding to the reality of the objects thought of. The use of *If*, as in asserting *If there are crows, then &c.*, implies the possibility of there not being crows; which of course is an extreme instance, since the negative alternative is with difficulty imaginable. Alternatives, however, may be of all degrees of probability, and all alike are covered by the introduction of an *If*. The uncertainty of an antecedent, combined with the assertion of its consequent as a certainty, supposing the antecedent true, is the essential character of all hypothetical judgments. This is amusingly illustrated by some doggrel lines of Lessing, entitled *Gewissheit:* [1]

---

[1] G. E. Lessing. *Sämmtliche Werke.* Ed. Lachmann. Vol. I., p. 42.

"Ob ich morgen leben werde,
Weiss ich freilich nicht:
Aber, wenn ich morgen lebe,
Dass ich morgen trinken werde,
Weiss ich ganz gewiss."

Which for the benefit of English readers I thus translate, or rather paraphrase:

'Shall I be alive to-morrow?
'Faith I cannot tell;
But, if I'm alive to-morrow,
That I'll have my glass to-morrow,
This I know right well.'

Thus the fact of alternative possibilities, which is concealed by the categorical, is brought into prominence by the hypothetical mode of assertion. And it must be remembered, that, what possibility is in objective thought, that contingency is in the real objects thought of. Possibility or conceivability, with all its degrees of probability in thought, is the subjective aspect of contingency, with all its modes of dependence on the varying play of conditions, in the world of real existents. Nor have we any other means of picturing contingency in real events than by reference to, and employment of, the knowledge, be it more or less, which we have of the probability of the conditions, by which those events are determined. Contingency is, in fact, read into the order of real existence, which is the Course of Nature, in a way precisely analogous to that in which real conditioning itself is read into it, namely, from the mode in which we reproduce in thought the simple sequences and co-existences of perception, under the influence of the desire for knowing. Our own uncertainty in picturing as real one out of two or more mutually exclusive alternatives, both or all of which are possible to thought, is what we call contingency in the real events, just as our own conception of the events which must occur, whether previously or simultaneously, if a given event is to occur, and without which it would not occur, leads us to characterise them as real conditions and conditionates.

We see moreover from what has been said, that the idea of possibility and its object, contingency, is not the only idea which the hypothetical mode of assertion brings to light. The idea of the conditionally necessary is equally essential to it. This also is a duplicate idea; the thought of what is conditionally necessary is the subjective aspect of that which is thought of as having conditions which bring it to pass in reality, that is, in the chain or course of real existence. Our idea of a necessary connection between realities is first attained by taking our own objective thought of them piecemeal, as it were, and throwing it out into separate and sequent parts; a mode of dealing with it which, as we have seen, Logic formulates as its processes of hypothetical judgment and syllogism. Thus it is that we finally come to conceive the whole panorama of our objective thought as reducible to a vast scheme of consequents and antecedents (as before to a vast scheme of genera and species), governed by the principle of *Ratio Sufficiens Cognoscendi*, which represents the whole order of real conditioning, or Course of Nature, as if governed in its direction from time to time, or from step to step, by a corresponding principle, the *Ratio Sufficiens Existendi*, and which would represent it in all its minutiæ, if only our detailed knowledge of its phenomena, that is, the panorama itself, could be made complete. So long as this is not the case, we are left to the expedient of selecting and adopting as provisionally true the most probable of two or more alternative thoughts which it is possible to conceive as true, that is, as representing objects or events which really exist, to the exclusion of others, which might have existed in their place.

Two out of the three concepts (or six, counting their contradictories) which are known as the Modal Concepts or Categories, namely, those of possible existence and conditionally necessary existence, have now been traced to their origin in that mode of dealing with phenomena in thought, which Logic formulates as hypothetical judgment and syllogism. The next question is, whether the remaining Modal Concept, that of simply actual or *de facto* existence, (the contradictory of which is non-actuality or non-existence), can be traced to the same origin. It seems evident that it can. It was shown in Book I., Chapters VII. and VIII., that our idea of the reality of an object thought of, as distinguished from that of its representation in objective thought, first arises on occasion of our finding our expectation of meeting a represented object deceived, and of consequently putting the question, What must happen in order that such an expectation should be realised and not disappointed? The instance illustrating this was that of a child being disappointed of seeing a pet dog in his accustomed basket. It was there shown, that occasions like these are the first occasions of our distinguishing objects of consciousness from the consciousness which contains the representations of them, or objects thought of from objective thought. And farther, that, out of our drawing this distinction, there arises a perception of the reality (in the full sense of the term) of those objects thought of which are found to be the condition of arousing immediate presentations in our trains of consciousness; both the objects conditioning and the presentations conditioned being classed as real existents in the large or general sense, and in that character distinguished from consciousness in its character of a knowing. The second step in the process now described was exemplified by analysing the perception of a bell.

Now the mode of thought which is employed in coming to conclusions like these is precisely that which is afterwards formulated as hypothetical judgment and syllogism. If I am to have a presentation of my dog (the child virtually though not explicitly argues) there must be something real in the basket to produce it. If nothing real is there, I shall have no such presentation. The presence of what we call the real dog is thus taken as a real *sine qua non* condition of his being actually seen. The assertion in thought of the *de facto* existence of the dog, as distinguished from, and as the real condition of, the immediate presentation of him, is thus virtually though not explicitly the conclusion of a hypothetical syllogism. In other words, judgments which, if formulated, would be formulated as conclusions of hypothetical syllogisms are the first existential categorical judgments, existential, I mean, as distinguished from simple categorical judgments *de inesse*, such as A *is* B, which assert the coalescence of two concepts, without any assertion of the real existence either of the concepts themselves or of their objects thought of. The concept *real existence* is thus a modal concept, and judgments which predicate it, which are called existential judgments, are arrived at in the first instance by the hypothetical line of judging and reasoning.

We may briefly summarise our results as follows, so far as the subjective side of the thoughts we are dealing with is involved, that is to say, so far as they appear in the movement and moulding of objective thought, apart from the conclusions to which they lead concerning the Course of Nature, which is their object thought of, and with which we have not in this Chapter to busy ourselves.[1] With this restriction, and regarding hypothetical judgment and reasoning as a whole, we may say that therein our objective thought exhibits three distinct phases, closely connected with each other, which, supposing them ranged in order of increasing complexity, are the three Modal Concepts, Categories, or Determinations;—namely, the thought of *actuality*, the thought of *possibility*, and the thought of *necessity*. The first is when we think of anything as simply real or existent. The second is when we think of anything as a possible alternative, or as possible to be or not to be. The third is when we think of anything as bound either to be or else not

---

[1] Those who may desire to see the Modal Concepts more fully treated, in dependence on the principle of Contradiction, though without their being specially connected with hypothetical judgments, are referred to the author's *Philosophy of Reflection*, Vol I. Book II. Chap. v. § 10, and Chap. vi. §§ 5 and 6.

THE FOUNDATIONS OF LOGIC.

to be, by the nexus of conditions of which it forms part. These concepts, by the aid of which we arrive at the recognition, that our knowledge is knowledge of one unique Order of Real Conditioning or Course of Nature, are perfectly general, and also perfectly indifferent to every kind of content, every place, every time. They apply to reality in all its modes, to states of consciousness as well as to Matter, to thoughts as well as to their objects,—in short to everything that has a *whatness*, however general, vague, or evanescent, by which it contributes to experience, and by which thought can lay hold of it.

Especially important is their being totally irrespective of the position of the facts, to which they apply, relatively to other facts in time, or in space, or in both together, which is the Order of Real Conditioning. For instance,—whether it is or is not now raining at the Antipodes; whether it was or was not raining at the Antipodes exactly a million years ago from the present moment; and whether it will or will not be raining at the Antipodes exactly to a day, a million years hence;—in all these cases, the true alternative (whichever it be) is strictly and equally a *de facto* reality, in relation to the Order of Real Conditioning, whether it belongs to past, present, or future time. It is also strictly and equally a matter of possibility or contingency, when related to our present knowledge of it; and also in the same way a matter of necessity, when related to our knowledge that it has *de facto* some place in the Order of Real Conditioning. What we do not know is,—which of the alternatives in any of the three cases is the true one, the raining or the not-raining. And this again, in every case,

BOOK III.
CH. IV.

§ 6.
Hypothetical Judgments and Modal Concepts.

is a matter of evidence, that is, of degrees of certainty in our knowledge. The highest degree of certainty attaches only to phenomena which are perceived and objectified as immediate presentations. In ascertaining the truth of all other phenomena there is always some admixture of inference.

Moreover these Modal categories are only possible in thought, that is, are conceptual not perceptual determinations. They possess logical universality, being based on the principle of Contradiction, by which Not-being is included in the Universe of Thought, as an ideal determination making Being a concept. Subjectively we embrace what *is not* as the necessary logical opposite of what *is;* without which conceptual negation, the object of which is simply the objective thought of the absence of all content whatever, the positive content, which we say *is*, would be a content of perception only, devoid of logical or conceptual significance. *Not-being* is very real in objective thought, and therefore also in Logic, while objectively, in the world of objects thought of, that which "is not" is Nothing, has no content, no *whatness*, and therefore no reality, and is wholly excluded from that which "is." Possible alternatives are involved, the moment we begin to apply the thought of simple existence, that is, to subsume any content, or *whatness*, or anything perceptual under that conception. We have then to consider whether the thing to be subsumed exists *or not*. To arrive at a conclusion on this point, we have to ask the two questions, *When* and *Why;* the *Whatness* of the content being given, and its present existence in the thought that represents it not being then in question. We ask the question *When*, because it is Time that mediates between that which now is and that which now is not, and enables us to subsume that which has been and that which will be under the notion of that which is, this being a general and indifferent conception. We ask the question *Why*, because Time enables us to do so in any given case, only if there are reasons for inferring, that there has been or will be a time in which the content questioned has been or will be present. And this inference we can only arrive at by applying the conception of the conditionally necessary, and subsuming the content questioned under it. Such are the nature and the function of the Modal Concepts.

Now since our knowledge is always limited, and we are spurred on by the desire of knowing more, or knowing better, than we actually know at any given moment, the second Modal Concept, the thought of possible alternatives, is the pivot on which the actual process of judging and reasoning turns, thereby coinciding, as it were, with the point of logical contradiction. We are always in the presence of alternatives possible to thought. We have at every moment to choose and adopt that alternative, in our objective thought, which seems the most likely to correspond to the reality of the object thought of, as a part of the real Course of Nature; we have to mould our objective thought into harmony with that Nature, the laws of which are *ex hypothesi* only partially and imperfectly known to us. It may be added, that hypothetical judgment and reasoning, of which the Modal Concepts of Actuality, Possibility, and Necessity, are inseparable adjuncts, and in which they are first

352 THE FOUNDATIONS OF LOGIC.

BOOK III.
CH. IV.
—
§ 6.
Hypothetical Judgments and Modal Concepts.

brought out into distinct apprehension, are the mode of thought which plays the most important part in all methods of Positive Science.

A word in conclusion must be said of the volitional character of thought, and of the assent which is involved in all choice between alternatives. Reasoning being admittedly a volitional act, it must clearly do something, alter something, make some change. What, then, does it alter? It alters the order and arrangement of the reasoner's objective thought in the first place; and then, consequent upon this, or more strictly consequent upon the neural processes upon which objective thought depends, and which we name and characterise by means of this their dependent concomitant, it alters the reasoner's own immanent and overt action. Except to the extent of that immanent and overt action on the part of the reasoner, and their consequences, it does not alter in any degree the objects thought of by the reasoning; that is to say, the Course of Nature, so far forth as it is the object known by the reasoning, is entirely unaffected. Knowing an object means knowing it as it really exists, independently of alterations which may be introduced indirectly by the knowledge acquired. It is the desire for this kind of knowledge which is the motive of speculative thinking or reasoning in pursuit of Truth; its having a selected motive makes it volitional, and the motive being desire for truth makes it speculative. The assent which we give to conceptions, judgments, or conclusions, in speculative thinking, is an assent determined by the desire for this kind of knowledge, and therefore is an assent determined solely by the evidence, and not by our wish that conceptions, judgments, or conclusions, of a particular kind should be true.

When an assent is given which is motived by desires of any other kind than that of pure knowledge, that assent is an act of choice which derogates from the character of being purely speculative reasoning, or thinking in pursuit of truth, which the process possesses, and makes it *pro tanto* a process of conduct in pursuit of good. It may be laudable, but it is not laudable as logic. It is in fact the perennial and copious fountain of fallacies of every kind. Conception, judgment, and reasoning, governed or deflected by any such heterogeneous desire, and the acts of assent which they include, have an effect upon the reasoner's own objective thought, and consequent action both immanent and overt, just as in the case of thought governed solely by the desire for knowledge. Moreover, like that kind of thought, they have no effect upon the real objects thought of. The Course of Nature goes its own way unaffected by them, except so far as the individual reasoner is concerned, and those whom his action influences, just as in the opposite case. The difference is, and it is immense, that the individual gets a distorted picture of reality. The two kinds of assent, therefore, must be kept carefully distinguished from each other.

The power which we have of giving or witholding our assent, alike in cases of attention, of judgment, and of reasoning, is undoubtedly great. If it is determined by anything else than the evidence within our reach, it may seriously affect the truth of our beliefs, though it can have no effect on the realities concerning which we entertain them. It may be a question, how far we are capable of believing in the truth of beliefs when they are not grounded simply on the available evidence, how far we are compelled to recognise them in self-consciousness, though not to avow them, as make-beliefs. It would seem that, the more closely we scrutinise our thoughts in the light of the distinction between the two kinds of assent, the more clearly must the difference between belief and make-belief be forced upon our awareness. There are certainly some facts which cannot be disbelieved, from which we cannot withold our assent, however strongly we may wish to do so. Such are all immediate perceptions of sense and emotion, and truths of the kind which are called self-evident. Intellectual assent again cannot be accorded to a logical contradiction, when once perceived to be one. But within these limits the power of giving or witholding assent has a wide field open to it.

It is to assent of the second or non-speculative kind that what has been called a Grammar of Assent belongs. Cardinal Newman's well known *Essay in aid of a Grammar of Assent* is an exhibition of the reasons which may lead us to assent to the doctrines of Christian Theology as true. But in the pursuit of speculative truth, based solely upon the desire of knowledge, there is no place for any such Grammar. A grammar of assent would there be identical with a treatise on the laws of evidence. The case is different in practical, moral, and religious matters, where a good life, not speculative truth, is the end in view, and where all speculative evidence is beyond our reach. All questions of comparative moral value come under this head, because comparative moral value is matter for practical estimate, and cannot either in the moment of choice, or even in retrospective judgments, be reduced to quantitative measurement, there being no common measure or unit of moral worth. Yet in these matters we are necessarily called upon, now to give, now to withold, our assent to doctrines concerning the nature and history of the world, of which our own moral estimates and actual conduct are a part. Many of the doctrines, to which we then assent, are assented to because they are the intellectual form, in which we explain to ourselves or others our sense of the transcendent value of conduct which is commanded by conscience; and our conviction of their truth depends mainly upon the closeness with which they represent our sense of that transcendent value. Assent of this kind is not an act of cognition, it is an act of faith. The speculative truth of the doctrines assented to is for us suspended upon the moral goodness of the practical aims or purposes, the realisation of which they afford us the means of imagining intelligibly, that is, in accordance with whatever system of ideas we may, at the time, be accepting as our philosophy.

It is not possible for the moral conscience to command a belief, that any doctrine is true in fact; because the knowledge of its corresponding or not corresponding to fact is itself a fact, which is independent of moral choice (which alone conscience commands), and the knowledge of which again depends, not on moral choice, but on evidence.

§ 6. Hypothetical Judgments and Modal Concepts.

What the moral conscience can do is this; in default of evidence, it can command our accepting and acting on a doctrine, as unhesitatingly as if it were known to be true in fact, supposing that doctrine to be, in our own individual case, owing to our previous training or other circumstances, essential to our keeping a firm hold of the aims and purposes of morality. And such a doctrine we may embrace with the whole energy of our undivided will, provided we know that, from the nature of our intellectual endowment, no positive evidence is attainable. But then its acceptance as a truth is an act of faith, and involves our consciously recognising that the truth of the doctrine is not matter of evidence and knowledge. We accept it unconditionally, indeed, so far as volition is concerned, but neither as an unconditioned or ultimate datum of experience, nor as a demonstrated truth in necessary matter. The fact that we embrace it unconditionally does not convert it into knowledge. The line of demarcation between the two kinds of assent coincides with that between speculative or logical and moral or ethical reasoning. The volitional act of assenting is an act of thought, but not necessarily an act of cognition, except so far as thought itself is the object cognised.

§ 7. The Limits of Thought as compared to Perception.

§ 7. There remains one point to which it is necessary to advert before quitting the present subject, a point which it would have been premature to insist on, until our brief survey of the whole province of conception, thought, and reasoning, in their essential features, was completed. I mean the comparative magnitude of the two domains, that of thought on the one hand and perception on the other. It has been pointed out that perception is a term which has two meanings, a wider and a narrower, in the wider of which it is equivalent to consciousness, and includes both perception modified and perception unmodified by conception. It is with this latter distinction, that is, with perception and conception as contradistinguished from each other, that we have now to do, and therein with the magnitude of the fields which they cover; the question being whether, when conception supervenes upon and modifies perception, it contracts, enlarges, or leaves unchanged, the field of time, or time and space together, occupied by the perception in its unmodified form. Or in other words, whether perception modified by conception, or perception unmodified by it, covers the larger field of consciousness. This question is important, because it involves the nature, origin, and logical justification, of our ideas of eternity and infinity, as opposed to what is merely indefinite in duration and extension, both of these opposites being alike opposed to what is simply finite in both respects. And the question is a logical one, because Thought therein, returning as it were upon itself, completes the comparison of its own nature and processes with those of its pre-supposition, perception, both being taken, not psychologically, but as two complementary modes of Knowing.

There is one way of understanding this question in which we see its answer as soon as it is asked, since it is plain that we can always think of or conceive a perception *as such*, adding nothing and subtracting nothing from its content, and so leaving the magnitude of its field the same. But this is not a case which just now concerns us, though I shall recur to it later on. It is not a case of modifying a perception, so as to make it into a conception, but of taking a perception as the object of a conception and yet continuing to think of it as a perception. In all such cases, I mean the *as such* percepts just mentioned, we are really re-modifying, or thinking back into perceptual form, what we have first modified into a conception by a prior act of selective attention, expressible by simply logical negation of everything else. The real question is whether, in a *first* act of conception, whenever it may occur, we contract, or enlarge, or leave unchanged, that content of perception to which we are then and there selectively attending. There is always some positive content, first of perception alone, then of conception, before us; and what we are now asking is, whether the act of judgment completing the act of selectively attending to that positive content, with a view to knowing it better, makes any change in the magnitude of the field which it previously occupied in consciousness as a knowing, or in that of the apparent area covered by consciousness itself.

The answer depends upon what is called the form of perception, as distinguished from the form of conception and thought. The form of perception, as already said, is twofold; all percepts whatever have duration of time as the formal element in, that is, occupied by, their content; and all visual and tactual percepts have some mode or modes of spatial extension, in addition to time-duration, as their formal element; that is, their content occupies a certain extent of some mode of space, as well as a certain duration of time. In all cases of perception, the two elements, formal and material, are inseparable; always, however, remembering, that it is only certain classes of perceptions which include modes of space in their formal element. Perception as a whole, including all its content of whatever kind, has thus the properties attaching to its formal, as well as those attaching to its material, elements. And the formal elements of perception, time and space, are those parts of it which are the foundation of the perception of magnitude, or out of which it originates. Particular magnitudes, of duration, of spatial length, surface, and volume, are brought into notice originally by perceived differences of quality in the contents which fill them; these differences serving to distinguish them from other percepts which are their context in the otherwise continuous formal element or elements, which are of no other than the same two kinds in all perception.

It is sometimes said, that perceptions of greater and less intensity, in sensations or feelings of any kind, are immediate and independent perceptions of magnitude. But though these perceptions are so closely bound up with perceptions of magnitude, when once the conception of magnitude has been acquired, as to seem immediate perceptions of it, they cannot be held to be independent sources of that perception or idea. The case is closely analogous to that of the supposed immediate perception of a "remote," that is, a visible and tangible real object, a perception which in truth requires the conception of sensibly solid objects to have been acquired previously. So also the greater and less intensities of feeling, which we perceive immediately, do not of themselves contain any intimation of, or foundation for, the idea of magnitude or quantity; but are differences of feeling lying wholly within the quality of the feelings experienced.

In support of this it must be considered, that the intensity of a feeling is something wholly different in kind from the duration of it, and also from the extension of it, supposing it to be a sensation of sight or touch. It is only when we have acquired from elsewhere the conception of magnitude or quantity, that we can in the first instance acquire the conception, that the intensity of feelings has magnitude, or is capable of degree, namely, by asking *how much* of a specifically given feeling is contained in a given duration, or given extension, and then calling that roughly estimated quantity its magnitude or degree of intensity. In other words, varying intensities of feeling are not perceived as varying magnitudes or degrees, until the perception of magnitude has been elsewhere acquired, any more than solid bodies are perceived as solid, until we have put together extended perceptions of sight and touch into that perception. The apparent immediateness of both perceptions, I mean magnitudes or degrees of intensity in feeling and solid bodies, is due to the fact that, in cases where these perceptions have been acquired and have become familiar, we instantaneously class (by association) newly given feelings of intensity, and newly given perceptions of sight or of touch, with intensities already perceived as magnitudes in the one case, and with groups of feelings already perceived as solid bodies in the other. The perception of magnitude or degree of intensity in feelings is thus an interpretation put

THE FOUNDATIONS OF LOGIC.

upon certain variations in their element of feeling, from applying to them ideas of measurement and quantity derived originally from the formal element alone.[1] I therefore put aside the consideration of intensity of feeling, as not bearing on the nature or origin of the perception or idea of magnitude. And I take up the thread of argument where it was dropped, two paragraphs above.

Now in order to compare magnitude with magnitude in any of these cases of different contents in the same continuous formal element, we require selective attention and thought. If the perception of magnitudes originates in the formal element of perception, in the manner shown, it is completed only by thought, in comparing one magnitude with another. The question, then, of the comparative magnitude of the fields covered respectively by perception and thought is, as already said, one for thought to decide, in retrospection on its own nature and processes as compared to those of perception. That is to say, we here and now, in scrutinising the foundations of Logic, which is the science of Thought, have to see how Thought deals and, according to its own laws, must deal with this question; without doing which we should be leaving one important domain or mode of Thought, namely, its reflective knowledge of its own nature, unexamined.

The question being so presented, one point at least contributing to the answer is plain. We have just seen, throughout this Chapter, that Thought is essentially limitation. In the first place it selects

---

[1] See this question again handled in my Aristotelian Address, *On the Conception of Infinity*, Nov. 1893, in the Proceedings of the Aristotelian Society, Vol. II., No. 3, Part I., pp. 6 to 8.

BOOK III.
CH. IV.

§ 7.
The Limits of Thought as compared to Perception.

and therefore demarcates a vast number of fields out of the data offered by sense-presentation and spontaneous redintegration, which, be it remembered, includes imagination, by gathering them into groups called concepts, on the basis of observed differences and resemblances in their perceptual content, groups or concepts which are general or universal, both in point of their comprehension, and in point of their extension over an indefinite number of particular instances; so that the whole continuous field composed of positive process-contents of perception might conceivably come before us again in the conceptual form thus imprinted upon it.

If this were all, the magnitude of the fields covered by perception and thought might justly be considered equal, being in fact the same field differently distributed. But there is another point to be taken into consideration, which is this: How does thought deal with the phenomenon of magnitude itself? Thought is essentially limitation; and it completes the conception of magnitude, originated by perception of differences of content in otherwise continuous duration and spatial extension, by holding fast and comparing the magnitudes, so originated, one with another. The measurement of given, or rather suggested, magnitudes is performed by thought, even when actual superposition is employed as the means of their comparison.

But here comes into notice a singular and important fact. In one respect, Time and Space escape all limitation by Thought. The formal elements of perception, time and space, have no final limit, no limit beyond which they are not perceived to extend, though the content of that extension beyond the last perceived limit may be specifically unperceived, and therefore the extension and content together, beyond the last perceived limit, may not be perceived as a positively knowable object. To show this, let us begin with the case of simple presentations. A presented difference in time-content has a time-content both before it and after it; a presented difference of space-content has a space-content both on one side and on the other. And the same holds good of positively represented or positively imagined differences in both formal elements. In these cases a specific content on what I may call the hither side of the difference, a specific content on its farther side, and the difference between them, are all alike things which are positively perceived.

But now consider the case of the whole objective-thought panorama of the positively known, knowable, or imaginable, real Universe, taken as one vast and complex percept. Conception and thought contribute, as already shown, to the formation of this panorama of objective thought, and give to it whatever definiteness of outline it may possess, which is what enables us to call it figuratively a panorama. As having or appearing to have an outline, it is the result of thought; and we have already seen that the final results of thought, as well as its original materials, are percepts.

Have, then, conception and thought assigned, or even established the fact of there being, real limits to this vast and complex percept, the panorama representing our whole positively perceivable or imaginable universe? By no means. For in its case a remarkable difference between the panorama itself and any of the percepts, or objective thoughts, included in it comes into view. These percepts or objective thoughts had a positively perceivable or imaginable context, beyond their own limits, on every side of them in time and space. But the panorama of objective thought itself, supposing it taken, in consequence of thought, as a single vast and complex percept, and so being placed by thought in the position of a specific content bounded by differences, has no context, and no limits, save what may be supplied by the circumstance of the positive conceivability of its content ceasing, and leaving its pure elements, time and space, unlimited, but empty of positively imaginable or conceivable content, beyond them. The positively imaginable or conceivable content of the panorama, therefore, when thought of in this way, has, as it were, a setting of pure and unlimited time and space, surrounding it in the case of space, preceding and following it in that of time.

The panorama of objective thought, when so conceived, is thus wholly unlimited in respect of its formal elements, time and space, but is limited in respect of its positively and specifically imaginable or conceivable content; this limitation being probably attributable to the fact of the want on our part, as human beings, of appropriate sense or brain organs, as well as to the feebleness of those we have, and not to any limitation in the possible modes of specific consciousness, or in the modes of reality perceivable by them, which the universe may contain. Our panorama of objective thought, therefore, considered in its full extent, that is, as embracing whatever its formal element time, or time and space together, may embrace, though beyond what we can positively conceive or imagine, has a content which escapes all limitation by thought, and therefore cannot, in point of its necessary magnitude, be compared to any given or merely conceivable magnitude; since all given or merely conceivable magnitudes are also conceivable as being bounded on both or all sides by differences of content either in time or in space.

The name for magnitudes which are of such a kind as to escape all conceivable limitation, by difference of presented or imagined contents bounding them, is *eternal* in the case of time, *infinite* in that of space; and what is now pointed out seems to be the only assignable origin of the two ideas of eternity and infinity, which would otherwise be entirely inexplicable. Both kinds of unlimited magnitude belong to the formal elements of perception, and both escape our powers of conception and thought, because these powers operate only by dividing or limiting perception on the basis of differences in the contents perceived. The field of perception, therefore, exceeds the field of conception or thought, in point of magnitude, by the whole extent of that pure time and pure space, which offer no differences for thought to fasten upon, and in virtue of which it is named eternal or infinite.

Eternity and infinity are originally and necessarily percepts only; and therefore, if we attempt to define the meaning or connotation of the general terms which denote and name them, it can only be by the very circumstance of their escaping the limitations of thought; time and space being taken as their proximate *genus*, and that circumstance, in time and space themselves, as their characteristic or *differentia*. That is to say, Time is eternal, and Space is infinite; and the meaning of eternal and infinite is learnt only from properties belonging only to Time and Space themselves. We thus obtain, it is true, conceptions of eternity and infinity, but thought does not obtain them by enlarging the field of the perceptions which it modifies, either by adding to them a not-time or a not-space, as if these logical forms were percepts, or by generalising them so as to include other modes or varieties of time or of space, which might possibly some day be discovered. They are conceptions of elements in perception as perception, and their characteristics are drawn from perception as yet unmodified by thought. The act by which we conceive eternity and infinity derives the content of those conceptions from the invariably occurring perception of an unlimited 'beyond' to every positive content which we perceive or imagine. It does not add an unlimited 'beyond' to a limited percept, but records the fact, that an unlimited 'beyond' attaches to every limited content of perception. As concepts they are founded in perception, and expressed by definition. They in fact signify the duration and the extension, to which no limit is possible or conceivable, so that the duration of Time is necessarily eternal, and the extension of Space necessarily infinite.

They are thus obviously different from finitude or the finite, both in time and space. But they are also essentially different from indefiniteness or the indefinite, in both its meanings. By the indefinite is meant, either (1) something having a particular concrete nature which is known to have a limit, while the *locus* of that limit is unknown, or (2) something having a particular concrete nature, of which it is unknown whether it has a limit or not. In either case it differs from that necessary infinity of pure time and space just spoken of, by the circumstance of including only concrete contents or objects the nature of which can be positively conceived, however meagre that conception may be, which is the means whereby thought apprehends and deals with them. But in the second case, that of the indefinite something, of which it is unknown whether it has a limit or not, an alternative is presented to thought, namely, the alternative of conceiving it either as in fact finite, or as in fact infinite; in adopting the latter of which alternatives we should be conceiving it as in fact, though not of necessity, sharing in the infinity of pure time or pure space, to whichever of these its nature was conceived as immediately belonging.

1. Examples of magnitudes which are indefinite in the first sense are found in mathematic, and we must remember that we have to do with the discovery of their limits in both directions—I mean both in the direction of increase, κατὰ πρόσθεσιν and in that of decrease or division, κατὰ διαίρεσιν,—in both of which directions their contrast with the necessary infinity of pure time and space will become apparent. We cannot, in fact, think away duration or spatial extension, so as to reduce the one to a point in time, the other to a point in space. In fact their infinite divisibility means this very thing, that no division annihilates any portion of that which it divides, however infinitesimally small the portion or

portions so distinguished may be. Every point in time or in space pre-supposes a duration or an extension which it divides, and which lies on both sides of it. There is no last point in division either of time or space, beyond, or rather perhaps within, which there is no duration or no spatial extension. Likewise there is no last point in the direction of increase, that is, no maximum, of duration or spatial extension, beyond which there is no duration or extension. And this is the meaning of their being infinite in the direction of increase.

There are, however, processes in thought, by which we may make a perpetual approximation, indefinite in the first sense of the term, to such supposed points, in either direction, though (since the supposed points are purely fictitious and imaginary) we can never attain them; and these processes consist in perpetually adding in the one case, and subtracting in the other, portions of time or of space, which may be infinitesimally minute, to or from given periods of time or given figures in space. If we follow processes of this kind, what we come to are magnitudes which are indefinite in the first sense of the term, namely, that of having limits the exact *locus* of which is unknown. Both kinds of processes alike pre-suppose the perceptual formal elements, time and space; particular portions of which, portions which are concrete in the sense, that limitations of those continuous elements, as well as the elements themselves, are involved in the conception of their nature, are the contents or objects with which, as processes of thought and conception, they deal.

THE FOUNDATIONS OF LOGIC.

BOOK III.
CH. IV.

§ 7.
The Limits of Thought as compared to Perception.

Mathematical methods, which are methods of conception and thought applied to the figuration of space, in which they constitute Geometry, and to acts divisive of time, in which they appear as Universal Arithmetic or Algebra, including the Infinitesimal Calculus, may be taken as adequate, for all practical purposes, to determinations of the Indefinite in its first sense, but not to the determination of Time and Space themselves; for these escape determination, both as being infinite, and as being the necessary pre-supposition of all determination of limits. It is a fallacy, due to defect of subjective analysis, to overstep this line of demarcation between the indefinite and the infinite; an error in reasoning of which we are made aware by the non-sense or unintelligibility which appears in the result.

Endeavour in thought to extend a closed figure, say a sphere, to infinity by continual additions to its magnitude. Its surface then approximates, in every part of it, more and more to a flat surface. But to suppose, that *at infinity* (as the possibility assumed *argumenti gratia* is called) it becomes a flat surface, is to destroy both its original nature as a sphere and its anticipated nature as a flat surface, and the bubble bursts into nothing at all. The result is neither a flat surface nor a curved one. The same flat surface cannot be at opposite sides of the sphere at once. Thus the contradiction which results when we endeavour to identify a closed figure, which is a limitation of space, with infinite space of which it is a limitation, is made evident. It can only become infinite by ceasing to be a closed figure. The truth is, that the sphere is a magnitude

BOOK III.
CH. IV.

§ 7.
The Limits of Thought as compared to Perception.

which may be made in thought inedfinitely great, by a succession of infinitesimal increments, short of that point at which it ceases to be a sphere at all. In other words, the *locus* of its limits as a sphere lies somewhere between its magnitude as originally given and its maximum magnitude as a closed figure, beyond which it would no longer exist as a sphere. The question is, at what particular increment we are to stop short.

Similarly with the endeavour to diminish a sphere to a point, which "has no parts and no magnitude," by gradual diminution or decrements. *At infinity*, as it is called, where the diminished sphere is supposed to coincide with the point which was its centre, it *ipso facto* ceases to exist as a sphere. It must therefore be considered as an indefinitely decreasing magnitude, the minimum limit of which lies just short of the point at which its circumference and its centre would coincide. What precise infinitesimal portion of space is to be taken as separating it from that coincidence, which would be its annihilation as a sphere, depends upon the purpose we have in view in calculating it.

The case is very similar with divisions and additions in counting, that is with, Number. "Unity," that is, counting *once*, so making an *unit* of whatever object-matter we may be engaged upon, is the given basis from which we start. If we take no particular object-matter as that which we are engaged in counting, but prefer to speak of Number or Numbers in the abstract, then, supposing we also wish to take units as divisible into lesser, and multipliable into larger, units, and therefore distinguish them, together with their fractions and multiples, as something counted or capable of being counted, from the acts of thought which count them, we must perforce in that case take Time itself, which is common and essential to all object-matters whatever, as our object-matter to be counted, and we must take our acts of counting it into units, their fractions, and their multiples, as acts divisive of Time, and having no duration by themselves. For Numbers in the abstract have the double character of being acts of counting, and of being units made by those acts, in one.

Accordingly, in all processes of counting we can advance so long as we can invent symbols, in thought, speech, or writing, to express the number of times we count or imagine ourselves to count *one*, and the various modes in which we can combine them. But still we cannot count till we have exhausted all possible numbers, as if they were a store waiting to be exhausted. For numbers, unlike Time and Space, are made by counting. So long as we count there are numbers,—and no longer. Counting is a special mode of thinking, that is, of limiting Time. There are no numbers in Nature. There is only their presupposition, time, with differences of its content which enable man to count its different portions, real or imagined, by dividing it in thought. Consequently the number of possible numbers is given only by a *processus in indefinitum*, and is an *indefinitum* of that kind which is known to have limits, because beyond the highest number which may from time to time be counted, there is always time remaining still to be divided by acts of counting as yet unperformed. Number itself is a creature of thought operating on and dividing its eternal presupposition, Time. Consequently an *infinitely great number* is a contradiction in terms; and an *indefinitely great number* is the only accurate general expression for the highest number that can possibly be reached.

2. As a representative and crucial instance of the indefinite in the second sense,— something concrete of which we are uncertain whether it has limits or not,—I take Matter, or the Material World, in its relation to the space which it occupies. I say in its relation to space only, because in its relation to time it will presently appear, that it must be conceived as having at least a beginning in time, and therefore, so far as its beginning was concerned, would be an instance of the indefinite in the first sense. Matter differs from purely mathematical figurations and numerations in being, not like them a construction of human thought by the introduction of imagined boundaries into space, imagined divisions into time, but a discovery made by thought of what may be called a doubly or trebly concrete, or composite, reality, presentable to sense, and thought of as real in the full sense of the term. It is not like numbers, which are made by counting, nor like geometrical figures, which are made by ideal limitations of space.

The discovery of it bears, it is true, the character of a construction in thought, inasmuch as we attain it by observing one by one the constant relations which different concrete or empirical percepts of sight and touch bear to one another, and inferring from them the existence of material substance with its inherent agencies. But inasmuch as this construction is everywhere governed by observing the *de facto* relations of given not ideally imagined percepts, we cannot but regard the material substance or substances which they form as existing prior to and independently of our observation, that is, of the attention and thought which we bestow upon the relations of the percepts from which we infer them. Matter, in short, must be regarded by us, either as a single real existent which is also a real condition, or as an aggregate of such real existents; and in either case as existing independently of our observation and thought.

Now we have already seen (Book II. Chap. I., § 7), that Matter has a minimum, that is, cannot be thought of as divisible *in infinitum*, like the space which it occupies; but that two portions at least of three-dimensional space are requisite, to enable us to conceive that force of coherence, without which Matter itself is inconceivable. And from this it follows, that Matter, though conceived as existing and operating independently of our observation of it, must nevertheless be conceived as dependent upon real conditions which are not Matter, and which are positively unknown and indeed positively inconceivable by us; because, compelled as we are to ask of all concrete or empirical realities *how* and *by what means* they came to exist, we find that the composition of Matter is neither self-explanatory, nor an ultimate datum of experience. Consequently Matter cannot be regarded as eternal *a parte ante*, but must be regarded as dependent upon the existence and operation of real conditions, the nature of which we cannot positively conceive. It bears the character which the authors of *The Unseen Universe*,

BOOK III.
CH. IV.

§ 7.
The
Limits
of
Thought
as
compared
to
Perception.

or possibly some earlier scientific authority, by a bold figure, attributed to the Atom, of being "a manufactured article."

Space, therefore, which, as an element of concrete objects, is infinitely divisible and infinitely extensible, plainly affords one of the constituent elements of Matter; and Matter as a real but conditioned existent has a minimum of spatial extension, below which it would not exist as Matter. But this says nothing whatever as to its upper limits, or its extensibility, as an existent independent of our observation, in the direction of increase, κατὰ πρόσθεσιν, nor, I may add, as to those of its duration into the future, or its eternity *a parte post*, always supposing its unknown real conditions to continue in existence and operative. So far, then, as necessities and alternatives of thought only are concerned, and apart from arguments drawn from the results of positive physical science, it is open to us to conceive the whole material world as a single vast atom, or minimum of Matter, which would have no maximum in the strict sense,—since a maximum implies limitation,—but would be found commensurate (supposing measurement possible) with infinite space; so that the whole infinity of space, and not a portion only, would then be conceived as occupied by Matter. If on the other hand we should conceive the material world as an aggregate of discrete material objects, whether minima or not, still no difference would be made by this way of conceiving it, so far as its magnitude is concerned. The aggregate would still be conceivable as having no limits in the direction of increase, short of infinite space, with which it could equally well be conceived as commensurate. For it would be thought of as a given and observable existent, independent of our actual observation, and not as an existent dependent on our imagination and thought, like mathematical numbers and figures, or subject to limitations which are necessarily, but solely, inherent in the processes whereby we attempt to conceive or imagine it.

Apart, then, I repeat, from conclusions of physical science, there is nothing on the one hand to compel us to regard Matter as a finite magnitude, having fixed limits, in the direction of increase, in comparison with infinite space, notwithstanding that the one is a composite real object, the other an abstract element, the finiteness of which in both directions is inconceivable. And on the other hand nothing compels us to regard it as infinite; since nothing is easier than to conceive Matter as finite in the direction of increase, whether we take it as a single vast object, or as an aggregate of objects. For our common-sense experience of separate masses of matter enables us readily to conceive it, in either case, as bounded by a void. In short, nothing compels us to conceive it as finite, nothing as infinite, in comparison with space, and in the direction of increasing magnitude; and yet, in reality, one of these contradictory conceptions must be true, and the other false. Matter cannot be both; it cannot be neither; it must be one of the two, exclusive of the other. It is therefore an instance of the indefinite in the second sense of the term; and is thereby also an instance of the limitation of our knowledge.

§ 7. The Limits of Thought as compared to Perception.

On the whole we see, that Matter may (though it need not necessarily) be conceived as infinite in spatial extension, and as infinite in duration into the future, counting from any given present moment. At the same time, this conception of it involves its being conceived as dependent on real conditions existing in time, which are not positively conceivable by us, and brings it into striking contrast, not only with the necessary eternity of time, but also with the necessary infinity of space, neither of which admits the conceivability of the contradictory alternative; since space, supposing its existence, cannot be thought of save as infinite in point of extension. Moreover, since Space is a necessary constituent of Matter, being its formal element, the existence of Matter in time future may be said to be doubly dependent. For Space, which is its formal element, must itself be conceived as conditioned in point of duration upon Time, inasmuch as it could not exist at all without duration, and carries with it, in itself alone, no evidence of eternity in time past, and no guarantee for its future duration, or permanence in time, beyond the present moment. Thus the only real ultimate in consciousness is its formal element Time, and that ultimate is necessarily infinite or eternal.

Now Time, taken as the sole ultimate and necessarily eternal element of consciousness or experience, is an element of perception simply, as distinguished from perception modified by thought. It is not introduced into consciousness by thought, when thought arises therein. The function of thought in regard to it is to attend to and fix divisions of it, divisions which are either offered by presented differences of feeling, or introduced ideally by imagining such differences, namely, differences between Numbers, when not offered by presentation. Thought *per se* has no content of its own but divisions, or dividings, either of consciousness in the concrete, or of its formal elements in the abstract. A division *per se* has no content, and therefore no magnitude, whatever. The act of selective attention in thought is an act of dividing ideally any content attended to from others; and in the act of judgment, which completes the act of attention, the place of the act of dividing is taken by the act of assertion, which is expressed by the copula, *is* or *is-not*.

If, then, the question before us was, whether perception alone or thought alone covered the larger area of the phenomena of consciousness, the answer must be, that perception covers its entire area, since it covers its entire content, while thought, having in itself no content, covers no area at all; for pure thought is pure division, and pure division is the exclusive opposite of magnitude.

But this result, though important, is no answer to the question proposed, which was, whether perception unmodified, or perception modified by or into conception, covered the larger area. To this question we are now in a position to reply. It is only perception unmodified that covers an area which is necessarily infinite and eternal. Perception modified by or into conception covers areas which are either (1) finite, and in this case are all included within the necessarily infinite and eternal extension of unmodified perception, or (2) are indefinite, in the sense that they may, for aught we know, be as a fact infinite in point of spatial extension, or in

BOOK III.
CH. IV.

§ 7.
The Limits of Thought as compared to Perception.

point of future duration; but if they are so, are still broadly distinguished from the necessarily infinite and eternal of unmodified perception, by the fact of their having only a conditioned and dependent existence, and therefore falling short of the extension of unmodified perception by that whole duration of infinite time, in which their real though unknown conditions must be conceived to exist. For space itself, though necessarily infinite in spatial extension, is not also necessarily eternal, that is, infinite in point of time-duration.—This, so far as I can see, is the furthest point to which we can attain, in answer to the question proposed at the outset; and this, with its consequences, is the contribution which Logic has to make to the solution of what is practically perhaps the most interesting question in philosophy, and the main problem of its Constructive Branch, namely, the nature and existence of an Unseen World.

I say with its consequences, because it is now necessary to recur to the case which was mentioned at the outset of the Section and there postponed, namely, where it was said that we could always make a perception the object of a conception, and yet continue to think of it as a perception. Eternity and Infinity are originally and necessarily perceptions, consisting in the fact, that in perceiving a limit we perceive a duration or an extension beyond it; so that whatever concrete or empirical object we perceive has a setting, the limits of which are not perceived. It is this fact, and not merely the fact that the limits of some concrete objects have not as yet been perceived, nor yet the fact that there are some concrete objects, of which it is unknown whether they have limits in some respects or not, which is at once the perception of eternity or infinity, and the *differentia* by which we conceptualise those perceptions. A *processus in infinitum*, which is necessarily a conceptual process, does not give, but on the contrary pre-supposes the perception of infinity, to which, as it were, it is the endeavour to attain. Consequently the concepts of eternity and infinity have the percepts of eternity and infinity as their objects. But this very circumstance precludes our supposing, that eternity and infinity, the 'unlimited beyond' of the percepts, are limited by our conception of them. It is essential to our conception to conceive them as they are in perception, that is, as unlimited; or in other words, to make the fact of their being necessarily unlimited by conception their *differentia* in defining them, Continuity being taken as the *genus* to which they belong. And thus it is in the nature of perception, that is, in any and every percept as a datum of experience, that what we afterwards call our conceptions of eternity in time and of infinity in space are rooted.

Our results, then, briefly stated are, that the forms of perception, namely, time-duration and spatial extension, are not only unlimited as immediate and ultimate data of experience, but that they are incapable of limitation by conception and thought; that limitation of this kind is always a limitation of parts within them; and that of this limitation they are a necessary pre-supposition. The forms of conception and thought, that is to say, the Postulates of Logic, the forms of judgment and syllogism, the direct concepts of *genus, differentia,* and *species,* and the modal concepts of *actuality, possi-*

bility, and *necessity*, supervene in volition upon the forms of perception, but never transcend them. They deal with the content of those perceptual forms by means of negation, limitation, and contrast, but neither discover nor create a content which is not subject to those perceptual forms. When Neo-Scholastics talk of anything being 'out of time altogether,' they do so only by tacitly or explicitly hypostasising thought as an energy which necessarily produces its entire content, time included, out of itself;—overlooking the fact, that a productive energy pre-supposes time as an element in its own existence, and thereby rendering the fundamental conception of their philosophy self-contradictory.

Two considerations are usually relied upon in attempting to show that the field of thought is wider than that of perception. The first is that of the power of generalisation, which undoubtedly makes its first appearance with the volitional act of conceiving. Generalisation admittedly includes and anticipates future and possible cases, which have never been data of experience, and in this way seems to transcend perception, to which all ultimate data of knowledge belong. But even generalisation has its limits. We can generalise again the already general conception of a perceptual form, can conceive the possibility that there may be forms of perception different both from time-duration and from spatial extension, for percipients differently endowed from man, just as for human percipients these two forms of perception differ from each other. But we cannot conceive such new forms, either as varieties of time or of space, or as not also having time-duration, that is, as being 'out of time altogether'; for that would be conceiving them not to exist, so contradicting the original conception, even while making it. The forms of time-duration and spatial extension, therefore, are each unique and ungeneralisable, and thus impose a limit upon the generalisation of new forms of perception. And if this is true of these two forms of perception, it is *a fortiori* true of whatever content we may conceive to occupy them. The conception of the Universe itself is subject to the form of time-duration. Its unity is, at the least, an unity in time. But the conception of the Universe is for this reason incapable of being generalised. It is not itself a logical universal or general term; it has a percept *as such* for its object. The term *Universe* implies the singleness of its object. There may be myriads of separate worlds, but there can be no separate universe. A second universe is a contradiction in terms.

The second consideration relied upon to show the greater magnitude of the field of conception is the logical form of Negation, or Contradiction, which is employed in all conceiving and judging; as when we select a particular content A, thereby distinguishing it from its purely logical contradictory Not-A, for the purpose of seeing what content, other than A so distinguished, and therefore provisionally and for a purpose included under its contradictory Not-A, in reality belongs to A and is predicable of it; a content, therefore, under which A must in judging be subsumed; as in the judgment A is B, where B is only provisionally included under Not-A, as a step towards arriving at a distinct and positive judgment concerning A. On this state of facts it is then argued, that perception gives us only

Being, while conception gives us Not-Being in addition. But here two things are forgotten, first, that Not-Being is not a concept having a content; and secondly, that the term *Being* is an instance of terms which have two senses, a wider and a narrower, of which the wider embraces the narrower (a particular Being in this instance) and its contradictory (not-this-particular Being), as opposites of each other. In this it is like the terms *consciousness, experience, perception,* and others. Not-being may be a particular determination, or negation, within Being in the wide sense, which latter is always originally given by perception; as when we say of coal, a particular Being, that it is not-white, which is a simple record of our observation of coal, and also supposes a previous knowledge of the meaning of *white*. Here, therefore, there is no enlargement of the field of perception by thought.

If again we attempt to take Not-Being as the contradictory of Being in the wide sense, here too there is no enlargement of field. For it will be found that we cannot realise Not-Being in thought, that is, cannot empty it of all content, without at the same time ceasing to think of it, or to be conscious of it at all. To be conscious, and *a fortiori* to think, is to be aware of some content in consciousness. The Not-Being of Logic, in the wide sense, or the Not-A of the Postulates, is a term describing the act of provisionally arresting a content of consciousness, for the purpose of comparing it with other contents, not a term describing any content of consciousness whatever.

The nearest approach we can make to realising pure Not-Being in thought is when we think of all particular content ceasing to exist, leaving only the abstract and unlimited form of time-duration present in thought, a form which a particular content might occupy but does not; the proper name for which privation of content is *Nothing*. There is therefore no production of a new concept, whether it be that of *Nothing*, or that of *Not-Being*, by thought; for *Nothing*, in this approach to realising it, is the empty perceptual form of time-duration, and *Not-Being*, taken without restriction, is simply a name for the act of selective attention to a content, when the content attended to is Being in its entirety. In speaking of Not-Being as a content, we are attempting to generalise from cases where some particular content is absent, and we have therefore something positive to negate, in contrast to something else positive which we perceive, to the supposed case where all content, all Being, is absent, which is impossible so long as we perceive or think at all; since we have already seen that generalisation is no substitute for perception, and never transcends it, by supplying a content of its own. *Being* is a perception which is incapable of generalisation. It is only particular Beings which can be generalised. Here again, conceiving by an act of thought presupposes perception and its form of time-duration. —These remarks are necessary to explain the true nature and function of Thought, but inasmuch as they thereby bring into consideration the relations of Thought to Perception, they also necessarily throw some light on the kind and degree of the knowledge or cognition which we can obtain of the Universe of Being.

CHAPTER V.

THE FOUNDATIONS OF POETIC. [1]

§ 1. I venture to anticipate that the subject which I propose to treat of next, the Foundations of Poetic, will not demand anything like so much space as I was compelled to devote to the Foundations of Logic, seeing that the science of Poetic has not yet, like Logic, been either organised or impugned in its entirety, or the various branches which belong to it finally recognised as subordinate parts of one comprehensive whole. I should therefore wish the present Chapter to be regarded as a contribution made to such a final organisation. The science of Poetic in its breadth, depth, and unity, though it has had a long pre-natal history, has still to be created. [2]

On the other hand, its nature, origin, and place among the sciences of practice, have been already pointed out in the concluding Section of Chapter

---

[1] Readers who may desire to see a somewhat detailed analysis and classification of the phenomena of sense, imagination, and emotion, which have served as the basis of the present Chapter, are referred to the author's *Theory of Practice*, Book I. Chap II., in Vol. I. pp. 56 to 334.

[2] The present Chapter was written, in all essentials, at least some considerable time before the publication of Mr Bosanquet's valuable *History of Æsthetic*, 1892. Mr. Bosanquet is apparently of opinion, that the Æsthetic, the history of which he writes, and which is mainly a product of Germany, has a solid foundation in the Hegelian Philosophy. That any foundations laid in that philosophy can be solid, is a belief to which I confess I cannot subscribe.

III. Towards the end of that Section it was shown, that there was a certain large class of desires, and actions founded on them, which might justly be called optional as distinguished from imperious, on the ground that they were neither imposed nor forbidden by moral considerations; and that the exercise of poetical imagination was a mode of voluntary redintegration, having some optional desire or desires as its motive. Moreover, as a mode of conscious voluntary action it necessarily falls under the survey of metaphysical or subjective analysis. It is thus found to be distinguished from pure thought, on the one hand, by its aim being a gratification other than simple truth of fact or correctness of reasoning, and from pure morality, or conduct in general, on the other, by its exercise being in every instance optional, that is, already permitted (though not enjoined) by the laws of morality. Poetic imagination, therefore, together with the different fields which it includes or governs, is the sum and substance of what lies before us in the present Chapter. It is at once an object-matter dealt with and the function dealing with it, which are the object-matter of the science for which I propose to retain the name *Poetic*, this science having its origin in the self-conscious reflection of individuals upon their own pursuit of those ends which they take as the ultimate ends or desires of their own poetic imagination.

Poetic, then, as a science which is a creature of self-consciousness, stands, or ought to stand, to Poetic Imagination just as Logic stands to Thought; that is to say, each science is an analysis and systematisation of a definite conscious function.

§ 1.
Nature and Range of Poetic Imagination.

Logic analyses and systematises Thought for the ultimate purpose of right reasoning; Poetic analyses and systematises Poetic Imagination for that of a more rational and complete enjoyment of a certain class of selected gratifications. Like Logic, too, its constitution is twofold, analytical and practical. It has first to discover analytically the nature, purposes, and methods, of poetic imagination, and then to throw that knowledge into a shape in which it can readily be consulted and utilised, whether by producer or by critic. Each of them is primarily a science of practice having a practical science founded upon it, although it must not for a moment be supposed, that the canons of Criticism, which is the practical branch of Poetic, have anything approaching to the authoritative character of the corresponding branch of Logic. As Conscience, not Ethic, is supreme in moral action, so here what may be called the poetic conscience is the ultimate arbiter of rightness in poetic production, not the canons of Criticism, which are themselves based on the judgments of the poetic conscience.

The first question, then, which meets us on the threshold of our present enquiry is this, What constitutes poetic imagination; or, Wherein does its characteristic difference as poetic consist? *Imagination*, taken simply, is the name we give to that mode of voluntary redintegration which differs from Thought by retaining, or immediately restoring, in its reproductions, the perceptual form of the imagery and its content offered by spontaneous redintegration, whereas Thought impresses upon them a new form of its own, namely the conceptual. Conscious selection is common to both modes of

THE FOUNDATIONS OF POETIC. 387

voluntary redintegration; but the interest, which is the motive of the selection, is always, in the case of imagination, an affectional interest (if I may use the word), that is, an interest of feeling, taken in the individual or particular object or objects to be dwelt on and reproduced, not the purely intellectual interest of discovering the general laws under which they fall, or of which they are instances. In imagination we always try to represent to ourselves how some individual scene or train of events would present itself to an actual spectator or participator in it, what feelings it would arouse in him, how the actions and events involved in it sprang from, or reacted on, the characters of the persons concerned in them, irrespective of the general classes or concepts to which they may be referred by thought, when we want to understand their laws, either as an addition to, or as a prerequisite of, the imaginative picturing of the scenes and events themselves. In a word, Imagination, whether employed in reproduction of the real, or invention of the fictitious, always aims at the representation of Persons and Things, Situations and Scenes, Actions and Events, in their concrete perceptual form, and as they appear or would appear in the ordinary common-sense mode of apprehending them, and not at their scientific or metaphysical analysis, or the discovery of the laws to which their analytically discerned constituents are subject. The kind of Truth which belongs to it is the result, not of scientific or metaphysical thought or reasoning, but of sympathetic Insight, sometimes misnamed Intuition.

But this differentiation of Imagination from Thought, both alike being modes of voluntary

Book III.
Ch. V.

§ 1.
Nature
and
Range
of
Poetic
Imagination

§ 1. Nature and Range of Poetic Imagination.

redintegration, is but preliminary to answering our present question, which concerns the differentiation of poetic from non-poetic imagination. Now just here it is, that our fundamental distinction between optional and imperious desires becomes significant. All imagination, being volitional, is set on foot and governed by some interest, that is to say, some desire affecting ourselves, the satisfaction of which is its end and motive. And this is a process which is constantly going on. Taken together with the transeunt or overt actions which it prompts from moment to moment, it is the staple of our conscious waking life, its main current or its main texture. When we are said to be doing nothing in particular, we are really feeling desires, framing imaginations, and speaking or moving in consequence. Now differences of kind in the desires which are the motives of imagination determine differences of kind in the imagination which is prompted by them. Poetic imagination, in the widest sense of the term, may be defined as that kind of imagination which is prompted by the foreseen pleasure taken in the exercise of imagination itself, irrespective of the particular object-matter which it is said to imagine, provided that the imagination of that object-matter is not forbidden by moral considerations. In poetic imagination we distinguish (though not necessarily recognising what we are doing) between ourselves as imaginative agents and ourselves as the Subjects of particular desires, and identify what we may call our true poetic self with the action of imagining, while leaving our ordinary self identified with the object-matter of that imaginative activity.

THE FOUNDATIONS OF POETIC.

What takes place is this. We wish to heighten the interest which we take in the representations of Persons and Things, Situations and Scenes, Actions and Events, which ordinary or non-poetic imagination supplies, in two large classes of cases; first, where the objects represented are themselves of a pleasurable character, including all cases of the ludicrous and the comic, and a heightened pleasure of the same kind is the motive of the imagination, and secondly, where the objects represented, though painful, disquieting, or terrible, in their own nature, including what is tragic as one extreme, yet do not involve our own individual fate or fortunes, or those of other real persons for whom we feel as for ourselves. And in both kinds of cases we wish to do this by a further exercise of imagination, having that heightened interest in view. We alter the situations, the circumstances, the actions, the powers, the characters, the thoughts and feelings, of the persons imagined, intensifying here, softening or obliterating there, comparing and contrasting one thing with another, until we have produced a new and coherent whole, a new imagination as we would have it, out of the imagination which we originally had, in short an ideal imagination out of an imagination simply.

The term *idealisation* in this sense describes in one word the specific difference of poetic imagination. And since this is throughout and necessarily imagination, its object is always the particular, never the general. Idealisation is always of an object, one or many, as imagined, that is, of some particular object or set of objects, while its essence consists in specialising that object or set of objects, since

BOOK III.
CH. V.

§ 1.
Nature
and
Range
of
Poetic
Imagination.

BOOK III.
CH. V.

§ 1.
Nature
and
Range
of
Poetic
Imagination.

only so can it either heighten its interest, or intensify its effect, at the same time keeping it an object of imagination as distinguished from thought. We can, it is true, reflect upon it as a case falling under a general law, but then we are not imagining it, but thinking about it in relation to its antecedents and consequents, its similars and dissimilars, and drawing a *Hence we may learn* from the consideration. Still less do we generalise the object itself. Generalisation is a process of conceptual thought, not of imagination; subsidiary indeed to imagination, as imagination in turn is subsidiary to it, but still not a part of imagination itself. Of what, or of whom, is Homer's Achilles, or Milton's Satan, a generalisation? Or how can either be generalised? They are on the contrary Idealisations; and one admitted charm of the Ideal consists in its uniqueness, in the *nihil simile aut secundum*. Poetry can only be called general, or said to seek or aim at the general, in the sense, either that things in general are its material, the Universe with all that it contains its object-matter, or that it has all mankind, if not as its producers, at any rate as its possible appreciators. It is from the Universe at large that our imagination first selects, then idealises, its objects; and the Ideal is the product of our poetic imagination, in its striving to heighten the interest inherent in ordinary non-poetic imagination, partly by direct modification of certain selected features, partly by removing features which have at the time no interest in themselves, or one which, if heightened, would interfere with the heightening of those originally selected; in all cases aiming at the gratification of the imaginative activity itself, not at the imagination of having our own personally felt desires of any other kind actually gratified.

This latter distinction, therefore, is necessary, as being, at the least, the companion-key to the most seemingly intricate problems of what is commonly called Æsthetic; indeed the existence of some of them as problems at all is owing solely to the neglect of it. The name *Æsthetic* itself is misleading. We too commonly take up questions belonging to a science so named as if pleasure or gratification simply was the end in view, and not one kind or class of gratifications only, namely, the gratification which we feel in the exercise of imagination, and which arises solely from that exercise.' And having thereby, to begin with, made Æsthetic commensurate with Hedonism in all branches of practice, and being consequently at a loss for the characteristic which justifies its distinct existence as Æsthetic, we have recourse in our embarrassment to some arbitrarily selected feature, either in the external world, such as Beauty or Grandeur, or in our reproduction of it, such as Fidelity of Imitation, or Insight into the Idea (as it is called) of natural objects or historical situations; and then, by erecting these into differentiating characteristics, create a science which lies open to endless objections and disputations, both as to the reality and as to the validity of the foundations on which it is erected.

Besides the uncertainty which is thus introduced into our conception of Æsthetic, the science itself, whatever may be taken as its *differentia*, is thereby brought also into collision with Ethic. For since the field covered by the two sciences is taken as exactly the same, each of them including all possible desires in its purview, and since the governing ends of both are admittedly ultimate, that is, pursued for their own sake alone, and not as means to any ulterior purpose, it is impossible to conceive either Æsthetic as subordinate to Ethic, or Ethic as subordinate to Æsthetic. Nor is it possible to find any third science capable of adjusting their claims and mediating between them, because any such science must be a science dealing with cases of choice simply as choice, which is the very character which, it has been shown in Chapter III., is borne by Ethic and by Ethic alone, as one of the two all-embracing sciences of practice, co-ordinate with Logic, the other member of the pair.

Consequently there is neither any issue from the difficulty raised by this mode of conceiving Æsthetic, nor any other way to avoid it than that which has here been taken, I mean that of limiting the scope of the whole science treating of poetic imagination in its widest sense, including its imagination of sense-presentations as such, which are the proper object of Æsthetic, by the special kind of gratification which poetic imagination aims at, namely, the pleasure which arises from its own exercise as imagination; while at the same time reserving to Ethic a negative voice, forbidding its pursuit in any case where that pursuit involves the infringement of any rule of morally right living. If this line of demarcation between Ethic and Poetic or Æsthetic is adopted, by allowing Ethic a negative control over them, a control consisting in forbidding some, but not commanding any, of the gratifications which require imagination for their enjoyment, then the domain of Poetic, or what is now called Æsthetic, will be co-extensive with that of an imaginative, artistic, and limited Hedonism. For the simple truth is, that, if the imagination could be exercised solely with the effect of its own gratification, without intensifying feelings and ideas, bad as well as good, experienced as personally affecting ourselves, and stimulating desires for other than purely imaginative gratifications, there would be little need for any moral control or ethical criticism, since there would be no difficulty in marking out theoretically a special domain, in which the principles and maxims of poetic imagination would reign with undisputed authority. Now since the principle on which this domain is demarcated and established is the distinction between poetic and non-poetic imagination, it follows that *Poetic*, not Æsthetic, is the only true name for the department of thought which deals with it; and this moreover is the name which Aristotle long ago gave it, a fact which I am glad to see recently brought into prominence by Professor S. H. Butcher's admirable work.[3]

Pleasures, then, of every kind, and pains of every kind, together with all kinds of circumstances which are their vehicle, imagery, or embodiment, are the object-matter of poetic imagination. But this object-matter in and upon which poetic imagination works, and which, because imagination is representational and depends on redintegration, belongs strictly speaking to the imagination, even when we actually see its vehicle in sense-presentation also; and moreover the desires, whether of obtaining the

---

[3] *Aristotle's Theory of Poetry and Fine Art.* With a Critical Text and a Translation of the *Poetics.* Macmillan, 1895.

*Book III.
Ch. V.*

*§ 1.
Nature
and
Range
of
Poetic
Imagination.*

pleasures or avoiding the pains, which that representation arouses; that is, all desires arising in the imaginative redintegration;—this whole object-matter must be sharply distinguished from the poetic imagination which deals with it, and from the purely poetic pleasure which that dealing with it affords. We must be able to detach both the pains and the pleasures represented as belonging to the object-matter, from the pleasure which either contemplating or imaginatively dealing with them affords; that is, we must detach them, as pleasures and pains to be obtained or avoided by ourselves, from our own pleasure in contemplating them, before we can enjoy the pleasure of purely poetic or purely æsthetic imagination.

The same object, say an object of sense, such as a flower, a landscape, a beautiful person, may yield both kinds of pleasure; but it is only so far as we detach the pleasure arising from the imagination of personally possessing and enjoying the object, whatever it may be, from the pleasure of simply contemplating it, that we can derive from it a purely æsthetic or poetic gratification. When a young Exquisite, in one of the most entertaining of modern novels,[4] exclaims, "All Paradise opens! Let me die eating ortolans to the sound of soft music!", we see at once that he is confusing these two kinds of pleasure, and expressing the lower in terms which are suitable only to the expression of the higher, the really æsthetic and imaginative pleasure. The contemptuous criticism to which such traits of epicureanism are justly amenable is the criticism, not of the moralist, but of the poet or

---

[4] *The Young Duke.* By Benjamin Disraeli (Lord Beaconsfield).

the æsthetician. It is the man of imagination who tells the gourmand that he ranks low in the scale of imaginative beings. To call in the moralist to tell him so would be doing the rogue too much honour. He is simply a comic personage.

All æsthetic pleasure in the first place, and then all strictly poetic pleasure, is founded, historically and psychologically speaking, upon pleasure inherent in some kind of object or action felt as immediately affecting ourselves; is engrafted, as it were, upon an utility or a service, which satisfies some natural want or personally felt desire of human nature; before by transcending that desire it becomes an æsthetic or poetic pleasure. All purely imaginative pleasure has its historical and psychological source in the represented and imagined satisfaction of desires, the pleasure of which imagined satisfaction is originally undistinguished from the pleasure of the act of imagining them, and is therefore originally identified with the imagination of actual possession or enjoyment.

But there is yet a deeper root than this, still speaking historically and psychologically, to which æsthetic and poetic imagination may in many cases be traced. I mean cases where a desire or pleasure of imagination of one kind is added to or engrafted on a desire or pleasure of imagination of another kind, both being felt as personally affecting ourselves, while only the latter is felt as the satisfaction of a necessary or unavoidable need. It is thus that the desire or imagined pleasure of gratifying the sense of flavours is distinguished from and then added to the desire or imagined pleasure of satisfying the pressing need of taking food simply. It is

BOOK III.
CH. V.

§ 1.
Nature
and
Range
of
Poetic
Imagination.

thus that the pleasure of personal adornment, or decoration of the dwelling, is added to that of satisfying the more urgent needs of clothing or of shelter; though here it is often maintained, that the pleasure taken in personal adornment has an origin of its own, quite independent of any felt need for clothing, or any other equally pressing necessity. If so, the desire for it will rank among ultimate desires and tendences; though the gratification of it will not of itself be an æsthetic pleasure, so long as it remains a pleasure undistinguished and undetached from that of personal enjoyment.

A similar phenomenon is found in the case of sounds uttered and heard as necessary means of expressing and communicating feelings and wants, upon which song and music are superposed as gratifications of the less pressing desire for melody and harmony. Similarly with the satisfaction of the sexual instinct and its supervening desire of beauty, nobility, or grace, in whatever these may be conceived to consist, in the objects of the impulse. The same with the expenditure of physical energy in bodily movements, which are a physiological necessity of our bodily structure and functions; energy which, when not exhausted by the necessary requirements of war, labour, or the chase, takes the shape of an imitation of these exercises in games and dances, the invention and development of which then become matters of imaginative art or skill. The same again with the development of the intellectual powers and their expression by picture-writing and articulate language: upon these necessities of thought and its expression are engrafted the play of fancy and its expression in tales, allegories, similitudes, riddles, jests, symbolical pictures and carvings, both of religious and non-religious significance, dramatic impersonations, and representations of real or imaginary scenes, histories, and incidents, whether of a serious or tragic, or of a ludicrous or humorous type. Again, the mere exercise of thought for its own sake may become a pleasure, even when it is known that it can lead to no result, as when a mathematician delights in filling up a few more decimal places in the expression for the incommensurable π, or the pleasure which a Neo-Scholastic might describe himself (in words slightly altered from the original) as deriving from thinking (of course *sub specie quadam æternitatis*) of everything in general and nothing in particular :

    Ich denke wie der Hegel denkt,
        Der in den Nebeln wohnet;
    Das *An-und-für-sich*, das mich lenkt,
        Ist Lohn der ewig lohnet.

Enough perhaps has been said to show the nature and importance of that transition, by which we pass from the imagination involved in dwelling upon simple desires and their gratification, first, to the imagination of more complex desires and gratifications, and then to the exercise of imagination itself, solely for the sake of the gratification inherent in its exercise, apart from our own personal interest in the objects imagined; which second step is the birth-place of æsthetic and poetic imagination.

The circumstance which at once enables and determines this transition, which results in the evolution of æsthetic and poetic imagination, is the fact, that desire is a redintegrative phenomenon

BOOK III.
CH. V.

§ 1.
Nature
and
Range
of
Poetic
Imagination.

which involves imagination of what might be, as well as simple retention or remembrance of what is or has been; or, briefly stated, that all desire is imagination, though not all imagination is desire of the thing imagined. Of æsthetic and poetic imagination, when so evolved, the Fine Arts and Poetry of Language in its highest forms are but the most highly refined and developed instances.

When these have been briefly surveyed, it will be found, if I mistake not, that certain desires and emotions, as actually and personally experienced, can be again taken up and incorporated with that poetic imagination from which, as actually and personally experienced, they have been distinguished, and that the poetic imagination of them thereby becomes the means of intensifying and enforcing them as part and parcel of that true self, with which poetic imagination alone was previously identified as the poetic conscience. The condition of such re-incorporation is, that the desires and emotions intended must be such as can make part of the true self as morally discerned, that is, as the object of volitional effort of the whole man, as well as being identified with the true self of poetic imagination. In such cases only it is, that the true self of the poet as poet, and the true self of the man as man, are one; or in other words, that the claims of his poetic and of his moral conscience are at once and equally satisfied.

Meantime we must not lose sight of the fact, that poetic imagination, whatever may be the case with that department of it which I have called æsthetic, not only includes the imagination of what is pleasurable, but extends to everything that has interest of any kind, even when that interest springs from what is painful or terrible. Every kind of object, every kind of action, every kind of feeling or emotion, painful as well as pleasurable, suffering, conflict, calamity, and misery, in every shape which is capable of being brought before us in imagination, may alike be the object-matter of poetic imagination; that is, any form or kind of them may become its motive, and be selected as the object of its idealising powers.

The reason is, that simply as human beings we cannot help taking an interest in whatever concerns humanity, and that, as said above in the case of pleasures, we know from our own experience something also of the meaning and significance of suffering and of conflict. But it is only in cases where we can contemplate suffering and conflict apart from ourselves and ours, only in cases where we do not feel their immediate pressure and impact, that this interest becomes, or can become, a motive for further freely performed imaginings, that is, acts of poetic imagination, which, by idealising, transform the imagination of pain into a pleasure.

I say by idealising, for in idealising scenes of suffering or of conflict, we mould and modify, not only the actions and events, but also the emotions, thoughts, resolves, and mental dispositions, of the actors, by imagining them to be such as enable the actors to sustain the conflict and endure the suffering with heightened energy and ennobling fortitude, and with clear comprehension of the situation in which they are called upon to suffer and to act. We imagine them, so to speak, as mentally and morally rising to the occasion, and endow them with something of our own imaginative sense of its moral grandeur and significance. In fact, by so idealising them we raise them to heroic proportions, and deprive those sufferings of their sting, which as suffering simply it would be impossible for us, without suffering, to imagine.

§ 2. From the foregoing account of the nature and objects of poetic imagination I return to the question of the point of view from which it is here treated. I mean its treatment as a case of volition selecting and adopting desires; by which we are placed at once, psychologically speaking, in the very heart and centre of the subject. Behind us, as it were, looking retrospectively, from the moment of volition, lies the whole complex material offered by sense-presentation and spontaneous redintegration, and before us lies the operation of poetic imagination, which is a special mode of voluntary redintegration. And this operation consists, first, in selecting for contemplation those parts of the material offered, which interest us solely for themselves as matters of contemplation, without any further motive than the mere contemplation of them affords; and secondly, in so altering and modifying them, by addition, retrenchment, or enhancement, that the gratification of contemplating them may be enhanced; but always without going beyond the pleasure of contemplating or dealing with them for their own sake alone.

Thus we have not begun at what some would consider the natural beginning of the subject, by pointing out that beauty, or any other special quality, is a quality immediately perceived in certain objects or collocations of objects of sense, in order to show in the next place how we are led by the pleasure it gives us to imitate it, surpass it, or produce its analogue, in works of our own. It may be true that beauty interests us immediately and for its own sake alone, but it does not follow, that all that so interests us is beauty. That is to say, the perception of beauty cannot serve as an explanation, or be the foundation, of the pleasure inherent in poetic imagination in its entirety. There may be many sources of poetically imaginative gratification. The true criterion of poetic imagination is not that the objects which it selects for contemplation are objects which we perceive to be beautiful, even in the widest sense of the word, but that they are objects, our interest in which arises in us uncompelled save by some intrinsic quality or qualities, apart from their producing any other gratification. By adopting our present central point of view we not only avoid hasty and embarrassing assumptions, and survey at once the whole possible range of poetic imagination, but we also see the necessary connection between its two functions, that of taking pleasure in contemplating what is offered, and that of creating new matter for pleasurable contemplation. For these two functions are naturally and closely connected by the simple fact, that poetic, including æsthetic, imagination is a mode of voluntary redintegration. It is at once the offspring of certain spontaneous desires, and the parent of the Arts by which new spontaneous desires of the same general kind are awakened and suggested.

Now the material which is offered to us by sense-presentation and spontaneous redintegration, under the laws of association, consists of two elements inseparably combined; first, its train of perceptual imagery, secondly the emotional content of that imagery; both of which have interest for us in their several ways. By Imagery is meant, as hitherto, not only visual perceptions and their combination, or perceptions of visible and tangible objects in combination, from which the name *imagery* is originally derived, but also all sense-presentations, to whatever sense they may belong, as they are reproduced and combined in redintegration; and that, whether the combination consists of perceptions of the same kind only, as in the case of sounds in music, or of perceptions of different kinds, as in the case of language, where sounds and visual and other perceptions, which are the meaning of the sounds, are closely united.

The imagery in this large, but yet psychologically strict, sense of the term, taken by itself, is again distinguishable, since it is derived from sense-presentations, into two inseparable elements, formal and material; the formal consisting of its figure, order of sequence, arrangement and proportion of parts, and the material consisting of the sense-qualities of all kinds, which occupy or are arranged in that figure, order, and proportion. The emotional content of the imagery, on the other hand, is not again distinguishable into form and content, but is itself a material element or constituent of a special kind, in the imagery taken as a whole, and is analogous, but also additional, to the material sense-element in the form of the imagery taken by itself, or in abstraction from its emotional content. This new or emotional content of the imagery is added in spontaneous redintegration, as already pointed out in Chapter I. of the present Book. And it may also be divided, according to what was there shown, into two classes, the personal and the pre-personal emotions, the former containing those emotions which we are said to feel towards persons, or rather which arise in imagery representing persons, such as anger, envy, shame, contempt, hatred, eros, love, religious emotion, and the latter those where, or so far as, persons do not make part of the imagery in which they arise, as in many forms of joy, grief, hope, fear, pride, despair. Both these kinds of emotion play an important part in differentiating the various kinds and degrees of Art and poetic imagination, but do not directly concern us at the present moment.

The main distinction between imagery derived from sense-presentation and the emotional content which it contains, or rather perhaps the division, founded on this distinction, between any imagery dwelt on alone and any imagery and its emotional content dwelt on together, is that which here concerns us; for in this distinction is found the first great line which divides poetic imagination as a whole, and consequently Poetic which is its science, into two chief departments, a lower which is Æsthetic, and a higher which is Poetic proper, that is, Poetic in a more restricted and special sense than that in which it embraces both departments, and gives its name to the science as a whole. In the general case, the imagery and its emotional content together are offered to volition by spontaneous redintegration, or by that and sense-presentations which are instantaneously taken up into it, so as to make parts of a single whole, bound together by association. The emotional content is the meaning or significance, of which the imagery, in which it is involved and brought before consciousness, is the framework, vehicle, or embodiment. But we can always, by abstraction, select either element as the special object of contemplation, and furthermore, in the reproductions or creations of Art, we can produce imagery the charm of which is wholly in itself, being wholly devoid of any extraneous emotional meaning or significance, to which it serves as a vehicle. This is often the case, for instance, in harmonies of colour, of shape or visible outline, of movement, of musical sounds, of proportion in solid masses of architectural structure, of colour, brilliancy, and shape, in the cutting, polishing, and setting, of precious stones. The gratifications which depend upon such abstract contemplation, or upon such isolated production of imagery alone, are strictly and properly æsthetic gratifications, or pleasures of the æsthetic imagination.

Such complete isolation, however, is impossible in the case of the emotional element, since all emotion requires some imagery or other, as its condition or vehicle. In order to bring into consciousness emotions from which poetic, as distinguished from æsthetic, gratification can be derived, we must select some imagery as the means of doing so; and the harmonies of this imagery must be such as to harmonise also with the emotions which we wish to arouse. As for instance the harmonies of colour, of form, of grouping, and of suggested movement or action, in a picture representing a real or imaginary group of persons, must not only not jar with, but must positively promote, the emotional meaning or significance of the group as a whole. They are subordinate but indispensable conditions of the total effect, which is of an emotional, that is, a strictly poetic character. By this dependence of the poetic or higher character on the æsthetic or lower, in works of Fine Art, the two departments are bound up into a single whole, which rightly takes its name from the higher department, which is that containing its τέλος and crowning glory, and by the requirements of which every kind of excellence belonging to the lower department must, in practice, be apportioned and regulated.

But although we may thus contrast the two departments of imaginative Art, æsthetic and poetic, as being devoted one to imagery alone, and the other to emotion subserved by imagery, it must not be supposed that pure imagery, the province of æsthetic taken alone, is wholly unemotional. The desire for æsthetic harmony, beauty, or charm, is itself an emotion, arising in the imagination and stimulating it, and its gratification by means of works of art, or by contemplation of natural scenes and objects, is in itself an emotional and imaginative gratification, though one which is *sui generis*. For in this case the emotional desire to be gratified is not a feeling additional to, or supervening upon, the imagery which is its vehicle, but is the desire for the heightening of some quality inherent in the imagery itself simply as imagery, that is, as a reproduction of sense-presentations.

Hence it is, that strictly æsthetic excellence of a high order can be appreciated only by those who by long study, or practice in producing or in watching it, have trained their perceptive powers to an exceptionally high degree of acuteness and subtilty. *Beauty* is the name for this inherent quality, including all its kinds and varieties, and in whatever imagery, natural or artificial, considered simply as capable of sense-presentation, it may be found. Emotional effects which supervene upon the imagery, on the other hand, require no special training of the perceptive powers, beyond what may be acquired by constant attentive observation of the scenes and incidents of ordinary life.[5] In all cases alike, however, the power of appreciation is identical, in one most essential respect, with the power of production; both are powers of imagination. In æsthetic the power of appreciating beauty is called, most inadequately, *Taste*; but there is no name at all for the corresponding power of appreciation in poetic. The power, for instance, of appreciating a play of Shakespere, a symphony of Beethoven, a landscape of Turner, a really great piece of sculpture, or a noble work of architecture, has no name by which it is at once connoted and designated. To call it the faculty essential to connoisseurship, or a branch of what, in judging Biblical literature, is nowadays dubbed "the higher criticism," is a clumsy periphrasis. For that which corresponds to it in production the most usual name is *Genius*. In appreciating production it is what I have spoken of above

---

[5] See G. F. Fechner's *Vorschule der Æsthetik*, Theil I., Abschnitt IX., for a full and admirable account of the way in which Association operates in giving emotional meaning to simple sense-presentations. This work from the hand of the illustrous founder of *Psycho-physik* is a valuable and thoroughgoing analysis of the phenomena and laws of imaginative or poetical Æsthetic, though it seems to belong to what I should call the "English-empirical" school of thought.

(Book III. Chap. III. § 6) as the poetic or imaginative conscience, a faculty which Genius also must possess as an essential ingredient.

§ 3. In order to take the next step in the differentiation of the field which is legitimately governed by poetic imagination, recourse must be had to a distinction which was mentioned in the foregoing Section as belonging to the imagery apart from its emotional content. I mean the distinction, which is found in every percept, between the inseparable elements of form and matter; time and space relations being the formal element intended, and the content of sensation, sound, colour, and so on, being the material. Though all the senses alike possess both elements in some degree, yet the degree in which the formal element is prominent is very different in different senses; and since the formal element is that upon which pleasures of admiration, which may properly be called æsthetic pleasures, in contrast to pleasures of enjoyment, are founded, we are at once enabled to mark off the perceptions of certain senses, including of course their images or representations, and refer them, notwithstanding that the pleasures belonging to them may be optional, to a lower and non-æsthetic region, and thus preclude them from being held to furnish, like the strictly æsthetic perceptions, an independent material to poetic imagination. Taste, smell, and the whole group of systemic sensations, are on this ground excluded from supplying the object-matter, or prescribing the aim, of imaginative creation. Their pleasures are pleasures of Enjoyment, Kant's *Annehmlichkeit*, and not pleasures of Admiration, Kant's *Schönheit*. See his *Kritik der*

Urtheilskraft, §§ 13 and 14, a passage to which I referred in my *Theory of Practice*, Vol. I., p. 69, when analysing the sensations, and endeavouring to bring out the importance of the foregoing difference between them. The three special senses, Sight, Hearing, and Touch, together with the feelings of effort and resistance which are so closely bound up with the latter, alone furnish the material element of perceptions which are capable of independent imaginative treatment; and accordingly it is only those objects which are the vehicles or embodiments of these perceptions, namely, pigments, audible sounds, and tangible objects, which can become the media of Fine Art, or the material in and upon which it works.

It is in the formal element of concrete sensation or perception that all proportion, all symmetry, all grace, all measurable intervals of time or tone or movement, are ultimately founded; and this is the chief and indeed wholly indispensable element in all pleasures of admiration, that is to say, in all Beauty. Taken alone, the material or sense-element of perception, or concrete sensation, yields only pleasure of enjoyment; the richest or purest colour, or sound, for instance, gives pleasure by its quality to sense only. And even contrast of colours or of sounds, however pleasing, cannot be called beautiful, unless some quantitative proportion in the contrast is perceivable, by which the pleasure is as it were intellectualised, and raised to the rank of a pleasure of admiration. The rich purple edging, sometimes seen along the horizon line of the sea, bounded by the sky above, and shading off below into the less deep blue of the nearer waters, would not be strictly beautiful apart from that form which it derives from its boundaries, and more especially from that long and distinct upper line, which divides it from the sky. Without this admixture of perceivable proportion, the pleasure continues one of simple enjoyment, like an agreeable coolness, or warmth, or flavour, or odour.

It follows, that those sensations which yield pleasures of enjoyment only are, not indeed wholly excluded from the domain of Fine Art, but are made therein wholly subordinate to the pleasures of admiration, which the special media, with which Fine Art works, may be made to yield. These special media, which as already said are pigments, sounds, and solid objects, are capable of a substantive treatment, by which beauty of proportion, in all its various modes, is either exhibited in or impressed upon them, and by which therefore they are made into products of Fine Art. But even then we are only in Æsthetic; the higher domain of more distinctly emotional imagination, the domain of emotion supervening upon imagery, which is the domain of Poetic in its stricter sense, is still not entered. Just as simple optional gratification of sense is subordinate to the laws and purposes of æsthetic imagination, so æsthetic beauty is in its turn subordinate to those of emotional and poetic imagination. Each higher domain has to accept, incorporate, and regulate the materials and the aims of the domain below it, which are indeed its own necessary pre-suppositions and limiting conditions.

The Fine Arts are thus determined by the different chief modes of substantive treatment, of which the media in which alone they can work are capable. Each of them takes its rise from some specific æsthetic pleasure derivable from that treatment. But this, though their immediate, is not their ultimate aim. As modes of poetic or emotional imagination, they have their ultimate end and guiding law in the combination of æsthetic pleasure with imaginative emotion, and in the more specific imaginative pleasure which results therefrom. As modes of poetic imagination, Poetry in Language, Music, Painting, Sculpture, and Architecture, owe their characteristic differences from one another, and the specific nature of the total effects which they severally produce, to the different relations which their two elements, imagery (including its æsthetic pleasure) and its emotional content, bear to one another in each of them. All alike produce their effect by combining these two elements into a single harmonious whole, though each combines them in a different way; but this again is primarily owing to the fact, that the media, in and with which they work, are different, and impose each its own limitations upon the *reproducenda*, that is, the total imagery offered by spontaneous redintegration, and upon the mode of bringing it before consciousness. Thus the poetry of language works with words, painting with colours, sculpture and architecture with solid masses of resisting matter, music with sounds not articulated into language. When the medium is selected, the main kind of effect to be produced is thereby determined also.

The next most obvious division of this group is into the imitative and the non-imitative arts; poetry, painting, and sculpture being imitative, that is, producing imagery which is moulded upon that of ordinary experience; while music and architecture are non-imitative, inasmuch as the sound-structures of the one and the mass-structures of the other are creations of imagery which have no prototype in the natural world, unless it be in previous creations of those arts themselves. In the imitative arts the imagery is an imagery of ideas, the non-imitative it is an imagery of pure sounds, or of pure figuration of solid masses, both of which are simple repetitions of sense-presentations with the aid of redintegration.

Coinciding with this distinction, which is drawn from the point of view of the producer, there is another which is drawn from that of the recipient, whether spectator or hearer. The imitative arts require much greater intellectual activity on the part of the recipient, in order to appreciate them properly, than is required of him by works of non-imitative art. In gazing at a noble building, for instance, the spectator, supposing him to have no technical knowledge of architecture, has simply to hold himself open to the impression which it produces upon him. Its beauty of outline, symmetry, proportion, grandeur, or elegance, will of themselves produce their effect upon his mind, without any attempt on his part to understand their meaning, or to estimate the problems which the architect has had to solve, or the difficulties which he has had to cope with.

So also with music. The succession of sounds, and simultaneities of sounds, the harmonies and melodies, the discords and their resolutions, and so on, speak a language of their own, that is, awaken emotional states of consciousness which stand in no need of further interpretation, and indeed the effect of which is marred, supposing the hearer be no musician, by any intellectual effort to understand them. You may indeed reflect upon the impression afterwards, but not at the time of receiving it. But the case is very different with the imitative arts, where the imagery is an imagery of ideas. Here it is requisite to understand the ideas, the words in poetry, the scenes, figures, and action, in painting and sculpture, as a condition of receiving the emotional impression which they convey, and so of enjoying the total effect of both the elements combined in the artist's work. Thus works, which, considered from the side of their production, are works of imitative art, are also works which, from the side of their appreciation, require an actively co-operating intelligence; while works of non-imitative art require, when considered from the side of their appreciation, an attitude of mind, studiously maintained indeed, but still one that is receptive merely.

Music and architecture are in fact devoid of imagery in the sense commonly attached to that term. The imagery of music consists solely in the sounds built up by the skill of the musician; that of architecture solely in the masses of solid matter piled together by the skill of the architect. I do not for a moment put the range of emotion commanded by architecture into comparison with the richness and subtilty of that commanded by music. The contrast between them in this respect is rather an instance of what was said above, as to the difference in total effect, produced by the several arts, being due to the different relations borne to each other by the imagery and emotional content, which their works combine; which difference again is primarily owing to the difference of the media in which they work, and of the senses to which those media appeal. The emotions which can be received from works of architecture, over and above those which are simply æsthetic, and attach immediately to their form, magnitude, proportion of parts, use of light and shade, and other structural qualities, (which again are to a great extent dependent on the particular variety of the specific kind of medium selected to work in, such as wood, iron, stone), are those of sublimity and awe, and a certain undefined feeling, when we are in presence of any work of real genius, of being in the presence of a living and personal being, who has of his own free will chosen and assumed that unique embodiment of enduring form which we see before us, and stands immovable as a silent but observant witness of the petty mortals who live their ephemeral lives around him.

The emotions which it is the special, though of course not the exclusive, property of architecture to arouse are thus few in number, but at the same time readily associable with others, and in this way extend over a wide range of thought and feeling. They have a certain vagueness, shown by the difficulty of analysing and defining them; which of course can only be done by assigning the images or ideas which constitute their framework. In the emotions of awe and sublimity, one essential element of the framework is undoubtedly the idea of power; another, I think, is that of mystery. When we feel awe, we have in our mind the idea of a power greater than our own, and possibly injurious, but the real nature and limits of which are unknown to us. This attribute of mystery distinguishes it from simple fear of power which we know to be injurious or hostile, but the nature or the limits of which we are also familiar with. In the emotion of sublimity we have the idea of mysterious power, but not that of possible injury, before us; the power being shown by the work performed or effect produced, and the mystery by the apparent absence of effort in its performance or production.

The frameworks of both these emotions, awe and sublimity, readily combine with the idea of personality, which is itself mysterious; and when a power which we feel as sublime is represented as exerted by a person for moral ends, we then have the emotion which is known as moral sublimity, or the moral sublime; our sense of its sublimity resting here also on the mysteriousness of the source, as well as on the degree, of the power, the latter being estimated by the effort which it would cost ourselves. For instance, as I have somewhere seen it admirably remarked, the intrepidity, and still more the joyful alacrity, with which a martyr faces torture or death for the sake of a noble or sacred cause, is felt as morally sublime, not because we think of him as making a great effort, or exercising an immense force of self-control, but precisely for the opposite reason, because, knowing the painfulness of the trial, we think of the ease with which he encounters it, the absence of effort in performing so difficult an action. The mystery, and consequently the sublimity, of the action lie in the ease or apparent absence of exertion on the part of the agent.

Music, we may with probability conjecture, owes its immense power of redintegrating the emotions in their entire range, without the intervention of the imagery of ideas, to there being a ramification of nerve-fibres transmitting the effects of minutely distinguishable sounds to all parts of the redintegrating portions of the brain, which are seats or centres of emotional feeling; while the sense-presented sounds themselves are not connected with visual, tactual, or other imagery of ideas, by any direct links of association. The emotions thus awakened would in this manner be extremely varied, and their changes would closely correspond with the minutest changes in the sound-imagery which evoked them. At the same time they would almost entirely escape definition or description, since no one of them would have any particular visual image or idea bound up with it; as would be the case, if their evoking sounds were parts of an articulated language understood by the hearers. Emotions in fact may be evoked by the most varied circumstances; any emotion, single in point of kind, say, for instance, grief or joy, love or anger, having a vast variety of possible causes as they are called, that is to say in reality, thoughts or ideas of various kinds, which are its framework or setting. The emotion also contains varieties within itself, minutely corresponding to the kinds, and varieties within the kinds, of its frameworks. But our only way to describe an emotion, and so render it definite, is to name a whole class or list of circumstances, in which either itself generally, or any one of its kinds or varieties, is found to arise. Now in music we are profoundly stirred by minutely varied emotions, unconnected with any imagery save that of the sounds which compose the piece of music which we listen to. The emotions so aroused may indeed often awake particular images or ideas, especially remembrances of past experiences; but the way to these images lies through the emotion, not the way to the emotion through the images. The reverse is the case with the imitative arts.

The necessary and original link of connection, psychologically speaking, between emotion and sense-presented musical sounds must undoubtedly be looked for in the natural cries to which we give utterance under the pressure of all varieties of pleasurable and painful feelings, whether of sense, emotion, or passion. Musical sounds, by their varieties of tone or colour chiefly, but also, in combination with these, by varieties in their pitch and loudness, recall these cries by similarity; and thus the basis is laid for the further elaboration of musical combinations, capable of stirring the emotions merely for the sake of the imaginative gratification involved in stirring them. On this topic I can hardly do better than refer to Fechner's work already cited, Theil I., Abschnitt XIII. 2. *Der directe Factor in der Musik,* pp. 158 to 177. Some other remarks of his, in the same work, on the impossibility, in the present immature state of psychophysical knowledge, of assigning the particular nerve-mechanism on which pleasure and pain depend for their existence as pleasure and pain, will also be found valuable, as well as what he says of the subsidiary position which all such psycho-physical explanations hold in sciences which, like Æsthetic, have particular branches of consciousness as their special object-matter. See Theil II., Abschnitt XLIII., pp. 263 to 272, for these remarks.

At the opposite pole to music, in respect of the relation between imagery and emotion, stand the two imitative arts of painting and sculpture. Their media, though different, are alike in conveying and arousing emotion by means of the imagery of ideas; and both arts alike are restricted, by their media, to represent a single moment in the course of a life, scene, or action, which thereby becomes fixed for ever as the centre of the whole, and as the point of departure from which we are challenged, as it were, to reconstruct the whole in imagination. In fact, the emotions to be aroused depend chiefly upon the imagination of the whole, in which the moment actually depicted or sculptured is but a single point, though that point is the point of origin governing the imagination. Hence the extreme importance, in both these arts, of selecting a typical or pregnant moment to represent, and of making it suggest the entire personality, or the entire action, from which it is taken.

The representation of persons, scenes, and actions, by the imitative arts gratifies the imagination by calling up emotions which interest us by resembling our own, without having the poignancy which they would have, if the case was really ours. A certain degree of verisimilitude is therefore a primary necessity in works of this kind. To depict or sculpture what purports to be a real person, scene, or action, and yet to depart flagrantly from what we know must be the truth of fact concerning it, destroys our interest in it as a real scene, and introduces discord instead of harmony into our imagination of the whole. In portraits and portrait-statues, therefore, and in historical painting generally, the limits of idealisation, as it is called, are comparatively narrow. The same law applies to that landscape painting which purports to represent real places, views, and passages of scenery. If, on the other hand, we know that the landscape painter means to depict an imaginary scene, or to use a real one simply as a theme on which to engraft his own ideas of beauty or sublimity, we readily follow him, provided only he keeps within the wider limits of what is physically possible.

But the most unlovely scenery, like the most homely face, may be rendered inexpressibly magnetic in a picture, without any departure from the plain truth of fact, by a painter of genius. The *Avenue of Middelharnis*, a landscape by Hobbema, now in our National Gallery (Peel Collection), representing a straight road running through the level and monotonously regular fields of Holland, is a striking instance, which is, I think, generally regarded as one of the great triumphs of landscape painting.[1] The effect is apparently wrought by using the upright parallel lines of two rows of pruned and scraggy trees to emphasise and yet relieve the characteristic flatness and uniformity of a tract of country in which the hand of man is everywhere visible. Yet by this simple and

[1] I remember hearing this pointed out, many years ago, by a distinguished critic and poet, to a party of visitors to the Gallery. [The late Professor F. T. Palgrave, taken from us since this note was penned.]

strictly realistic treatment the scene is idealised, and the spectator made to feel, without the use of language, the inalienable loveableness inherent in every portion, however homely, of the habitable globe. The genuinely imaginative character of this treatment is evident from the fact, that, though we are made so to think of the landscape, we are not for a moment inspired with a wish to visit it or to live there.

The limits of idealisation, again, are still wider in figure painting, than even in imaginary or freely treated landscape. Here the painter is not restricted even to what is physically possible, provided his intention is manifest, either to take a subject from mythology, theology, or romance, or to originate out of his own imaginative stores some fresh embodiment of supernatural agents, or some new intervention of supernatural power. Some of the noblest paintings in the world belong to this class, Michael Angelo's fresco *The Creation of Eve*, on the ceiling of the Sistine Chapel in the Vatican; Guido's *Aurora*, also a ceiling fresco; Titian's *Assumption of the Virgin* at Venice; and Raphael's *Sistine Madonna* at Dresden, for instance. The painter is here restricted to apparent possibility only; that is, he must avoid producing the impression that the persons or actions depicted are impossible. If, as is universally allowed, it is a legitimate and fertile source of poetic gratification to give the rein to imagination in depicting such scenes at all, then the painter may also challenge our imagination to follow him in depicting them, so long as the laws which govern imaginary, as distinguished from physically real, possibility are obeyed, and continue uninfringed.

While the general fact, that poetic gratification is the gratification of an optional desire, thus in some cases makes reality, or truth of fact, the limit of embellishment, or what is commonly called idealisation, there are other cases in which the same general fact demands that we should use idealisation to impose limits on the representation of reality. There is no doubt that simple and exact imitation of nature gratifies a desire of imagination, as when we take pleasure in the reflection of objects in water or in a glass. At the same time the desire for it, though strictly imaginative, and the gratification therefore artistically legitimate, does not arise from any emotional content supervening on the imagery; and the pleasure of it must therefore be held to belong to æsthetic, not strictly poetic, imagination. It involves moreover a distinct perception of the difference between the reality and its representation. A work of imitative art which could be mistaken for the real object imitated would not permanently gratify the imagination. For the work would then seem to be part of our own real environment, and as such to be possibly an object of desires of personal possession or enjoyment on our part, by standing in real relations to ourselves; and even this expectation it would disappoint on closer inspection. Just as in the contemplation of real objects, persons, and scenery, our æsthetic and poetic gratification rests on abstracting from their use or value in satisfying desires of actual possession or enjoyment, so, in works of art, to present them as realities would be to undo this abstraction, and compel us to perform it over again, before we could derive æsthetic or poetic pleasure from the contemplation of them.

Statuary, from the obviously solid nature of the media which it employs, and from its appealing in consequence to the sense of touch as well as sight, comes in many cases very near to the extreme limit of allowable reality. I mean cases where it is of life size, and not placed in such positions or surrounded by such accompaniments as absolutely preclude the suggestion of its being the reality which it represents. This, I apprehend, is the really valid ground of the objection to coloured statues, and not the idea that statuary would be thereby trespassing on the sphere of painting. The addition of colour would be no trespass, but a legitimate and valuable combination, supposing the main principle, above stated, of all fine art were not infringed. It would seem that colour, and even metallic ornaments and trappings, may with great advantage be used to enhance the effect of statuary, in certain positions and circumstances, and especially when the statuary is part of the adornment of architectural work; provided always that every possible suggestion of reality is avoided, and provided also that portrait-statues, which are τέλη of themselves, are not used simply as pieces of ornament, or for the merely subsidiary purpose of enhancing the effect of the buildings in or about which they are placed. Portrait-statues, when properly placed in noble buildings, or in open spaces, may and often do add to the effect of the environment in which they are placed in a different way from this, namely, through the medium of association. The environment and the statue give additional value to each other. The environment becomes a shrine, enhancing the effect of the statue, without any loss of its own dignity; the statue enhances the effect of the environment by association with the personal emotions which are called up by the character whom it represents.

In the Poetry of Language we have an art the medium of which is of a mixed nature, namely, words conveying meaning or ideas. It is mixed, because words are sounds capable of producing a musical effect, as well as of conveying meaning. But of these two elements in its medium, the meaning is the most fundamental and important, inasmuch as, without it, words would be reduced to vocal sounds, which would be a kind of music, and therefore incapable of serving as the foundation of another art separate from music. On the other hand, language conveying meaning, and in virtue of conveying it, is the independent and underived element in it as the medium of poetry, making it as it were the stem on which its musical element is engrafted. Nevertheless it does not become the medium of poetry, or even of its æsthetic department, until some use is made of its musical element. When emotion is conveyed by language having meaning, in combination with some use of the musical element, however slight, some form of poetry is the result. But this need not involve the development of the musical element into any form of metre or verse. We then have poetry in the form of rhythmical and cadenced prose. It should be remarked, however, that in popular usage the term *poetry* is restricted to verse compositions, and opposed to compositions in prose. This may have its convenience as a popular mode of speaking, and is no doubt favoured by the alliteration in the two names. Nevertheless, as determined by the analysis of poetic imagination, and its relation to its vehicle, language, the true opposite to prose is not poetry but verse.

In all poetry, therefore, the element of sound is subsidiary to that of meaning, and is used to give it a directly emotional effect, over and above that which is derived from the imagery of ideas. The musical element is the source of accent, cadence, rhythm, metre, verse, alliteration, assonance, and rhyme, in poetry. It is also the parent of one distinct kind of poetry, the lyrical, used as directly expressive of emotion, as distinguished from those kinds which convey emotion indirectly by description, narration, or dialogue. In these latter kinds, where poetry is more directly imitative, it has an immense advantage over the other imitative arts, painting and sculpture, in that it is able to represent the whole of a life, or the whole of any series of actions and events, and therein to illustrate one part of the action by another, belonging either to another period of it, or to other scenes and actions extraneous to the one in hand, and is not restricted to the presentment of a single moment in a single action. It can also represent the same action from different points of view, and can give the reflections of the poet, or of the persons whom he introduces, upon their own actions, ideas, motives, and feelings. It is, in short, as universal in its range as language itself, which is its medium.

It is in poetry, therefore, that we most clearly see what is meant by the gratification of imagination, which is the distinctive purpose of all æsthetic and poetic art. What is essential to it is, not that the ideas presented, or their accompanying emotions should be beautiful, or strictly true to an actual reality, or noble, or refined, or sublime, but that they should be interesting to beings who are capable of entertaining similar ideas, and experiencing similar emotions, in their own case. It is essential to this interest that we should not be directly concerned ourselves in the scenes, actions, or events represented, or have part ourselves in the emotions of which they are the imagery. It is impossible to derive poetic gratification from a catastrophe, however magnificent in its circumstances, or heart-stirring in its emotional effects, if you yourself or those dear to you, or any living beings with whom you are in sympathy, are actually involved in it. In other words, the interest which you feel in it, if it is to be æsthetic or poetic, must be at once intrinsic and not compelled. Poetry and the other Fine Arts are essentially, in the producers the exercise of energies, in the recipients the stimulus of functions, which aim at nothing but their own inherent gratification; and if in any respect they begin to aim at instructing, or at conveying a moral, or any kind of practical or scientific doctrine, in that respect, and to that extent, they cease to bear the specific character of Poetry and Fine Art. I do not say, that they wholly cease to bear that character; and owing partly to the intellectual character borne by all poetry of which language is the vehicle, the line dividing the two kinds of purpose is often very difficult to trace. In some cases also, as already noted, a complete combination of the two, in spite of their recognised distinctness, appears to be effected. But this is a point to which we shall have to return in a later Section.

The degree in which æsthetic or poetic gratification can be derived from presenting, or having presented to us, realistic or imaginary horrors and deformities, either of sense, of ideas, or of emotions, varies with different persons, and with different states of education and refinement. But it may, I think, be laid down as an universal rule of art, that, whenever anything is introduced which is felt as a horror or deformity, it can only be done by making it subservient to the total effect of the whole work, and not allowing it to dominate, or imprint its own character upon the impression resulting from the work as a whole, which in that case would forfeit its claim to be a work productive of poetic gratification. When pleasure is taken in the representation of horrors or deformities for their own sake; that is to say, unless they are obliterated and resolved, as discords in music, in or by the total result to which they are made to contribute; the pleasure so taken in them for their own sake is always the gratification of a desire felt as immediately affecting ourselves, a desire springing from some natural or necessary appetite or passion, and not of a desire for any additional grace or excellence in our mode of representing or imagining them. Many of the pleas which are sometimes put forward for what is euphemistically termed "realism," in cases of this sort, rest upon defiance or forgetfulness of this cardinal distinction. Quite apart from any objection which might lie against such cases on moral grounds, it should never be forgotten, that pleasures of the imagination simply are one thing, pleasures of the æsthetic and poetic imagination are another.

BOOK III.
CH. V
§ 3.
The
Fine Arts.

It will not here, I think, be necessary to apply this, or the other distinctions which have been set forth above, to the various subdivisions of the Fine Arts, or to the arts subservient to them, or to the combinations of one branch with another; to Vocal and Operatic Music, for instance, to Dancing, to Dramatic Acting, to Recitation, or to the various Decorative Arts, which are special applications of painting and sculpture, as well in separation as in combination. It is sufficiently obvious that the main distinction or law, which defines and governs the Fine Arts, must extend to all their parts, combinations, and ministrants, so far as these are contributory to the main purpose of the whole system which they compose or support. The main and governing end or purpose of a drama, for instance, apart from the imaginative pleasure involved in producing it, is to produce, both in those who read it and in those who see and hear it acted, a certain emotional and imaginative effect. To be acted is not its main purpose, any more than to produce statues or pictures is the main purpose of sculpture or of painting. These are the means, special to those arts, by which their main purpose, the production of an emotional and imaginative effect, is attained. So also both the acting and the reading of a drama are alike means, though widely different means, by which its ultimate end is reached. In reading a drama, you have to imagine, if possible, the actual presentment for yourself; in seeing and hearing it acted, you take that actual presentment from others.

Yet it should not be forgotten, that what we must now logically treat as subordinate or ministerial departments of Fine Art were historically prior to its complete development, and as it were the seed out of which it sprang. Dancing and Acting were prior conditions of written Dramas; Buildings and their Decoration the prior condition of Architecture; rude singing and ruder instrumentation the prior condititions of Lyrical Poetry, and the intricacies of modern Music; Ornamentation of buildings, weapons, tools, and utensils, the prior condition of Painting and Sculpture. The Fine Arts which now, as modes of emotional and creative imagination, stand as it were erect, independent, and sovereign, giving law to their subordinates and ministrants, have sprung from beginnings which were indistinguishable from those of the subordinates and ministrants, on which they now impose their laws. Yet from first to last of this marvellous history, the same fundamental distinction, characteristic of its nature, is discernible, as the general fact or law which has governed its whole development, and separated Fine Art in all its branches, whether sovereign or subordinate, from arts which minister to simple utilities, and to necessary but less exalted requirements of human nature; I mean the twofold fact, first, that all desire arises in and pre-supposes imagination of something which can be actually presented only in the future, and secondly, that man is endowed with the capacity of taking pleasure in and desiring the exercise of imagination for its own sake, apart from the prospect, or even of the imagination, of himself sharing in the scenes, actions, or objects imagined, and irrespective of the time, past, present, or future, to which their imagined existence or enactment may be referred. The strengthening and development of his own imaginative power is the only part of this desire, which is actually experienced as personal to himself.

§ 4. The law of what I may call non-selfish gratification, then, on which I have so much insisted, is a law which differentiates poetic imagination, in all its branches and works, from other functions and departments of human activity. It is now necessary to say a few words concerning another law which, while operating within this sphere, serves to bring it into connection with man's other functions and spheres of action. This law is nothing but the expression of the most universal condition to be observed, in order to secure the gratifications which we have been considering. It has been appealed to already in several parts of the foregoing Section, and the facts therein mentioned and described furnish some of the evidence on which it is founded. It may be called the Law of Harmony, meaning thereby, not the harmony between a work of art and the desires which it gratifies, which would be only another name for the fact of their gratification, but a harmony attaching to works of art themselves, and constituting their most essential characteristic. It may be considered as falling under two heads, (1) harmony between the several parts or features of a work of art *inter se*, whereby they together produce the effect of an accordant and united whole, and (2) harmony between a work of art and the environment in which it is placed, or the circumstances in which it is to be enjoyed.

These requirements are nothing more than the appearance in the sphere of poetic imagination, and in application to its productions, of that universal requirement of man's rational nature, which has been shown, in earlier Chapters, to lie at the root of Conception and Thought, and indeed of all Voluntary Redintegration, namely, the need of escaping the pain of disorder and disappointed expectation. We have already seen in Chapter IV., how this requirement operates in determining the forms of conception, judgment, and reasoning; namely, by making conceptual unity the condition of all reasoned knowledge of matters of fact, whether general or particular. But this is its operation in a domain where the ruling volitional purpose is to discover and know what the Course of Nature is, not to enjoy the imagination of it, or effect alterations which may heighten that enjoyment. To enjoy the imagination of certain objects, and to produce further imaginative enjoyment of certain kinds, are the purposes of æsthetic and poetic imagination. In effecting both purposes, thought is involved, as a necessary though subsidiary factor. It is obvious, therefore, that the principle of avoiding the pain of disorder and disappointed expectation, upon which all Thought as a volitional process depends, must be a primary essential in all volitional processes, whatever their specific purpose may be, in which Thought is an essential ingredient. In other words, only those natural objects and those art-products can be productive of æsthetic and poetic pleasure, which satisfy the condition of having their own parts and features in harmony with one another, and of being themselves in harmony with the environment to which they belong.

The difference between the two cases, of harmony in thought and harmony in poetic imagination, is simply a difference in the standard and criterion by which the harmony is judged; a difference which depends on that of the ends aimed at by thought taken by itself on the one hand, and by poetic imagination involving thought on the other. In poetic imagination we attend to and produce only what satisfies, or promises to satisfy, the desire of heightening certain kinds of imaginative pleasure. We move, in each particular instance, within a certain limited field of perceptions, and perceptual modifications, of sense, form, imagery, and emotion. But this in no wise alters the stringency of the law, that harmony between our selected and combined perceptions is an essential condition of their giving us imaginative pleasure. To neglect this rule is to destroy the pleasure which we anticipate and aim at; notwithstanding that what constitutes harmony will be decided very differently by different persons, and the judgments prevalent in one state of society and culture very different from those prevalent in another. The only ultimate standard of harmony, for every individual, consists in the gratification of his own perceptive and imaginative powers. At every step which he takes in this imaginative process he is guided by what I have called his poetic conscience, that is, the immediate perception which he has of that step harmonising or not harmonising with those already taken, and of its conducing or not conducing to the harmony of what is as yet a future dimly foreshadowed whole.

But he has no decisive or final perception of its poetic or artistic rightness, until the whole work is complete, when the harmony of the total effect produced is again the final criterion of the poetic or artistic rightness of the gratification which, in the process, it has afforded to his perceptive and imaginative powers, and of that which it will continue to afford them as a completed whole. The criterion of the artistically right exercise of these powers lies within the perceptive and imaginative powers themselves.

At the same time, and chiefly for this very reason, these powers are highly educable, and the very recognition that harmony is the fundamental law of their gratification is an effective means of educating them, inasmuch as it affords an irrecusable principle of criticism, by reference to which individual judgments can be compared with one another. It is to the main constituents in the composition of any work of art that the question of harmony is first put, when we criticise it. These, as already said, are, first, the imagery, secondly the supervening emotional content; of which again the imagery is divisible into form and sense-content, and the emotional content into personal and pre-personal emotion. The first question is, Does each of these constituents, the imagery and the emotional content, yield a harmony between its own parts? The second, Do the two constituents, taken each as a whole, harmonise with each other? Then comes the final question, Does the work as a whole harmonise with the surroundings, with which it is intended to be associated?

BOOK III.
CH. V.
§ 4.
The Law of Harmony.

These remarks describe the application of the principle from the point of view occupied by the percipient or critic of works of art; the artist or producer deals with the question in a different way. Imagination does not go to work by first distinguishing the elements, of which whatever it produces must consist, and so criticising, if I may say so, the product before it is produced. It instinctively feels that harmony is essential, and operates on its lines as the living motive of its own nature as an action. Just as a reasoner reasons logically without waiting to analyse his reasoning into concepts, judgments, and syllogisms, or enquiring what are the middle terms of the conclusions which he successively draws, so the imaginative artist, without analysing his imaginations, as he proceeds, into form and content, imagery and emotion, or stopping to consider in what the harmony belonging to them must consist, simply gives rein to his imagination, though attentive at every step to the gratification which he receives from it as a conscious activity, of which harmony is the inherent and necessary law.

In this imaginative action he is governed by his own special preferences and peculiar insights; and thus his treatment of any subject in imitative art, or the creation of any musical or architectural structure in non-imitative, that is to say, the movement of his imagination in dealing with its material, becomes stamped with the character of his own individual personality, which individuality of character is known as *Style*. Style is the exponent of the artist's originality, and affords in some degree a measure of his imaginative power, on the growth and development of which its changes are dependent. When his power ceases to develop and expand, while the artist still continues to produce, his style becomes fixed, and tends to degenerate into Mannerism. This may be considered as stereotyped style; he then imitates himself. Moreover the style, and still more easily the manner, of an imaginative artist can be imitated by others. But what was style in the originator is not style in the imitator, since it is not the exponent of his own imaginative power. Neither in the imitator is it capable of degenerating into mannerism. If it degenerates, it degenerates into Caricature, and usually into caricature of the mannerisms of the originator.

§ 5. In thus briefly touching upon style and mannerism, in which poetic imagination is caught red-handed, so to speak, in the act of dealing with the material which it selects and with the works which it produces, we come round once more to the producer's side of the subject, and now, by putting producing agency and its product together, can see the object-matter of Poetic as a single and complete whole. There still remains, however, one aspect of the subject, which it will be well to consider more particularly. I mean the relation in which the exercise of imagination for the purpose of its own gratification stands to the feelings and ideas which are its object-matter, and by idealising which its own purpose is attained. Does it tend to promote and enforce them as realities by treating them in that idealising manner, or does it tend on the contrary to affect them with its own character of comparative unreality, by

§ 5. Relations between Artistic and Non-artistic Imagination.

making their capacity for ministering to imaginative gratification seem to be their principal or possibly their sole function? In short, the relation which poetical imagination bears to the rest of human activity, and the development of other purposes and powers, is the subject before us. Several questions of great interest in the theory of art belong to this border-land.

It has been shown above, that æsthetic pleasures are originally, in most if not all instances, engrafted upon some utility or other, the attainment of which is pre-supposed as their condition. It is true that the products of the principal Fine Arts, in their full development, stand in a great degree independently on their own footing, not resting on the prior satisfaction of any specific non-imaginative need; but even here there is one notable exception, namely that of architecture. Unless a material structure satisfies the natural wants, principally shelter, for which it is primarily erected, and is serviceable in the way of common utility and convenience, it cannot be a work of architecture, however beautiful, graceful, noble, or imposing, in its outline and proportions. The knowledge of its unserviceableness in point of utility would be in conflict with our enjoyment of it as a work of fine art, by making it produce the impression of unsatisfied need. A triumphal arch, for instance, erected in an open plain, not spanning some important avenue, either at its entrance or some marked point in its course, would strike us at once as a mere waste of skill and labour, and entirely destroy the pleasure we might otherwise derive from its architectural qualities. The same is true of decorative art in all its branches. All Fine Art, then, we may say, is founded originally in satisfied utility, and in some cases continues dependent upon it to the last. It is conditioned by the utility out of which it arises, and with which it is contrasted. And thus, when we look at the Fine Arts in their full development, a distinction is plainly to be drawn between those which continue throughout to be conditioned upon the prior satisfaction of some specific non-artistic utility, and those which are cut loose from such specific dependence, and have a free self-centred existence of their own.

§ 5. Relations between Artistic and Non-artistic Imagination.

But even those arts which belong to the second member of the above division, arts which have an independent and self-centred existence of their own, are subservient to ends which are of a non-artistic nature, and become so by means and in virtue of their own artistic qualities. They can be used for purposes which are not their own, that is, are not purposes of poetic gratification, but which they necessarily though incidentally promote by attaining their own purposes, and consequently without their works ceasing to be genuine works of fine art. These works may therefore be said to combine utilities of two kinds, the first represented by those ends or purposes, upon the satisfaction of which they were originally founded, though now cut loose from that foundation, and the second by those the satisfaction of which is dependent upon them, and is attained by making use of their artistic character. Not that this circumstance is necessarily confined to arts of the second member of the above division, that is, to arts which have

§ 5.
Relations between Artistic and Non-artistic Imagination.

an independent and self-centred existence. It may be met with in both members alike; but it is only in the latter that questions of importance in the domain of Poetic are distinctly brought before us.

To begin, however, at the lower end of the scale, and with a case which, strictly speaking, is not even of æsthetic rank, the production of attractive flavours in gastronomy not only gratifies the optional desire for new and refined satisfactions of the sense of taste, but as a stimulus to appetite, in cases where the taking of necessary food is repugnant, and especially in illness, it becomes itself a ministrant to health.

Amusements also, and games requiring strength or skill, both outdoor and indoor, which were originally invented and developed from motives of passing the time, that is, occupying the imagination agreably, become the means of fostering such degrees of strength and skill as may be afterwards efficiently employed in the most serious services; as we see recognised, for instance, in a favourite, though apocryphal, English dictum, to the effect that the Battle of Waterloo was won in the Playing-fields of Eton. Moreover recreations and diversions of all kinds, and change of scenes and occupations, as in travelling, have a beneficial effect upon health and vigour, roughly proportionate to the degree of enjoyment which they afford, whether they are or are not resorted to for health's sake in the first instance.

Coming to a higher level of the scale, painting and sculpture, both in decoration and in independent works, owe to their artistic qualities the power which they undoubtedly possess, of subserving ulterior purposes which were not among the motives out of which they originated, or by which they were developed. Historical painting, for instance, becomes useful as an exact and reliable record of scenes and events, costume, manners, and so on; thus subserving the serious and non-artistic purposes of history and knowledge. The same with portrait-painting. So also, in sculpture, with sepulchral and other monuments. They become useful as records and documents of facts. They stimulate patriotic and family feeling, the love of honour and renown, and bind the generations each to each. Yet these are not their immediate purpose, or essential to their character, as works of fine art.

So also in architecture, which is the sole instance of a main department of fine art continuing to the end to be conditioned upon its satisfying non-artistic and imperative needs, it is plain that the emotions of awe and sublimity, which it is its special prerogative to arouse, are emotions which readily combine with and may be used to promote religious or patriotic feeling and resolve. Yet religious or patriotic feeling or resolve is not the immediate purpose of art; and as desires, or mental acts, in the persons who feel or form them, they are not simply imaginative, but serious and moral desires and volitions, affecting us immediately and personally.

The same is true also of music, many kinds of which, belonging both to its higher and its lower flights as judged by an artistic standard, subserve the non-artistic purpose of stimulating and sustaining, at one time religious emotion, at another

§ 5. Relations between Artistic and Non-artistic Imagination.

patriotic or martial ardour; I mean the feelings themselves as actually and personally experienced, not their echoes, which belong to art, and are luxuries of poetic imagination. Music as an art-product possesses the latter as its own, and subserves the former as an extraneous result, though it may itself have arisen out of the desire and effort to intensify, by expressing, the very same personally felt emotions which, when completed as a work of art, it again subserves and promotes. The artistic enjoyment of a personally felt emotion, which is the purpose of art, is one thing, the intensification of that emotion as a permanent factor in life and conduct, is another. It is only the desire for artistic enjoyment which properly belongs to the domain of poetic imagination.

The essential characteristic of all artistic, that is, æsthetic and poetic, gratification consists, as already said, not in the specific nature of the feelings or emotions expressed, as feelings or emotions simply, for all feelings and emotions alike, with their imagery, are the materials or object-matter with which art is concerned, but in the nature of the pleasures which are inherent in imagination as an action or activity, and which constitute the purpose of our imaginatively dealing with and expressing them. When an emotion is felt as a matter of personal experience and concern, it is no longer felt as belonging to the domain of art, and is no longer a poetic gratification, however closely the two characters may be combined in it. When on the other hand it is felt as a pleasure solely in its character of an echo or reflection of what might be felt as a matter of personal experience and concern, then it is that it becomes and is felt as a poetic gratification belonging to the domain of art.

But in this latter case, supposing it to lead to our actually experiencing the same emotion as a matter of personal concern, the art to which it belongs is then subserving a purpose extraneous to its own ; and this it does without ceasing to be art, that is, without ceasing to give the artistic pleasure of the echoed emotion, at any rate to persons in whom the experience of the real or actually felt emotion is not aroused. The feelings with which we listen to sacred music in religious services, or to the performance of sacred Oratorios, Handel's *Messiah* for instance, are cases illustrating what is intended. For even supposing the same person to be sensitive alike to the real and to the echoed emotion, it is doubtful whether he can be alike sensitive to both at one and the same time, whether he does not experience an alternation between the two sensitivities, while listening to the whole.

When we take the case of poetry as an art employing language alone as its medium, we find that the services rendered by purely artistic qualities and perfections to ends extraneous to art become at once more numerous and more easily traceable. This is plainly owing to the poetic medium, language, being the universal medium of expressing and communicating ideas. In prose, to begin with, the beauties of cadence and rhythm, of well-balanced sentences and well-rounded periods, of movements slow or rapid, solemn or abrupt, in harmony with the ideas and feelings which they convey, the artistic employment of opposition and climax, in short all the devices of Rhetoric, are

BOOK III.
CH. V.

§ 5.
Relations between Artistic and Non-artistic Imagination.

adopted and applied, not for gratification only, but with the ulterior and dominant purpose of effectively persuading; as in legal pleadings, political harangues, and so on. But persuasion to take this or that practical decision, or to adopt this or that course of action, is no purpose of any poetic or imaginative art, which is devoted solely to please, though to please in a special manner, and the ends of which in their own sphere are self-justifying and ultimate.

In verse again, to begin with its humblest services to purposes other than its own, we see its forms employed as a *memoria technica*, to keep within call of memory simple facts of history or chronology, as in *Thirty days hath September*, etc., and *The Romans in England once bore sway*, etc.; or simple maxims, such as the *Rule of the Road;* or bits of proverbial folk-lore, such as *The Oak and the Ash*. Next there is its use in epigram, and in giving pungency to raillery, retort, jest, sarcasm, ridicule, and satire; all of which gratify some real and actually experienced feeling, over and above the gratification of the purely imaginative desires of poetry, and gratify it by using that poetic gratification as a means.

Next to this we have some more general purpose aimed at by greater and more systematic employment of similar artistic means, as in Didactic poetry of many different kinds; philosophic or scientific, as in Empedocles, Parmenides, Lucretius, Giordano Bruno; satirical, with a moral purpose, as in Juvenal, Persius, Pope, Johnson; political, as in Dryden; biographical, as in Wordsworth's *Prelude;* and so on. Yet to teach, instruct, plead

THE FOUNDATIONS OF POETIC.

a political cause, elevate the moral tone, depict mental growth, are no purposes of poetic art, which aims solely at gratifying desires of imagination, and finds in that gratification its sole reward.

Lastly in some of the very highest works of emotional and imaginative poetry we find a moral and religious purpose aimed at, and bound up inseparably with the effect which they aim at and produce as works of imaginative art. Dante's *Divina Commedia* is a marvellous and, on a great scale, so far as I know, the only instance of this close and inseparable combination. It is parallel in this particular, though in a far more complex art, and on a very much larger scale, to Handel's *Messiah* in music, which latter leans moreover on the aid of interpretative words, which do not strictly belong to music, in order to interpret and enforce the significance of pure sound.

The specific character of the *Divina Commedia* seems to consist in the equal intensity with which the poet feels the two desires, first of heightening both for himself and for his readers the real and actually felt religious emotion, together with those ideas which are to him its essential framework or embodiment, and secondly of heightening the imaginative representation which is their echo. For him the two purposes are inseparable, alike ultimate, and mutually sustain and subserve each other. The man and the poet are one. Yet the length and complexity of the poem, with its varied imagery, scenes, incidents, and didactic discourses, facilitate the discrimination of the two equally dominant purposes, by necessarily requiring the alternation of passages, in which now the one purpose, now the

BOOK III.
CH. V.

§ 5.
Relations between Artistic and Non-artistic Imagination.

other, is principally operative. Nevertheless, the unity of the whole is not thereby destroyed. For in the case of a poem which we can read, lay aside, and again recur to, reading different parts at different times, we are not compelled to keep both kinds of purposes in view together, and consequently not compelled to choose exclusively between them. The poetic beauty can be enjoyed at one time, the dominant religious emotion, which it is equally the poet's purpose to bring home to us, can be felt at another; and yet, on reviewing the whole in memory, the unity of the whole and the relation of its constituent purposes can be perceived and appreciated. The unity of any poem of great length becomes manifest only on reflection, and after comparison of its several main portions with one another.

There are, however, also poems on a smaller scale in which a didactic and a poetic purpose are so fused together, that it is difficult to say which of the two is dominant in particular passages. At one time we read them for poetic pleasure, at another we are personally affected by them as exhortations; and again on reflection we seem to see the didactic purpose half hidden from sight, half shining through the poetic form and beauty of the whole. Such a poem is Wordsworth's *Laodamia*. Here the didactic purpose shining through the poetic beauty of the narrative seems to be that of contrasting the imperishability of the highest kind of wedded love with the perishable nature of its necessary earthly accompaniments. But poems of this kind, I mean those in which the religious, moral, or even merely didactic purpose is equally dominant with the purely imaginative gratification, of which this is but one out of innumerable instances, plainly show, that æsthetic and poetic imagination, though guided by motives which have a purely imaginative character, has no isolated domain, is no isolated direction, of mental activity, but at all points blends with, influences, and is influenced by, the ordinary wants and wishes of human nature. It wields in fact, and may wield either for good or evil, an enormous power over the thoughts and feelings of men.

Perhaps, putting lyrical poetry aside, the most characteristic note of the most highly imaginative poetry of modern Europe, as distinguished from that of Greece in its classic period, and in a less degree from that of Rome, is its tendency to be autobiographic. True, there are exceptions; but for the most part the Greek poets aimed at imagining or celebrating the deeds and sufferings of their personages, while keeping their own personality in the background; those of modern Europe aim at giving utterance, through their personages, to their own feelings, character, and ideas. How the world appears to themselves is what they are ever striving to exhibit and express.

Shakespere was great enough, in spite of this modern tendency, to revert to the antique model of aloofness, owing to his marvellous power of identifying himself with his personages, and feeling and thinking with their imagined personality; a power so great that, even in the Sonnets, some of which, if ever poems did, bear the apparent impress of emotion personal to the author, he has been supposed by some to be speaking only in an assumed character.

Still there is a great difference. In the modern, and pre-eminently in the Shakesperian drama, it is the feelings and thoughts of the personages concerned in the action, from the least to the greatest, or their character as known in their own self-consciousness, that are the main object of the delineation, though this is exhibited by means of their participation in one continuously woven action or series of events. The main purpose is no longer that action or series of events itself, as of itself calculated to impress the spectators, though necessarily seen as mirrored in the self-consciousness of a few personages, who are the principal agents concerned in it, as in Greek Tragedy. The centre and pivot of interest has shifted from the contemplation of a heroic action, to that of the personalities of the actors; a change which carries with it, *inter alia*, the permission to mix tragic with comic scenes in the same drama, and the abrogation both of the rule of the unities of time and place, wrongly held, as Professor Butcher shows,[1] to rest on Aristotle's authority, and also of the prohibition to present the actual circumstance of killing on the stage, this latter circumstance being now considered to be one of the most effective means of exhibiting character.

The general adoption of the religion of Christianity, which marks the beginning of the modern world, involved the equally general adoption of that which is commonly characterised as the subjective point of view. The Delphic and Socratic Γνῶθι σεαυτόν became thenceforward the dominant tendency of all poetical, as of all other kinds of intellectual activity. The feelings and

---

[1] Work cited, pp. 267 *sqq.*

ideas of the individual, to which he now strove to give imaginative utterance, were often most profound and intense, as well as of deep personal interest. But this made no difference with respect to the law, that all poetic imagination is the pursuit of a gratification inherent in imagination itself. The matter to be uttered might consist of personally experienced feelings and ideas, though they were painful or even torturing; yet the utterance of them in poetic form did not cease on that account to be a luxury. To hold them, as it were, at arm's length, contemplate them from a distance, and exhibit them in their true nature, strength, and value, as estimated by the contemplator, however painful or urgent they might be, continued to be a process which was its own reward. Witness those beautiful and touching lines of Coleridge, entitled *Constancy to an Ideal Object*. (Poetical Works. Vol. II. p. 90, edit 1847.) Still more perhaps was this the case, when the feelings or ideas which demanded poetic utterance were in themselves a pleasure and delight. Only that here it becomes almost impossible to discriminate how much of the total effect, either upon the poet or upon his readers, is due to the strength of the inspiring feeling, how much to the art and skill of the inspired poet. "I am one," says Dante, in reply to Buonagiunta's question, whether he saw before him the author of the Canzone beginning

Donne, ch'avete intelletto d'amore,

"I am one who mark when Love inspires, and in that fashion which he dictates within, go setting it forth:"

> "Io mi son un che quando
> Amore spira, noto, ed a quel modo,
> Ch' ei detta dentro, vo significando."
> (Divina Commedia. Purg. XXIV. 52.
> Mr. A. J. Butler's edition and translation).

Well does Bianchi say in his note on the passage, "In these few words the whole art of poetry is comprised." And whenever, as by Dante, religious emotions and ideas are taken as the subject of poetry, and this method is employed in their imaginative treatment, the inevitable result is, that poetry becomes the handmaid of religion, and that the service which it renders is the greater, in proportion as the poet's insight into the facts is deeper, his imagination more vigorous, his diction more precise and trenchant. For then it is that he more surely evokes in others the ideas and feelings which have been the source of his own inspiration, and in evoking invests them with the glamour of his own imaginative presentment.

END OF CHAPTER V.

IN BOOK III.